ORGANIC THINKING

A STUDY IN RABBINIC THOUGHT

BY

MAX KADUSHIN

BLOCH PUBLISHING COMPANY
NEW YORK

ISBN 0-8197-0018-5

PRINTED IN THE UNITED STATES OF AMERICA
PRESS OF THE JEWISH PUBLICATION SOCIETY
PHILADELPHIA, PENNA.

TO THE MEMORY OF

CHARLES GARFIEL

ר' שמריהו בהר"ר מרדכי גרפיל ז"ל

PREFACE

SOCIAL values or ideals cannot be coördinated into a logical system. Whenever this has been attempted, religion has been constricted into dogmas and ethics hardened into the rules of the doctrinaire. Logic has its rightful place, to be sure, in these enterprises of the human mind and spirit, but when it seeks to lay the foundations of conduct its efforts are futile when they are not harmful. A well-ordered, logical, hence uniform, system negates that very complexity which is the chief characteristic of human motives and conduct. It takes no account of the differences between individuals, nor of the uniqueness of every ethical situation. In short, it runs counter to all the forces and factors that make the human scene human.

Every historic group possesses its own distinctive traditions, every individual his own peculiar character, every ethical situation its own unique quality. If no order whatsoever inheres within such variety, then any attempt to study human institutions were foredoomed to failure. On the other hand, should we impose a logical order upon these institutions, then the variety which distinguishes them disappears from view. Is there no alternative here between chaos and logic? This study demonstrates, I believe, that there is an alternative; and that in discovering it we come upon an articulation of thought and values more complicated than that which can be devised by logic, complicated and flexible enough, indeed, to allow for both the variety of mankind's traditions and the distinctiveness of the individual's character. The study which resulted in this discovery was that of a great, historically-evolved tradition, rabbinic thought. A careful analysis of the pattern of rabbinic thought proves not only that it gave room for the variations of individuals but that such variation was inevitable. A comparison with primitive mentality serves to indicate that this type of thinking is an abiding feature of man's mental life. This type of thinking, therefore, is universal, whilst local in content and individualistic in configuration. It is not logical but organismic: Each organismic pattern of thought or organic complex has its own distinctive individuality,— each social pattern and each individual variation of it.

The proof that organic thinking is a genuine phenomenon, not an artifact, rests with the actual analysis of rabbinic literary material, to which so many pages of this book are devoted. Rabbinic thought is concerned with numerous rabbinic concepts, terms peculiar to itself. These concepts are certainly not united in logical fashion and their relationship with each other defies diagrammatic representation. Instead, every concept is related to every other concept because every concept is a constituent part of *the complex as a whole*. Conversely, the complex of concepts as a whole enters into the constitution of every concept; and thus every concept is in constant, dynamic relationship with every other concept. Rabbinic thought, hence, is organismic, for only in an organism are the whole and its parts mutually constitutive. Indeed, the rabbinic organic complex affords an instance wherein the organismic process can be viewed with exceptional clarity. Since we are dealing with definite concepts, terms, it is merely a question of tracing these terms through all their interrelations. A clearly discernible pattern will then emerge, firm enough to supply the necessary cohesion, yet remarkably elastic, even fluid. The elastic, organismic qualities of the concepts enable them to canalize experience, to give it order and harmony without loss to its richness and variety, in fact, to evoke rich variety by virtue of the subtle, flexible order. But we must not imagine that the complicated structure renders organic thinking a difficult feat. Breathing is effortless though it involves a complicated structure. So with organic thinking.

The theory that an aspect of man's mental life is organismic dovetails with our knowledge of other aspects of man's nature. That man's body is an organism has, of course, long been known. His psychological constitution, it has recently been discovered, is organismic as well. A man's emotional life, Freud has shown, is an integrated whole, and Gestalt-psychology has demonstrated that his sense-perceptions are "organic and dynamic". These discoveries, then, support our own theory. Unless man's mental life is absolutely divorced from the rest of his nature, his mental life, too, his concepts, must possess an organismic aspect. To argue, therefore, that organic thinking represents a pre-logical stage of thought which civilized man has outgrown, that it is not something native to man as man, is to argue against all that we know of man's constitution. The fact is, we shall learn, that organic thinking and logical thinking are complementary to each other. Logical thinking of the most rigorous sort is essential to, and exists within the framework of, organic thinking.

The theory of organic thinking can prove helpful in social studies generally and particularly in the study of religion. Organic concepts are to be found, apparently, in any historically-evolved tradition, religious, national or economic. Such social traditions our theory renders more amenable to analysis. We have an hypothesis to start with and a method for the examination of material, and we already know those features of the complex as a whole characteristic of all socially inherited organisms. We even possess some clues as to the nature of the differences that must distinguish one organic complex of this kind from another. But whatever the value for other fields, our theory is especially relevant to the study of religion, in which field it offers a new orientation. The study of religion has been wrongly oriented in respect to both psychology and philosophy. The unusual personalities, the saints, the ascetics, the mystics who see visions and hear locutions, have been of primary interest to the psychology of religion; and when it has analyzed religious phenomena exhibited not in individuals but in groups, the phenomena were out of the ordinary, bizarre, abnormal. When associated with religion, the term "psychological" has acquired a connotation similar to that of "pathological". By means of the theory of organic thinking, however, we have been able, in this work, to describe the religious experience shared by all the members of the folk, by the common man and the spiritual leader at once, religious experience as a factor in the ordinary, normal course of every-day life. "Normal" mysticism assumes the place in our regard which "abnormal" mysticism, now seen to be dependent on it, had occupied. Old problems take a new turn, among them the relation of ethics to religion and of religious folklore to magic.

The new orientation makes for a complete reversal in our attitude toward philosophy. Instead of examining the sphere of religion in the light of philosophy, we must do exactly the opposite. There can be no real amalgam of philosophy and religion, no sound philosophy *of* religion, for the reason that in any philosophical system all the ideas are related to one another in tight logical sequence whereas religious concepts are organismic, non-logical. A religious complex of concepts therefore cannot be made part and parcel of a philosophical system.* Apparent similarities between religion and philosophy are only verbal similarities. The organic experience of God, we shall learn, has nothing in common with philosophical concepts of God. But, since philosophy or metaphysics purports to describe the order inherent in the universe, it can be supported or else refuted

*This view, expressed in other terms, was held by the late Charles Garfiel.

by the order exhibited by any sphere of knowledge, any sphere of science. If there can be no philosophy of religion, there is, this study demonstates, a science of religion. According to this science of religion, the sphere of religion exhibits an organismic order. The organic traits of religion afford us here, then, a means for testing the validity of contemporary philosophies of organism.

Rabbinic thought is organic thinking *par excellence*. That alone is why the coherence or order of rabbinic religious thought has, to the student of rabbinics, long been a vexing problem. The solution throws new light on cognate problems. The relations of the Bible to the Midrash, folklore to theology, and rabbinic thought to medieval Jewish philosophy become more clear. Rabbinic concepts which may have been hitherto obscure emerge with enlarged meaning. These matters, of special interest to the student of rabbinics, have wider bearings. The analysis of rabbinic thought is an excellent point of departure for the study of organic thinking. Brought forth by the examination of rabbinic thought, the general principles of organic thinking are illumined and exemplified by the data of rabbinic thought.

The nature of this inquiry is such that the general problems of organic thinking cannot be taken up apart from the data supplied by rabbinic thought. Discussions pertaining to the more general problems, however, will be found in the first and last chapters of the book, and the delineation of rabbinic concepts proper in the two intervening chapters. The more technical discussion of the rabbinic terms is, for the most part, restricted to the first two sections of the second chapter. For the sake of smoother reading, the Notes have been placed in the back of the book, but this does not mean that they are wholly reserved for the interested specialist. Conclusions essential to the description of organic thinking itself are often drawn from details properly left to the Notes. The transliteration of Hebrew words is in accordance with the usage of the Jewish Encyclopedia, except for the name "Seder Eliahu" wherein I followed the precedent set by the editor of the critical edition, M. Friedmann. The Indexes serve both the present work and my earlier study, *The Theology of Seder Eliahu: A Study in Organic Thinking.* The General Index is both epitome and proof of the central thesis. It demonstrates at a glance the organic interrelation of all the rabbinic concepts. Moreover, such is the organic quality of the complex that even concepts I have apparently dealt with only incidentally appear in the Index with a wealth of detail and with definitely marked individualities.

I wish to express here my gratitude to Professor Louis Ginzberg whose teaching and writings have placed all students of rabbinics in his debt. I am especially indebted to him for his kindness in annotating my manuscript with many helpful comments and valuable suggestions, most of which I have incorporated in the Notes and marked with his initials. His illuminating remarks there on the text of Seder Eliahu, which include numerous emendations, are made more accessible by means of a special Index.

I desire also to thank Alice Seltzer Max for assisting with the manuscript and Voltairine Feingold for helping with the Index.

MAX KADUSHIN

Madison, May, 1938.

CONTENTS

PAGE

CHAPTER IV

On the Organic Complex

CHAPTER I

INTRODUCTORY

I. The Problem of Coherence

"THERE is (thus) a zone of insecurity in human affairs," remarks William James in his essay on The Importance of Individuals, "in which all the dramatic interest lies; the rest belongs to the dead machinery of things. This is the formative zone, the part not yet ingrained in the race's average, not yet a typical, hereditary and constant factor of the social community in which it occurs."[1] While stressing the importance of individuals, James does not mean to deny, of course, that "the race's average" is the matrix of such individuals. A few sentences back, he qualifies his assertion that any man's virtues and vices might be just the opposite of what they are by adding "compatibly with the current range of variation in our tribe." But James does pass over here the essential problem of how the "zone of insecurity in human affairs" relates to the "typical, hereditary and constant factor of the social community in which it occurs." In the realm of values, the problem is to discover the principle of coherence which renders them a typical and constant factor of the social community and at the same time makes possible for them a degree of inconstancy or indeterminacy in the lives of individuals. The coherence or order inherent in such values cannot be that of logic for that would leave no room for indeterminacy. Perhaps the "zone of insecurity" will be less shrouded in mystery when we begin to perceive that "the race's average" cannot be dismissed as "dead machinery."

The problem of the coherence of rabbinic theology[2] appears to be precisely that which we have just raised with regard to values in general. Any representation of rabbinic theology as a logical system, such as Weber's *System der Altsynagogalen Palästinensischen Theologie*, is bound to be a distortion. Careful scholars agree with Schechter who says "that any attempt at an orderly and complete system of Rabbinic theology is an impossible task."[3] Instead they aim at "letting Judaism speak for itself in its own way,"[4] to use Moore's words, and therefore, for the most part, merely offer collected data on rabbinic concepts or attitudes in the form of centos of rabbinic passages on these themes drawn from various sources. The very fact, however, that disparate passages drawn from rabbinic sources that were composed at different periods and under divergent circumstances can yet be brought together so as to elucidate a rabbinic concept — that fact is proof positive that rabbinic theology possessed some kind of unity, some sort of coherence. And this is, indeed, the conclusion of the great masters in the field. Schechter insists that "Rabbinic literature is, as far as doctrine and dogma are concerned, more distinguished by the consensus of opinion than by its dissensions," and points out that there is remarkable agreement in doctrine not alone among Rabbis of the same generation but even between Palestinian teachers of the first and second centuries and Babylonian authorities of the fifth and tenth, "though the emphasis put on the one or the other doctrine may have differed widely as a result of changed conditions or surroundings."[5] Bacher states that in both method and content haggadic literature was already well developed at a very early period, and that, therefore, it is more correct to speak of the *enlargement* rather than of the *development* of the Haggadah.[6] If, during the later centuries of rabbinic religious thought there was enlargement rather than development, the pattern of rabbinic theology must have remained the same. Yet, as Bacher goes on to say and as Schechter also recognizes, there was no complete submergence of differences among the individual teachers. On the contary, the individual Tana or Amora expressed to the full, in the haggadic statements he uttered, his personality and the tendencies peculiar to himself.[7] The principle of coherence of rabbinic theology, then, must have been such as made for unity of thought over great stretches of time and still gave room for differences due to changed circumstances and to the divergent proclivities of individuals.

Since rabbinic theology and social values in general present the identical problem as regards coherence, the former would seem to be but a special case of the latter. Now once we penetrate to the principle of coherence, avenues will be opened up for the investigation of other problems of rabbinic theology. We shall thus go on to learn more about the characteristics of rabbinic values; the rôle of logical thinking in rabbinic theology; the relation of rabbinic theology to the Bible and of rabbinic theology to rabbinic ethics; and the rabbinic experience of God. If rabbinic theology is but a special case of social values in general, the more we shall learn concerning the coherence of rabbinic theology and cognate matters the greater will also be our knowledge of the valuational life in general.

II. On Method and Text

Despite the conviction of the modern authorities that rabbinic theology does possess some kind of coherence or unity, a conviction not only expressed but implicit in their treatment of any aspect of rabbinic theology, they have made no attempt to describe this coherence. It may be that the method employed in the analysis proved an insurmountable handicap. In culling rabbinic literature for the purpose of explaining rabbinic concepts, attention is centered upon the particular concept under discussion and diverted from other concepts which may be involved. Furthermore, when the passages culled are juxtaposed in the presentation, the original settings of the separate statements may often be ignored. What is not taken account of then is the connective tissue between the concepts or, more accurately, the inherent relationship between the concepts.

In the present study we avoided this difficulty by sifting, examining and endeavoring to classify every statement contained in one rabbinic work. We were forced, therefore, to reckon with *all* the concepts involved in any single statement and with *all* the passages mentioning any given concept. Under these circumstances the endeavor to classify the concepts at length revealed the inherent relationship between them. It will not be necessary, however, to present here an analysis of all the concepts in the book. The description of a fairly large number of them will be sufficient to establish and illustrate the principle of coherence, and will also afford material for the discussion of problems on which that principle sheds light. Moreover, when once we are aware of the principle of coherence we may even use the method of culling various rabbinic sources for the exposition of any concept to advantage. Such an exposition is certain to be richer in detail than one based on a single rabbinic source.

The rabbinic text we have analyzed is Seder Eliahu Rabba and Seder Eliahu Zuṭa. The only critical edition of this text is that of M. Friedmann; and when Seder Eliahu is here referred to by page it is always to that edition.[8] Various difficulties present themselves in any attempt to establish the date and provenance of our text. Seder Eliahu is mentioned in the Talmud and described by the ʻAruk, a talmudical dictionary of the twelfth century.[9] But according to the ʻAruk's description, the Rabba should contain three large divisions and thirty chapters and the Zuṭa twelve chapters. Our text, however, has no large divisions at all, and the Rabba contains thirty-one chapters while the Zuṭa has twenty-five. Further, even granting that the dates mentioned in the text are later interpolations,[10] on the basis of internal evidence some parts seem to have been written before and some parts after the close of the Talmud, some passages refer to an author in Palestine and other passages certainly imply a land outside of Palestine. These considerations have led to a number of contradictory theories. Some scholars, insisting that our Seder Eliahu is not the one mentioned in the Talmud, say that it was written in Babylon; others take it to be a product of the gaonic, post-talmudic period; and still another scholar declares the author or compiler to have been a man named Eliahu who lived in Palestine in the sixth or seventh century. Friedmann, basing himself on the talmudical story, advances the view that Seder Eliahu is the result of direct religious experience on the part of Rabbi 'Anan and others, and that, in the main, it must have been written before the close of the Talmud and after the composition of the Mishnah. In attempting to adjust the text to the description of the 'Aruk, he characterizes large sections similar in style and content to the rest of the book as later interpolations, and further excises the last ten chapters of the Zuṭa, without doubt written at a late period, from Seder Eliahu proper and dubs them "Additions to Seder Eliahu Zuṭa."

New evidence adduced from Genizah fragments enables Louis Ginzberg to state that Seder Eliahu was at one time composed of a Mishnah, or rather Baraita, which was composed early and a Talmud, or commentary, which was added later, certainly after Talmud Babli. We should not be surprised, therefore, if some passages reveal an earlier and some a later origin. Our text not only confuses Baraita with "Talmud" but is very much shorter than the original Seder which the 'Aruk apparently describes. In the course of our discussion, we shall point out instances where traces of Mishnah and commentary can still be discerned, corroborating Ginzberg's theory.[11]

III. The Organic Character of Rabbinic Theology

The coherence we find in Seder Eliahu consists of an inherent relationship between the concepts and is therefore a mental coherence. All the concepts employed bear an organic relationship to one another, interweaving with each other so as to produce a definite, though an extremely flexible, pattern. In using the term "organic," be it recognized, we do not mean to surround it with that aura which it assumes in fascist vocabulary where the term is vague, unbuttressed by demonstration, as well as honorific. We propose to depict in some detail the order which the rabbinic concepts exhibit, *to demonstrate*, that is, the existence of this order, and then to indicate why it can only be characterized as organic.

There are four fundamental concepts in rabbinic theology — God's loving-kindness, His justice, Torah, and Israel. We wish to emphasize that these four are fundamental not because they are the most important. Other concepts — the sanctification of the Name and the World to Come, for example — are certainly as important as those we have called fundamental, if importance here implies being essential to the rabbinic world-outlook. The fact is that rabbinic concepts are not like articles of a creed, some of which have a position of primary importance while others are relegated to secondary rank. All rabbinic concepts are of equal importance, for the pattern would not have the same character were a single concept missing. We have, however, called God's loving-kindness, His justice, Torah, and Israel fundamental concepts because all the rabbinic concepts are built, woven rather, out of these four.[12] To demonstrate this we must be permitted what is in effect a brief résumé of our earlier study, *The Theology of Seder Eliahu*.[13]

Every rabbinic concept is constituted of the four fundamental concepts. For instance, the sanctification of the Name occurs, that is, God is recognized by the world as the one true God, when Israel demonstrate their readiness to die as martyrs for this truth, when Torah is exalted before men, when God's absolute justice or His love is vindicated.[14] Likewise, *Malkut Shamayim*, the sovereignty of God (not the *kingdom* of God),[15] is accepted by Israel upon themselves by declaration, and by the study and practice of Torah, and by the recognition of His love and justice.[16] Though the two concepts are very much akin, both having to do with the recognition of God, sanctification of the Name, *Ḳiddush Hashem*, refers to the effect upon others whereas *Malkut Shamayim* refers to the subjective acceptance or acknowledgement of God by individual or nation. The kinship in idea, however, brings with it similarity in other things. *Malkut Shamayim* is affirmed by declaration; *Ḳiddush Hashem* is achieved by declaration, as well.[17] *Ḳiddush Hashem* possesses an obverse in *Ḥillul Hashem*, the profanation of the Name; *Malkut Shamayim* possesses an obverse in "strange worship," the acceptance of strange or false gods,[18] a perverse worship that will disappear *le'atid labo* when mankind at large will perforce recognize the sovereignty of God.[19] Since the two concepts are so greatly similar, they naturally blend into one another occasionally. The destruction of idols is sanctification of the Name,[20] and martyrdom is crowned with an affirmation of God's sovereignty. We shall find in rabbinic theology other examples of kindred concepts which also blend into one another at times yet which are distinguished, again like the two concepts just described, each by its own individual features.

The inherent relationship between all the concepts, to anticipate a later discussion, is of such a nature that every concept must pcssess its own distinctive features, no matter how closely related it may be to another concept.

The Rabbis' conception of nature and their use of angelology conform to the four fundamental concepts. Notions of a fixed physical order and natural law are absent in rabbinic theology. Everything in nature — heaven and earth, the sun and the moon and the stars, insects and beasts — serves as a vehicle for the fundamental concepts. Rain falls and grass grows because of God's love for man; noxious animals performing their mission are agents of God's justice; Israel's twelve tribes are mirrored in the twelve stars and constellations in the firmament; and when God created the world "He consulted only the Torah."[21] As to angelology, there is no occasion in rabbinic theology when angels appear otherwise than in the service of a fundamental concept. The angels, with their complaints against man, serve to bring God's loving-kindness toward him into stronger relief; they are the instruments of God's justice, both in reward and punishment; they help to emphasize the transcendence of Torah; and they accentuate that God's special concern is with Israel. Though names of angels are found, and other details that lend concreteness to the angelology, neither the constitution nor the number of angels is a fixed and dogmatic affair. Angelology, then, is employed but as background for the fundamental concepts.[22]

The "independent attributes" and the anthropomorphisms are also incidental to the four fundamental concepts. By "independent attributes" of God we mean the attributes of eternity, omniscience, humility, omnipresence, creativity and the like, "independent" in the sense that they are additional to the fundamental concepts. Additional they may be but dissociated they are not. God employs His omniscience to aid His mercy and loving-kindness; His humility is associated with Torah; His ways of truth apply to His just recompense; and His universality is joined with His election of Israel.[23] Anthropomorphisms are confined to the fundamental concepts and to the independent attributes associated with the latter. God's "hands are stretched forth to receive those that repent," an expression of His loving-kindness; He will consent to walk with the righteous in Paradise, an anticipated reward; He devotes one-third of the day to the study of Torah; He weeps over the tragedies of Israel.[24] Out of reverence, the Rabbis refrain from employing the biblical terms for God, and instead have many terms of their own. A number of these names or terms derive from the fundamental concepts, and the multiplicity of the rabbinic names for God is thus no mere idiosyncracy of rabbinic theology.[25]

Besides entering into the constitution of all the other concepts, the four fundamental concepts are constitutive of each other, inextricably intertwining with one another. The concept of God's loving-kindness, for example, possesses several aspects or sub-concepts: Providence, or the loving care for the welfare of every individual;[26] mercy or forgiveness in the moral sphere;[27] repentance and atonement; and prayer. We shall indicate the organic interpenetration of the fundamental concepts in the case of repentance and in that of prayer. Repentance refers to the complete change of heart not only on the part of the sinner weighed down by the consciousness of specific wrong-doing but on the part of every individual who determines to live the good life. The ability to repent is given man because of God's love; if he repents, he is rewarded, if not, he is punished — in either case there is the infallible operation of God's justice. The means of his reconciliation with God—atonement—are to be found in the study and practice of Torah and association with Israel and the Patriarchs.[28] A sub-concept of atonement is vicarious atonement, the doctrine that an individual Israelite atones through the sufferings visited upon his person for the sins of all Israel; and this doctrine, incidentally, intertwines with the concept of God's justice, for the ideas of corporate personality and corporate responsibility which underlie vicarious atonement also underlie, as we shall soon see, the concept of corporate or collective justice.[29] Prayer is effective because of God's love: God "hears prayer immediately" since He is "merciful and gracious, full of great compassion." Israel, Torah, and God's justice and love are frequently combined into one theme in prayer; Torah is the authority for the prescribed prayers, and sets down their order; Israel is saved by prayer; God's justice, besides being invoked or extolled in prayer is counted on when reward is expected for reciting prescribed prayers. The Rabbis fully realize the danger of mere ritualism lurking in prescribed prayer and seek to overcome it in various ways, one of which consists in the rule to engage in Torah before one "stands in prayer."[30]

The concept of God's justice, sometimes personified, also has its various aspects or sub-concepts, each of which depicts God's justice as universal in scope. One such concept is the justice due the individual, the belief that whatever befalls anyone, for good or evil, comes as recompense for his own acts, with the moral temper of the individual taken into account. An elaboration of this kind of distributive justice is the concept of "measure for measure," poetic justice, frequently employed by the Rabbis to supply ethical causes for afflictions mentioned in the Bible. Corporate or collective justice is another aspect of the concept of God's justice, an aspect which permits the Rabbis to regard reward or punishment for the deeds of an individual as visited by God not only upon him alone but upon others as well. The Rabbis resort to this concept of corporate justice in their resolution of the problem of evil; and when employed in their accounts of how the fathers' good deeds affect the children's welfare and vice versa, the concept appears in its special forms of Merit of the Fathers and Merit of the Children. The contradiction between the concept of corporate justice and that of the justice due the individual as well as the ethical evaluation of both by the Rabbis will be dealt with in this study later on. At present we need only recognize that the two concepts imply two different apprehensions of individuality. As several rabbinic passages reveal, corporate justice implies that the individual is not merely a person but that he is merged into a kind of corporate personality of which he is only one link, as it were.[31] All the individual persons composing the corporate personality participate in, and must share in the consequences of, any action by any component member—in other words, there is corporate or collective responsibility.[32] With the remaining aspect of the concept of God's justice—chastisement, or corrective justice—we shall demonstrate the interweaving of the concept of God's justice with the other fundamental concepts. According to the Rabbis, chastisements are sent by God in order to correct and purify men, and hence there are also "chastisings of love," an interpretation the Rabbis are particularly apt to place upon the afflictions of the righteous. By the same token, God chastizes Israel because of His love for them, "For whom the Lord loveth He correcteth, even as a father the son in whom he delighteth" (Prov. 3:12). He that is engaged in Torah knows how to accept chastisement properly, and, indeed, Torah may be efficacious in enabling him to avoid chastisement altogether. The aspects of the concept of God's justice touched on above combine with the other fundamental concepts in a similar manner.[33]

The concepts of rabbinic theology thus exhibit a definite pattern. The four fundamental concepts interlace with each other and with the rest of the rabbinic concepts. This is again demonstrated, and perhaps in even stronger fashion, in our discussion in the present volume of the various aspects of the concept of Torah. We shall notice that not only do the fundamental concepts intertwine with one another but that a full description of any fundamental concept actually involves all the concepts of rabbinic theology.

The pattern inherent in the concepts of Seder Eliahu is not confined to that Midrash but is characteristic of rabbinic theology in general. The theology of the Mekilta possesses the same pattern, as we hope to show soon in a forthcoming study, and the Mekilta, an early, halakic Midrash, is indubitably representative of rabbinic thought. The conclusion that the pattern of concepts we have traced here is typical of rabbinic theology in general does not really stand in need, however, of such verification. As is illustrated by the relation of Seder Eliahu to other rabbinic works,[34] there are numerous parallel passages in various rabbinic sources. How could these passages have been placed in different haggadic books unless the concepts embodied are the same in haggadic literature generally? And if the concepts are the same, the pattern most likely is the same. This consideration is supported by two more. According to Ginzberg, whose theory is substantiated here in a number of instances, our text was written or compiled during the entire rabbinic period; and it can be taken, therefore, to be representative of that period. Finally, the kind of unity which both Schechter and Bacher saw in rabbinic theology, a unity presupposed in any modern treatment of the subject, can be accounted for only by the principle of coherence informing the pattern we have described.

IV. The Coherence of Organic Thinking

The coherence of rabbinic theology can only be characterized as organic. Rabbinic theology is a unitary pattern or complex of concepts wherein the four fundamental concepts are interrelated with each other and with all the rest of the rabbinic concepts. Without coherence, or relation to other concepts, no concept can possibly possess meaning. But the coherence between the rabbinic concepts is not such that one concept proceeds from another in inferential fashion. Instead, here the integrated pattern or complex as a whole supplies coherence, relationship with the other concepts, meaning, to each of its individual constituent concepts. The relationship of the rabbinic concepts to one another consists, therefore, in the relationship of each to the whole integrated complex—an organic relationship. Our conclusion, then, is that the rabbinic concepts are organic concepts and their pattern or complex an organic complex. Being thus a mental organism, a thought-organism, this organic complex provides us with an example of organic thinking.

The coherence of organic thinking renders the "zone of insecurity" or indeterminacy a characteristic alike of rabbinic theology and of social values in general. Since no rabbinic concept inevitably follows from any other concept, any given situation is not necessarily interpreted by a single combination of concepts. The same concept, as we have learned, can be combined with any of the four fundamental concepts; hence it happens not infrequently that the same or a similar situation may be given several interpretations "contradictory" to each other. Thus, at one time the Rabbis declare that because God loves the scholar's devotion to Torah He deliberately withholds from him wealth which would distract him from study,[35] and at another time they affirm that wealth is the reward of those who study Torah.[36] The first statement combines Torah with the concept of God's love; the second, Torah with the concept of God's justice. Furthermore, a situation may be interpreted differently by the various sub-concepts of the same concept, and so again different interpretations may be based on a common ground. The organic complex, therefore, is flexible, allowing for divergencies in interpretation either wide or subtle without losing thereby its essential unity. Fluid yet unified, the organic complex gives room for differences in temperament among individuals, even for different moods in the same individual, for the stressing of different concepts in different historical periods — in brief, for all those differences which may distinguish one midrashic compilation from another. We shall take up these matters at greater length under the caption, "The Fluid Character of the Complex."[37]

Organic thinking and logical thinking are not mutually exclusive. Two distinct orders of thought, two distinct types of coherence, they are at one in that both make for the integration of man's mental life. We shall learn later on of the tremendous rôle which logical thinking plays within the framework of the organic complex. The only occasion for conflict between organic and logical thinking occurs when an attempt is made to supply logical coherence to the organic concepts, and the organic complex, we shall also learn, brooks even this attempt to a limited degree. An out-and-out attempt, however, to erect a logical, hence dogmatic, structure of values or beliefs is utterly out of keeping, as we can see even now, with the organic complex. It is organic coherence, not hard-and-fast logical consistency, that permits the development and expression of individuality.

A striking feature of organic thinking is its concreteness. Though often mentioned by name, the rabbinic concepts are very seldom found without an exemplifying situation. Indeed, since the concepts interpret for the Rabbis the concrete situations of every-day life, the concepts are usually imbedded, as it were, in those situations. Our theory of organic thinking bears the same relation to the concrete complex of rabbinic theology as grammar does to a language, and, like grammar, can best be grasped through the actual analysis of a good sample of the literature. The analogy — it is probably much more than that — goes even further. Just as the rules of grammar always have reference to a specific language, so the implications of the theory of organic thinking have reference to a particular organic complex. Before turning to the consideration of these implications, let us then, by means of the detailed analysis of a concept, first become more familiar with the theory and with the organic complex itself. The fundamental concept of Torah as exhibited primarily by the text of Seder Eliahu will be our theme for the next two chapters.

CHAPTER II

TORAH

I. Torah as a Fundamental Concept

Very often "Torah" is a general term for the Pentateuch, the Prophets, the Writings, the Mishnah, Halakot and Agadot; yet it designates, as well, a verse or a statement from any of these divisions.[1] "Torah" is thus applied to the whole or to any part.

Now Torah is not merely a concept; it is a fundamental concept. There is no distinction, as we have stated before, between the fundamental concepts and the other concepts as regards belief.[2] The Rabbis believed firmly in all the concepts of their theology. The four fundamental concepts, however, are "the vantage-points from which the Rabbis viewed the world." All the other concepts, therefore, are built out of these four. It is to be expected, then, that the four fundamental concepts should be particularly vivid and colorful, that they should possess more varied aspects than do the others if only for the reason that, in a way, they include all the rest. The two fundamental concepts with which we have dealt in our earlier study were the two manifestations of God — His loving-kindness and His justice — which actively affect the world, and which the Rabbis felt at the very core of their being. No less fervently and in a fashion no less real did Torah and Israel well out of their experience, and necessarily so since all the four fundamental concepts are organically united.[3]

Torah, then, ought to be particularly rich in significance to the Rabbis. And this expectation is in every way fulfilled as we examine the texts. Where other concepts are personified in order to gain vividness, Torah assumes almost the character of a personality, and, in addition, is at times given a mystical turn. It is made a factor in the creation of the world. It is held to contain the life-principle of humanity, and to confer upon man his genuine status. It is employed as the standard of the measurement of the worth of other concepts. As one of the four fundamental concepts, Torah is stressed sometimes above and sometimes below Israel, and like Israel it is held to be holy.

Torah is not only personified, but possesses the qualities of a personality. It is one of the escorts of Israel, together with God and the prophets. When God shall judge the Nations of the World and Israel, they will be gathered in the valley of Jehoshaphat, the king; "and *Shekinah* will be in front of them (i. e., of Israel), and the prophets behind them and the Torah on their right . . ."[4] Between Torah and Israel there is an indissoluble bond: they take mutual joy in each other, as would two inseparable friends. "Just as Israel do the Torah in this world and rejoice in it so the Torah rejoices in them forever."[5] God, who took counsel only with Torah when He created the world,[6] loves the words of the Torah more than all who live and all He created. Why? "Because they weigh Israel over to the side of merit, and train them in *mizwot*, and bring them to the life of the World to Come."[7] Thus, in all its relations with Israel, Torah comes in the guise of friend, benefactor and teacher. Torah possesses, also, admirable traits that we associate with saintly personalities. It is modest, making no sound, since "the words of the Torah are like milk and like oil which, when poured from vessel to vessel, the sound thereof is not heard".[8] As toward the whole people of Israel, Torah serves as friend to the individual when he has most need of a human companion. When a person starts on a journey without anyone accompanying him, he ought to engage in the Torah, which will then be his invisible companion.[9] There seems to be also a suggestion of personification in the statement: "On that occasion (i. e., in the World to Come), the Holy One blessed be He will bring forth the Torah and place it in His bosom . . ."[10]

A tinge of mysticism, we may have noticed, colors the concept of Torah. There is one most secret chamber of the Torah which God did not reveal to Israel.[11] The Torah, one of the five possessions which God made especially His own in His world,[12] He pondered over nine hundred and seventy-four generations before the world was created: "and every single word that the Holy One blessed be He brought forth and established in His Torah . . . He searched and explored and tried and tested it two hundred forty-eight times corresponding to the two hundred forty-eight members of the human body, as it says, 'The words of the Lord are pure words, as silver tried in a crucible', etc. (Ps. 12:7). And after that the Holy One blessed be He brought it forth and established it in His Torah. And were it (i. e., a single word) to stir from its place even a little, that would cause the destruction of the entire world."[13] The words of the Torah and the structure of the world have thus a mystic interdependence. But even one letter had a cosmic potency; with the letter ב, the first letter in the Torah, God created the world.[14]

The Torah was among the six things created before the world.[15] By means of it, indeed, God created the world. He consulted only the Torah, which, on that occasion served Him as an artisan: " 'Then I was by him, אמון' (Prov. 8:30) — Read not אמון, but אומן, artisan, like an artisan who is engaged in his craft."[16] Further, after creation, heaven and earth could not endure were it not for the words of Torah and Israel.[17] And Torah is placed on a par with the entire world in the statement that both were created for God's glory.[18]

The words of the Torah, themselves forever alive,[19] contain the life-principle of humanity. In the homily just cited, the oft-quoted simile of water is used; elsewhere Torah is spoken of as the fountain of life, with God before creation.[20] Torah is also identified with "the tree of life" in Gen. 3:24, by analogy with Prov. 3:18.[21] Hence, it is the Torah that gives man "life in this world and in the World to Come."[22] "Just as it is impossible for a man to be without bread and water even one day, so it is impossible for a man to be without words of the Torah even one hour."[23] No greater boon, therefore, can be conferred than instruction in Torah, no matter how slight it be, for "everyone who teaches his fellow one verse or one *halakah* or one word it is as though he places life before him."[24] It would be a mistake to think that when the Rabbis ascribe this quality to Torah it is purely metaphorical. " 'And the tables were the work of God, חרות upon the tables' (Exod. 32:16) — read not *ḥarut* but *ḥerut*: no one is free unless the Angel of Death has no power over him."[25] Attributing thus life-giving properties to the Torah, the Rabbis declare that it was God's intention that every nation accepting the Torah "should live and exist (here) forever and ever;" and that it was only because of Israel's sin with the golden calf that this did not come to pass.[26]

Torah alone endows a man with true worth or raises him to genuine dignity. Nothing so well reveals the fundamental democracy of rabbinic theology as does the concept of Torah. External circumstances, social position, in no way decide what shall be a man's rightful status. Torah alone, within reach of all, decides. In a homily reminiscent of the last one quoted, and playing again upon the word חרות in Exod. 32:16, the Rabbis say, "Read not *ḥarut* but *ḥerut*, for there is no freeman except he that labors in the Torah."[27] The highest estate possible for man is that of Torah; it is greater than the priesthood and than royalty.[28]

In order to describe this estate, the Rabbis borrow from the symbols of royalty: "And in what shall a man glory in this world? Let him glory in the crown of the Torah . . ."[29] And it is Israel's pride that upon them, of all the nations, has been conferred this lofty rank: "For Thou hast magnified us and exalted us and sanctified us and praised us and crowned us with the words of the Torah — from one end of the world to the other."[30]

Torah is, for the Rabbis, the great ultimate standard of comparison, other qualities in the world being judged in its light. "Thou canst not find any good quality which the Holy One blessed be He has created in His world that is as great as Torah."[31] When the Rabbis wish to extol charity, they say that it has been made equal to Torah,[32] and that it has been compared to Torah;[33] when they desire to give repentance its place in the scheme of things, they declare its importance to be equal to that of Torah.[34] The entire course of history is so strongly affected by Torah that one of the three great epochs into which this world's existence is divided is characterized as "Torah": "For the entire existence of this world is to be six thousand years—two thousand years of chaos, two thousand years of Torah, two thousand years of the period of the Messiah."[35] Indeed, in this world-schema, Torah is central, the years of chaos having reference to a world which had not accepted Torah, and the period of the Messiah to the dawn of the new era coming as reward for Torah.

We ought not to try to find doctrinal differences between the statement that Torah is the highest of all values and the opinions that other qualities, charity and repentance, are equally as noble. There is no gauging of valucs through mathematical instruments. What can be remarked is the fact that no quality is ever placed on a higher level than Torah, and that Torah is used as the standard of measurement of the worth of other concepts.

Nor do we find doctrinal differences when the Rabbis come to consider the worth of Torah as compared to that of Israel. To be sure, one fundamental concept can sometimes be stressed above the other, Torah being sometimes subordinated to Israel and vice versa. Torah is plainly subordinated to Israel in the conversation our author had with a man "in whom there was Bible but no Mishnah", and who wished to know which of the two whom he loved so greatly — Torah and Israel — should precede the other. "I said to him: It is the habit of men to say, 'Torah precedes everything'. . . but I should say Israel precedes."[36] If Israel precedes Torah, the reason is that while Israel is central, Torah is an instrument for training Israel. The passage which explicitly states that the people of Israel come first follows another conversation in which the man "in whom there was Bible but no Mishnah" asks why the words of the Torah are more beloved of God than all who live and all things that He created. "I said to him: My son, because they weigh Israel over to the side of merit, and train them in *miẓwot,* and bring them to the life of the World to Come."[37] Taken together, the two passages, following one another, leave no room for doubt that our author, on this occasion, emphasized Israel as against Torah. It is not unlikely that the occasion was one in which our author felt called upon to implant the love for Israel, so outstanding a characteristic of the Rabbis, in a man to whom rabbinic teaching — the Mishnah — was unknown. But a similar recognition of the rôle of Torah as dependant upon Israel occurs not in any special pedagogic situation. The Quality of Justice hints that the world was created for the sake of the Torah, not for the sake of Israel, to which God replies, "Even the Torah was given only to Israel."[38]

Yet there are other homilies in which Israel is subordinated to Torah. Israel's raison-d'être is the Torah; had they not accepted it, they would have been destroyed. "When our ancestors stood at Mt. Sinai, the Holy One blessed be He . . . said, 'Perhaps Israel will not accept My Torah upon themselves, as the Nations of the World did not accept it upon themselves, then the decree against them will be sealed, and they shall perish — from this world and from the World to Come.' "[39] Important though Israel be, when God comes down "from the highest heaven of heavens" to dwell among them, it is "for the sake of the Torah they did."[40] One of our authors makes, among other claims for Israel on God's mercy, the plea that "if, God forbid, Israel should perish from the world then Thy Torah will perish from the world."[41] In this appeal, Torah is central, and Israel secondary, important only because necessary for the preservation of Torah. Similar in tone, apparently, is an interpretation of Ps. 137:5: "If I forget thee, O Jerusalem, may my right hand forget" etc. The Rabbis interpret this verse as uttered by God and, adducing from Deut. 33:2 that the "right hand" refers to Torah, take it to mean that God says that if He should forget Israel He would have to forget the Torah also since Israel is necessary for the preservation and promulgation of the Torah.[42] In still another homily Israel and Torah are given equal distinction: Were it not for Israel and the words of the Torah, heaven and earth could not endure.[43]

Rabbinic theology, organic complex that it is, allows for just these differences of opinion without thereby losing its essential unity. "Doctrinal differences", on the other hand, is an idea quite foreign to rabbinic theology, possessing a credal and philosophic connotation whilst rabbinic theology is thought of another order. We have an example here rather of the flexibility of rabbinic thought, permitting emphasis sometimes on Torah and again on Israel, in comformity with the mood and situation of our authors. It is an expression of thought not hardened according to formulae but fluid and fresh as the living experience that engendered it, and like that experience having its own organic unity.

Between Torah and Israel the Rabbis see an exclusive, inherent relationship, the exclusiveness of which is broken only at some detriment to Torah. "It was the (original) intention of the Holy One blessed be He to give the holy Torah (only) to (the) holy (people of) Israel; and when it was given to Balaam, the son of Beor, he misused it immediately."[44] The common bond between Israel and Torah consists in their both being holy. "The beauty of holiness" (Ps. 29:2), the Rabbis say, refers to a verse of the Bible or to an *halakah*,[45] in other words, to Torah. In the hands of others than those inherently qualified for it by the common bond there is always the danger that the Torah will be misused.

We have seen that the concept of Torah possessed an exalted, vital and cosmic significance for the Rabbis. We have now to prove what we have hitherto assumed, namely, that "Torah" is a generalization, that it is often used as a designation for the religious texts and laws and homilies as a whole which are then enumerated, and for single verses, statements or laws. We shall also learn, however, that "Torah" has a specific meaning, as well, and that then it refers to the Pentateuch alone. Following that discussion, we shall consider whether Torah as concept includes both instruction in Torah and the practice of laws and commandments or whether it refers to instruction alone.

The terms "Torah" (תורה) and "the words of the Torah" (דברי תורה) are used interchangeably in Seder Eliahu, as can be remarked from the quotations below in which both terms occur indiscriminately.

The following passage clearly designates "Torah" or "the words of Torah" as inclusive terms for the religious texts and laws and homilies as a whole: " 'And, behold, there appeared a chariot of fire and horses of fire which parted them both asunder' (II Kings, 2:11) . . . fire refers to Torah . . ."[46] This passage takes "a chariot of fire" to refer to "the Torah, the Prophets and the Writings"; "horses of fire" to "Mishnah, Halakot and Agadot"; derives by analogy with Ps. 19:8 that "fire refers to Torah"; and declares that Elijah and Elisha were therefore "engaged in words of the Torah", and hence that the Angel of Death had no power over them, "parted them both asunder" meaning that the Angel of Death could not get to them. Here "words of the Torah" and "Torah" are used interchangeably as inclusive general terms for the Pentateuch, the Prophets, the Writings and the Mishnah, Halakot and Agadot.[47] Another instance of the same use of the terms, and of the interchangeability of "Torah" and "words of the Torah": "Happy is the man that makes himself like unto an ox for the yoke . . . and sits and meditates upon the words of the Torah every day continually; thereupon . . . his Torah becomes an inalienable part of him (ותורתו בתוך מעיו). 'Happy are ye that sow beside all waters, that . . . the feet of the ox and the ass' (Is. 32:20) —'waters' refers to Torah . . . If a man studies the Torah, the Prophets and the Writings and Halakot and Midrash . . . thereupon the Holy spirit rests upon him and his Torah becomes an inalienable part of him."[48] To "sow beside all *waters*" is to "meditate upon the words of the Torah", for "*waters* refers to Torah" and "all waters" to all the divisions of Torah. Again: God established a covenant with David that he be expert in Bible and Mishnah, in Halakot and Agadot. The proof-text is II Sam. 23:5, and the Rabbis conclude from another phrase in the same text that "the words of the Torah were kept in him forever and ever."[49] "The words of the Torah", then, refers to Bible, Mishnah, Halakot and Agadot. We shall give but one more of many possible instances: "Every single sage of Israel in whom there are the words of Torah in truth has in his heart a hundred thoughts of the Bible, a hundred thoughts of the Mishnah and a hundred kinds of answers (i. e. discussions) of Talmud."[50] Again "the words of Torah" are equated to Bible, Mishnah and Talmud.

Being an inclusive term for all the smaller divisions together when these are enumerated, Torah is also a designation for the two large divisions of Bible and Mishnah. "Happy is he in whom there is Torah and sits and studies Bible and Mishnah . . ."[51] Torah, here, is Bible and Mishnah. Hitherto we have deliberately gone into a number of passages at length in order to demonstrate the manner in which the Rabbis employed the term "Torah"; it would be, however, useless and tedious to engage upon the same meticulous treatment further in our attempt to discover other applications of the term. Hereafter a few illustrations will be given, but the bulk of the passages in support of the argument will be merely indicated in the notes, with attention drawn to both terms—"Torah" and "the words of the Torah".[52]

The Pentateuch, the Prophets and the Writings (Ketubim) are the three divisions of the Bible. Though not enumerated by their names, they are referred to by the number "three", and designated thus collectively as "Torah": " 'Chief of the three' (II Sam. 23:8) — For thou (David) shalt be chief to My Torah."[53] "The words of the Torah" frequently refers to the Bible alone. The Rabbis declare that "the words of the Torah are everywhere given twice (כפולין)", and then give examples from Exodus and Deuteronomy, and also from the prophet Ezekiel.[54] The Rabbis used the Bible as a source for legalistic and homiletic interpretations, to which fact this homily must refer: "To what may the words of the Torah be compared? To the way in which when a skin is given a man he tans it, stretches it, until it comes out a beautiful handiwork."[55] Here "the words of the Torah" again refers to the Bible. And those "who do Torah" are, we learn, they who, on the Sabbath, study the Pentateuch and the Prophets.[56]

The Prophets are regarded as "the words of Torah". The man "in whom there was Bible but no Mishnah" was disturbed because, though a definite time was fixed for the end of the first exile, none was fixed for the end of the last, the present exile. Our author tells him that we can "only pray . . . and find one door in the words of the Torah from all the doors opened for us through His servants, the prophets."[57] Here the Prophets as a whole are spoken of as "the words of the Torah"; elsewhere the same term is employed in reference to particular verses from the Prophets.[58] Another passage introduces Josh. 1:8 by the statement, "Have I not written thus for you in My Torah."[59]

In one passage, the phrase "From what has been written in the Torah" introduces a statement from the Mishnah of Abot.[60] In another passage "a student who was not expert in Halakah" declares that he longs that "Torah should come upon me, and Torah does not come upon me,"[61] Torah, in this case, apparently being applied to Halakah in general.

Single verses of the Bible or a single *halakah* are designated as Torah. "If thou seest one in whom there is no Torah . . . teach him one verse (from the Bible) or one *halakah* . . . for there is no naked in Israel but him in whom there are no words of Torah."[62] He who possesses neither Bible nor Mishnah but just reads one verse (Gen. 36:22) all day "the reward of Torah is in his possession."[63] "Words of the Torah" is the term applied to the discussion of one *halakah*.[64] By now it is abundantly evident that, as we have said, "Torah is very often a general term for the Pentateuch, the Prophets, the Writings, the Mishnah, Halakot and Agadot; yet it designates, as well, a verse or a statement from these divisions."[65] Torah is a concept, a generalization; "it is applied to the whole or any part."[66]

Though used as a generalization, "Torah" nevertheless often stands also for the Pentateuch alone, and thus possesses, as well, a specific meaning. In the oft-recurring phrase, "the Torah, the Prophets and the Writings",[67] "Torah" has this specific meaning, the phrase as a whole referring to the entire Bible with "Torah" designating the first division, the Pentateuch. Hence, it is possible for the Rabbis to employ the term "Torah" in order to designate the Pentateuch in contradistinction to other parts of the Bible—in contradistinction to the Prophets, in one instance. The question is raised whether the Gentiles will be present in the days of the Messiah, and our author answers affirmatively regarding those nations that did not oppress Israel, giving proof-texts from the Prophets. Then he goes on to say that they will not be present in the *'Olam Habba*, explaining, "Leave the words that I told you at first and seize on the words of the Torah which are of more weight (חמורין) than the words I told you at first." These "words of the Torah" consist in an interpretation of Exod. 12:48, which enables him to prove his point by means of a certain hermeneutic rule.[68] In another place "the words of the Torah" also stands for the Pentateuch as against the Prophets.[69] "Torah" and "words of the Torah" are thus interchangeable terms even when standing for the Pentateuch alone as against the other parts of the Bible. We notice, again, the use of the term "words of the Torah" as referring to verses from the Pentateuch — not in opposition to other parts of the Bible, it is true — when Moses on command of God consoles Israel "with words of the Torah", the latter consisting of the laws in Num. 15:2 ff.[70]

Like all generalizations, the concept of Torah may cover matters not yet known or experienced. "Search it," says Joḥanan, the son of BagBag, "and search it again, for it contains everything."[71] The Rabbis regarded their interpretations, legalistic or homiletic, not so much as elaborations but as implications imbedded in the Scriptures which needed only to be drawn forth.[72] There are always deeper recesses in the Torah than those already discovered: "The Holy One blessed be He has a chamber among the innermost chambers in His Torah", and so, too, have the learned.[73] That the Torah is not yet complete, that final decisions on that which is permitted and prohibited, on the pure and the impure, have not yet been made is apparent from the homilies concerning the academy in the World to Come. "The Holy One blessed be He will sit in His house of study and the righteous of the world will be sitting before Him, and they will engage in discussions upon Bible, Mishnah, Halakot and Agadot; and they will say on the unclean that it is unclean and on the clean that it is clean — on the unclean as becoming it, and on the clean as becoming it."[74] Thus, Torah is a concept covering not only known but matters also to be known in the future. It is a generalization under which individual facts not at present before us can ultimately be subsumed. We shall soon discuss the general nature of these "unknown facts".

When "Torah" is mentioned, do the Rabbis have in mind just instruction and study or does the term cover both study and the practice of the laws and commandments of the Torah? Friedmann declares that the term means only the study of Torah and not the practice of the *mizwot*; and he attempts to prove this from other sources rather than from our text itself.[75] There is sufficient proof, however, from Seder Eliahu that the term can convey the ideas of both study and practice. "The Torah gives life to those that do it (i. e., study it — עושיה) and to those that keep it (שומריה)"; "to keep" the Torah surely means to observe and practice it.[76] Perhaps statements even more clearly referring to practice are the following: "Jacob our father observed the Torah (קיים) before it was given", and proof of this is found in his doing away with the foreign gods, thus observing the First Commandment;[77] the learned who quarrel with one another, "whose hearts are toward the Torah and who (nevertheless) observe not (מקיימין) the Torah, their only sentence can be Gehenna";[78] "Everyone who recognizes (i. e., knows) the words of the Torah and transgresses (ומעביר) them is absolutely wicked."[79] Certain commandments, to be observed, were given Adam and the generations immediately following him; they are referred to as Torah in this statement, if we agree with Friedmann that it speaks of the generation of the Deluge: "The world was destroyed that first time only because of faithlessness towards Torah".[80] Again, as Friedmann points out, the following passage refers to the whole world, not merely to Israel: "Because of the words of the Torah (people) are chastized, and because of the words of the Torah, (they) are healed."[81] Surely "words of the Torah" here denote deeds, practices, as indeed the subsequent passage on that page proves. The term "Torah", then, can denote both the study of Torah and the practice of the laws and commandments of the Torah.[82] It seems to me that in those homilies in which Torah is given a poetic grandeur, as in most of the passages cited above to illustrate what significance Torah had for the Rabbis, "Torah" conveys the totality of its meanings — as religious instruction and as precepts and laws that must be followed.

What no doubt misled Friedmann is the undeniable fact that, although "Torah" can convey the ideas of both study and practice, in the vast bulk of the statements where the term occurs it does have reference to the study of Torah. A summary of these passages would well-nigh be a summary of the entire text of our Seder.[83] "Doing Torah", a phrase found so frequently,[84] does not mean the practice but the study of Torah; and Friedmann quotes the passage which helps to render its meaning unequivocal: "Every one that does the Torah (עושה התורה) through suffering and that does the *miẓwot* through suffering (בצער)"[85] . . . The phrase can only mean the study of Torah for as it is mentioned here it is distinct from the observance of commandments and laws; above we also noticed the phrase and a similar dichotomy—"those that do (Torah), and those that keep it."[86] The Rabbis so often place Torah in one category, and *miẓwot* or Good Deeds in another that we cannot but feel that usually when they mention Torah they refer to the study of Torah, even if the context is ambiguous. Torah and *miẓwot* are distinct in the homily which compares all the *miẓwot* a man does to the light of a candle only whilst Torah lights the world from end to end;[87] and the dichotomy is mentioned in many other places.[88] Sometimes the two categories are "Torah" and "Good Deeds";[89] and there are times when the term "the study of Torah" (תלמוד תורה) is employed outright and placed in one category, with "Good Deeds" in the other.[90] We can, therefore, assume that, by and large, when the Rabbis use the term "Torah" they refer to the study of Torah, unless the context distinctly refers to the observance of practices or laws.[91] We shall discuss Torah as practice when we take up "Torah as Law and Ethics".

In this section we have shown that Torah is a concept, and that as a concept it covers even individual facts to be known in the future. We have seen that Torah, as a fundamental concept, has the deepest significance for the Rabbis. We concluded that we can safely assume that ordinarily the term "Torah" refers to the study of and instruction in Torah though it can convey the idea of the practice of the *miẓwot* of the Torah, as well. We have not yet defined completely, however, the meaning of "Torah", for we have not described its content (though touching on it) nor that which gave it distinction and character, its authorship. This we shall do in the following section.

II. Content and Authorship of Torah.

The chief distinctive feature of Torah consists in its having been revealed by God. According to the Rabbis, the Torah has been revealed by God in part directly, and in part indirectly — through Moses and later through the divine inspiration of the learned.

God is the Author of the Torah. In a homily quoted above,[92] and to be found rather often in Seder Eliahu, God is said to have "searched and explored and tried and tested all the words of the Torah two hundred and forty-eight times", and this took place "nine hundred and seventy-four generations before the world was created."[93] The number two hundred forty-eight corresponds "to the two hundred forty-eight members of the human body",[94] the Rabbis apparently implying by this the necessity of "whole-bodied" or as we should say "whole-souled", concentration on every word of the Torah by man in imitation of God. And the number nine hundred seventy-four is explained by this passage: "Nine hundred and seventy-four generations before the world was created the Holy One blessed be He established all His words for the sake of the seed of Abraham, Isaac and Jacob, saying, 'When will the time come when I shall hear My words from their mouths.' "[95] According to Seder Eliahu the Torah was created one thousand generations before Moses — that is, nine hundred and seventy-four generations before the world was created — for the sake of Israel; it was destined for them before the world was created. What the Rabbis wish to convey in these passages is the tremendous, indeed absolute, authority every word of the Torah should have, since every word and phrase is the careful product of the divine Author. Not man alone but the existence of the whole created world hangs on the Torah, even on the proper place of a single word of it.[96]

It is important to recognize that this careful authorship is not limited to the Bible. " 'Thine eyes . . . shall behold a land stretching afar' (Is. 33:17) — that refers to Halakot which were in the mind (בדעתו) of the Holy One blessed be He nine hundred and seventy-four generations before the world was created."[97] "Halakot", as we shall see, is a technical term for the laws derived and formulated by the Rabbis. In fine, God is the Author of the whole Torah as it was conceived by the Rabbis. The word Torah, in numerous places, is preceded by a possessive pronoun — "His" or "Thy" or "My"— indicating the divine authorship, which, in fact, gives Torah its character.[98]

God revealed the Torah directly to Israel at Sinai, and Israel accepted it.[99] He chose the wilderness of Sinai that He might grant the Torah in public, for the whole world to know;[100] and there gave them the Ten Commandments.[101] This was, apparently, the only part of the Torah given directly to all of Israel, in public. God Himself wrote and gave the Ten Commandments, an idea that the Rabbis express by forming an Aramaic notarikon from the letters of the first word אנכי: "I Myself wrote (the Ten Commandments); I gave (them)".[102] Again to emphasize their authorship, the Rabbis, taking Deut. 33:2 literally, declare that the Torah was given with His right hand,[103] and raise the question whether it was not also written with His right hand.[104]

At Sinai Israel received far more than the Ten Commandments, though the rest was given indirectly with Moses as the intermediary. "Moses . . . went up on high and received the Torah;"[105] and he seems to have acted as the amanuensis: "Did I (God) not write thus in the Torah through Moses . . . ?"[106] Israel, as the Bible tells us, feared and trembled and asked Moses to teach them, saying to him, "Speak thou . . ." (Exod. 19:16, 19; 20:18, 19),[107] whereupon Moses first reassured them and then placed before them the laws of damages and all civil laws.[108] Moses, then, besides writing the Torah at the dictation of God, also taught it in detail to Israel.

As transcribed by Moses, the Torah is perfect. The Rabbis were fully aware that there is much repetition in the Bible, but they did not, of course, attribute this to the presence of various versions. Instead, they declared that it is a rule "that the words of the Torah are everywhere given twice", listing a large number of examples, most of them laws in Exodus that are repeated in Deuteronomy, though showing other examples as well, including one from a Prophet, Ezekiel, which introduces the whole discussion.[109] This repetition, say the Rabbis, was made necessary because of the recalcitrancy of Israel: "You render them (i. e., My words) commands that are not commands, (and make of) gatherings no gatherings. I commanded you when you went out of Egypt (i. e., in the Book of Exodus); I commanded you in the book of reproofs (i. e., Deuteronomy). I gathered you together four hundred and eighty years, until the Temple was built; again I gathered you together four hundred and ten years, after the Temple was built."[110]

None of the forty-eight prophets who prophesied to Israel, including Moses, ever added any law by his own authority to those written in the Torah.[111] The Torah, with its laws and commandments, proceeds entirely from divine authority.

There are two great divisions in Torah: one is called "the written Torah" (i. e., the Bible), and the other, "the oral Torah", transmitted by tradition. Our text puts it that "there is twice Torah".[112] This oral Torah, the Mishnah,[113] was the subject of an argument between one of our authors, and a man, evidently belonging to an heretical sect that disputed the divine authority of the oral Torah, who knew Bible but no Mishnah. Our author's argument makes clear how the Mishnah derives from the Bible, and how, therefore, it shared in the latter's prestige. "He said to me, 'The Bible was given us at Sinai; the Mishnah was not given us at Sinai'. And I said to him, 'My son, were not Bible and Mishnah both given by God?' "[114] And thereupon our author presents his proofs, which consist of a parable, instances from his opponent's own religious practices, and at the end the application of the parable. The parable has to do with a king who had two servants whom he loved dearly and to each of whom he gave a measure of wheat and a bundle of flax. The clever servant made bread out of the wheat and a cover out of the flax; the foolish servant did not do anything. When the king came home and asked to see what he had given them, the clever servant was naturally preferred whilst the foolish one was left in shame. The application of the parable is withheld until after the man who knew Bible but no Mishnah made several important admissions. "I said, 'My son, if I find you in the midst of the Mishnah of the learned (i. e., acting upon it), your words will be false?' He answered, 'Yes' ". Upon inquiry, it develops that this man recites seven benedictions in the '*Amidah* of the Sabbath, and eighteen in that of the other days; that he recognizes the law that seven men should read the Torah on the Sabbath, and at *minḥah* on the Sabbath and on Mondays and Thursdays, three; that on the seven species of food he recites two benedictions and one on the other species; and that he recites four benedictions at grace after meals. "I said to him, 'My son, and do we have these (laws) from Mt. Sinai, and are these not but from the Mishnah of the learned? But when the Holy One blessed be He gave the Torah to Israel, He gave it to them only as wheat from which to make fine flour, and as flax from which to make a garment: It was given (for example) in general propositions followed by particular terms, in particular terms followed by a general proposition, in two general propositions separated by particular terms. It says (for illustration), 'And thou shalt bestow the money for whatever thy soul desireth' (Deut. 14:26) — that is a general proposition; 'for oxen, or for sheep, or for wine, or for strong drink' (*ibid.*) — those are particular terms; 'or for whatsoever thy soul asketh of thee' (*ibid.*) — that is another general proposition. This contains an inference drawn from a general proposition complemented by a particular term, and an inference drawn from a particular term complemented by a general proposition.' "[115]

We see in this exposition so admirably suited to the purpose, two grounds for regarding the Mishnah as having divine authority. Granting that the Bible possesses this authority, the practices of the people who observed the Bible and who, we infer, observed nothing that was not commanded by it, must also in some way derive from the Bible and must thus have had the sanction of divine authority. This argument blends into the second one in which several hermeneutical principles are presented, together with some illustrations, elucidating the method by which the Bible is interpreted, by which, in other words, laws may be derived from the Bible. The Bible contained all these laws implicitly; it has been worded in accordance with certain hermeneutic principles; and we have only to apply these principles in order to make explicit what has always been implicit. The Mishnah is the product of this authoritative interpretation, and hence, it also proceeds from God. Only the rabbinic interpretations can bring out the latent beauty and hidden implications of the Bible: "To what may the words of the Torah be compared? To the way in which when a skin is given a man, he tans it, stretches it, until it comes out a beautiful handiwork."[116] At Sinai God vowed that He would give them the complete, perfect Torah (תורה תמימה) —"everything arranged and ordered before them like goblets of water and tables filled with all the delicacies of the world."[117]

One of the three aspects of the oral Torah or the Mishnah are the Halakot. As ordinarily used, this term means the laws derived by the Rabbis without regard to their sources in the Bible.[118] Yet these laws are, of course, to be considered as imbedded in the Bible for they must be derived from it. " 'There is no speech, there are no words, neither is their voice heard' (Ps. 19:4) — that refers to Halakot,"[119] the Halakot, or laws of the Mishnah, being only silently present in the Bible, and it is only the rabbinic interpretation which evokes them. Now it is apparent why, as with the Bible, God had in mind Halakot nine hundred and seventy-four generations before the world was created.[120] The Halakot were implicit in the words of the Bible He had tested and explored.

Why were not these laws stated explicitly in the Bible? To another man "in whom there was Bible and no Mishnah" and who came and questioned the statement that washing of the hands is a biblical ordinance, our author gives this answer: "We have many matters, and they are important, and Scripture did not need to say them (explicitly). For this reason did He (God) impose them on Israel: He said, 'Let them (Israel) separate them (i. e., derive those laws from the Bible) in order to increase their reward.' "[121] This is not the only reason given as we may expect from explanations made after an historical process has long been established. There is the parable of a king who made a very small courtyard with an even tinier exit that led to the great plains where he held court, thus to test who it was that both loved and feared him and who it was that only feared him; and the application of the parable, understood from the proof-texts, is that he who only fears God remains with the Bible, but he who takes the trouble to emerge from that into the oral Torah both fears and loves Him.[122] Our text, then, gives two explanations — that Israel receives reward for deriving the laws and that the oral Torah was deliberately made difficult to derive in order to test Israel.[123] According to Seder Eliahu, the Mishnah, or more correctly, the laws of the Mishnah, were already well known in Israel by the end of the First Exile, at least: Referring to the generations who lived from the time the First Temple was destroyed to the time the Second Temple was built, our author says, "Were not the Torah, the Prophets and the Writings with them, and did they not discuss the dialectic of Torah (פילפול תורה) by means of them;" and then he further states emphatically that God did not leave a single thing in the world that He did not reveal to Israel.[124] The belief that the oral Torah, the dialectic of Torah, was contemporary in some sense with the written Torah has behind it some historical plausibility, as we can infer from the fact that a number of the laws in the Bible are extremely general and needed at once amplifying detail to be observed at all.[125]

As was noticed above, the oral Torah is not closed. In the World to Come, God and the righteous will engage in discussion on all branches of the oral Torah, "and they will say on the unclean that it is unclean and on the clean that it is clean — on the unclean as becoming it, and on the clean as becoming it."[126] And again: "Thus did the Holy One blessed be He say to Israel: My sons, study the Bible and study the Mishnah and increase (in study) thereof, until I Myself shall come and say to you on the clean that it is clean and on the unclean that it is unclean — on the unclean as becoming it, and on the clean as becoming it."[127] The oral Torah is thus conceived as not yet complete, final decisions being withheld until the World to Come.

The oral Torah is not closed, not only because God will ultimately render final decisions, but also because the learned here and now add to it by divine inspiration. Of a man who conducts himself in conduct and study according to twelve specified rules (which include kindness, devotion, great social sympathy and piety) it is said, "The Holy

Spirit is in his words";[128] and "every one of the learned in whom there is the word of Torah in truth and is concerned (literally, sighs) over the lack of glory of the Holy One blessed be He and over the dishonor of Israel all his days . . . the Holy Spirit is in his words."[129] We may remark that an indispensable condition to divine inspiration appears to be close application to the oral Torah already given. This is made even more clear in the following passage, partially quoted above: "Happy is the man that maketh himself like unto an ox for the yoke and like unto an ass for the burden, and sits and meditates upon the words of the Torah every day continually. Thereupon the Holy Spirit rests upon him and his Torah becomes an inalienable part of him. 'Happy are ye that sow beside all waters, that . . . the feet of the ox and the ass' (Is. 32:20)—'waters' refers to Torah, for it says 'Ho, everyone that thirsteth, come ye for water' (*ibid.* 55:1); what does 'beside *all* waters' mean? If a man studies the Torah, the Prophets and the Writings, and studies Halakot and Midrash and spends much time in study and little in business, thereupon the Holy Spirit rests upon him and his Torah becomes an inalienable part of him."[130] "All waters" refers to the Bible, Halakot and Midrash; and this list would seem to comprise the whole Torah since the word "all" is emphasized. We shall touch on this point later.

We may state, then, that the divine inspiration or the Holy Spirit descends upon him who has already absorbed Torah. What such a man initiates will have divine sanction. But he cannot initiate anything unless it be to find new interpretations in the Torah. As to him "that renews the words of the Torah", it is as though "they made him know (these things) from heaven."[131] To "renew the words of the Torah" means to find new interpretations in it as can be gathered when we are told that it is in the houses of study that the Torah "is renewed",[132] and that there are those "that renew the Torah every day continually",[133] an impossible feat unless it refers to the daily study which may bring forth fresh interpretations or new laws. Now when these interpretations or laws are valid, they are regarded as drawing forth meanings always implicit in the Torah; hence what has been discovered is divine truth, and the discoverer is thus speaking under divine inspiration, has been told these things "from heaven". Viewed from this angle, we can understand why the Rabbis, interpreting Jer. 4:20, say that "My tent" (i. e., God's) refers to the houses of study:[134] they are the abode of the Holy Spirit. The Rabbis, we have thus seen, considered divine inspiration to be limited in their own day only to new interpretations of the Torah as made by men expert in the dialectic of the oral Torah. The "unknown facts" which the term "Torah" covers are then in theory implied in the Torah from the first. Conversely, it appears therefore that what is not in the authoritative texts, or what cannot be validly derived by the rabbinical method of exegetical interpretation, is not Torah.

Let us conclude our sketch of the content and authorship of Torah by examining more closely the terminology used for the various divisions of Torah. The study of Torah is very often described by the phrase קרא ושנה in which קרא refers to the study of the written, and שנה to the study of the oral, Torah,[135] the phrase being a shorter form of קרא את המקרא ושנה את המשנה (he studied — lit., read — the Bible and studied the Mishnah).[136] When מקרא and משנה are used together in one phrase, the former refers to the written and the latter to the entire oral Torah.[137] There are times, also, when קרא stands alone and indicates the written Torah;[138] and when משנה by itself refers specifically to the laws and not to the entire oral Torah.[139] Another designation for the written Torah is the one enumerating its three large divisions — the Torah, the Prophets and the Writings (Ketubim).[140] The whole Torah, written and oral, with its main divisions is given in the phrase משנה מדרש הלכות (or מקרא) תנ"ך ואגדות.[141]

Now although the full phrase, enumerating all the divisions, occurs most often, at other times when it is obviously desired to denote the entire Torah, only a partial list is given. Thus where the Rabbis describe the learning of David,[142] Elijah and Elisha,[143] the righteous in the World to Come[144] and the learned of their own day,[145] the phrase given is משנה הלכות ואגדות (or מקרא) תנ"ך. This is possible because some of the divisions overlap. The Mishnah is a general term for the whole oral Torah; and its three main divisions are Midrash (מדרש), Halakot (הלכות) and Agadot (אגדות).[146] Midrash is the interpretation of the Bible together with law which results from the interpretation;[147] Halakah, the plural of which is Halakot, is the law itself without the interpretation;[148] and the Agadot contain all the matter of the oral Torah that is non-legal[149] — moral instruction and the theology we have been studying, as well as other matters. Hence it is possible for "Midrash" to be left out at times if the rest of the terms are present, or for "Mishnah" to be omitted under the same conditions, and even for both to be omitted, for the content of the oral Torah would still be mentioned in either case.[150] It is, indeed, possible to mention only the Bible, Halakot and Midrash and still refer to the content of the whole Torah,[151] for Midrash may include Midrash Haggadah, agadic interpretations of Scripture also.

The term "Talmud" (תלמוד) occurs four times in our text, and it is hardly possible to say that it is equivalent to Midrash in those contexts.[152] "One hundred answers of Talmud"[153] must refer to questions raised upon the Mishnah of R. Judah; "Mishnah, Midrash, Halakot and Talmud and Agadot,"[154] is a phrase containing both terms; and "those that know Talmud" (בעלי תלמוד) are set over against "those that know Mishnah".[155] The fact, however, that this term occurs so seldom here ought to be ample proof that a large part of our text comes from mishnaic times. We ought to recognize also that in the second example the term is suspect, and that the last example quoted is from the "Additions", at one time part of the "Talmud" of the "Baraita" of our Seder.[156]

We can, at the last, offer a definition of Torah more adequate than before. Torah is a fundamental concept of the utmost significance to the Rabbis; as a concept, it is a designation for the Pentateuch, the Prophets and the Writings, and Mishnah, Midrash, Halakot and Agadot — for each division, each book, each verse, statement or law, as well as for all collectively. The Bible is the written Torah; Mishnah, Midrash, Halakot and Agadot constitute the oral Torah; and both the written and the oral Torah have been revealed by God, the latter indirectly. As a concept or generalization, Torah includes individual things to be known in the future: God will give final decisions ultimately, and meanwhile the properly qualified learned can, by divine inspiration, discover new interpretations of Torah. But the new decisions and interpretations are all implied in the Torah in the first place, since that gives them validity or the right to be included in Torah. What is not now included in or derivable from the authoritative texts mentioned, hence, is not Torah. The term "Torah" as used by the Rabbis ordinarily refers to the study of and instruction in Torah though it can also convey the idea of practice of the *miẓwot* of the Torah.

From all this we can gather that the word "Torah" strictly applies only to the Bible and to the rabbinic studies (including laws) we have mentioned and also to new interpretations which are the result of the rabbinic dialectic. It is not enough to say without further qualification that the distinctive feature of Torah is that the Rabbis regarded it as knowledge given by God. All knowledge, including the skills necessary for a livelihood,[157] were conceived as being the gift of God. Torah is that particular kind of knowledge revealed by God to Israel at Sinai, recorded in the Bible and interpreted by the Rabbis. This does not, however, complete the definition of the term "Torah." We shall find an additional characterization in the section, "The Efficacy of Torah," and still further implications in the next chapter.

III. The Study of Torah[158]

When one engages in the study of Torah, he lifts himself, as it were, from man's estate to perform a function of God's. "The Holy One blessed be He, the King of the kings of kings . . . one-third of the day He studies Bible and Mishnah . . . "[159] The knowledge of Torah, together with the practice of the virtues, effects a change in the status of an Israelite and, though not of the priestly caste, he becomes a very priest of God: "he becomes worthy to offer up a burnt-offering upon the altar."[160] The study of Torah imparts to a man spirituality and gives his life a divine purpose.

The Rabbis regard, therefore, the study of Torah as one of man's primary duties. They view the good life as consisting of Good Deeds, but they generally link the admonition to do Good Deeds with the admonition to engage in "the study of Torah", an association which, as we shall see later, is not fortuitous. "Thus has the Holy One blessed be He said to this (i. e., every) man: My son, (during) the days that I have placed thee upon the face of the earth, do thou Good Deeds and (engage in) the study of Torah, and keep thyself far from transgression and from an unsightly thing."[161] Such injunctions, urging both the doing of Good Deeds and the study of Torah, are scattered throughout the Midrash, whether in a guise similar to the passage just quoted,[162] or as an explanation of how man can "acquire his Father in Heaven"[163] or as rising out of the contemplation of man's function in the world and his destiny.[164] Nevertheless, though it be true that the direct injunction to study Torah occurs but seldom by itself,[165] this by no means indicates that the study of Torah is aught but of primary importance. The discussion which now follows is an attempt to describe how all-important, all-pervasive was the study of Torah: It offered the greatest joy, demanded complete dedication to itself, shaped careers, permeated manners. Finally, in the next section, when we come to consider the efficacy of Torah, we shall be able to see from another aspect why the study of Torah loomed up as so important in the Rabbis' view.

The study of Torah was, to the Rabbis, a means of delight without end. So great was the joy they apparently felt when at study that they conceive the bliss of the World to Come in terms of it. The occupation of the righteous in the World to Come will be "séance" (ישיבה), and they have already been given "a portion of study" in this world.[166] It is in study at the synagogue and houses of study where the Torah is renewed that one can find new joy daily.[167] From an analysis of the statements in which the Rabbis urge this joy upon us or give expression to it, its source would appear to be two-fold. It rises in the first place, from their conviction that the Author of the very words and phrases over which they pored is God. To prize any other joy but that of Torah — the joy of "silver and gold and precious stones and pearls", for example — is to prize something ephemeral, for that joy ends with a man's death; therefore, "What joy can a man have in this world? Solely in the words of the Torah."[168] And because God is the Author of Torah, there enters into the joy of its study a mystic element, a consciousness of a reciprocal joy on the part of Torah: "For just as Israel do the Torah in this world and rejoice in it so the Torah rejoices in them forever."[169]

This intimate apprehension that Torah was indeed the word of God was, however, only one of the factors contributing to the joy of its study. Always strengthened by this factor, no doubt, the joy partook also of the zest to be found in keen mental activity. The Rabbis in describing the delights experienced in the study of Torah must perforce have recourse to analogies drawn from the enjoyments and satisfactions of the physical senses, as is generally the case when we attempt to tell of mental delights; but these very analogies reveal the vividness and demonstrate the reality of the sheer mental, intellectual joys they experienced. They are particularly fond of depicting the joy of the study of Torah in figures which call up the delights of exquisite foods — old wine, delicacies, dainties. "Better is the pondering over the words of the Torah and the words of wisdom . . . than the old wine of a king (kept in) hidden chambers;"[170] the Torah given to Israel was "like goblets filled with water . . . and tables full of all the delicacies of the world;"[171] and for the divisions of Torah the Rabbis find apt the rich allusions to food in Song of Songs 5:1 — "my myrrh with my spice" is taken to refer to the Torah, the Prophets and the Writings, "my honeycomb with my honey" to Midrash, Halakot and Agadot, and "I have drunk my wine with my milk" to Good Deeds and the study of Torah.[172] It is the love they bear the Torah and the joy they find in it that also prompts the Rabbis to compare it to a woman.[173]

The study of Torah brings joy into men's affairs and human relationships. It enhances the feeling of brotherhood among two brothers who dwell and study together.[174] It helps to make the Sabbath holy, to make it joyous.[175] It brings consolation to those who have reason to despair: When Israel despaired after the incident of the spies, God told Moses to console them "with words of the Torah."[176] It was but natural, then, that the Rabbis should be grateful for this joy and should urge a similar gratitude on the part of all who study. "When a man studies the Torah, the Prophets and the Writings and knows (sufficient) to answer (questions) about them, he should keep them in his hand (i. e., remember them) and bless and praise and magnify and exalt and sanctify the name of Him who spake and the world came to be, the Holy One blessed be He. And there is no need of saying regarding him who studies Halakot."[177]

If a man ought to thank God for the knowledge of Torah acquired, it is because at bottom such knowledge is a gift from God. That is to say, not only the ability to study but the actual acquisition of the content of the Torah are precious bounties from God. "If you have done for Me My will in My Torah every day continually, I will give you full speech in clear Torah (i. e., Torah that is clear to you) so that no one will be able to upset them (i. e., your words)."[178] Despite Israel's sins, which indeed God passes over and forgives, He never "withholds from them the words of the Torah."[179] The Midrash frequently declares that it is God who in His mercy gives the learned their "study of Torah" as well as, incidentally, their Good Deeds;[180] and from the context, "the study of Torah" seems to connote both application to studies and knowledge of the contents of the studies. Of course, this divine gift is at its rare highest when, as the result of merit, the Holy Spirit rests upon the learned.[181]

To every man with normal capacities, however, God has granted the possibility to study Torah. Far from being the intricate, esoteric knowledge open to the privileged few, Torah calls into play but the ordinary capacities every man exercises in his every-day calling; and it is upon this fact that the duty to study Torah from which no one is exempt, and of which we have spoken above, is based. One of our authors met a man who scoffed and mocked, apparently arrogant in his ignorance of Torah, and who, when asked how he could answer to God for his neglect of Torah, replied, "My master, I have arguments (דברים) that I can offer to my Father in heaven on the day of judgment: I can say to Him, 'Discernment and knowledge were not given me from heaven.'" Our author, however, finding that the man was a fisherman said, "My son, if to throw nets and to bring up fish from the sea, discernment and knowledge were given thee, for the words of the Torah concerning which it is written 'But the word is very nigh unto thee' (Deut. 30:14) — (for them also) were not discernment and knowledge given thee?" The argument in this instance seemed to have been effective for the fisherman grieved and wept, and the Rabbi comforted him.[182] Nonetheless, the Rabbis were quite aware that the intellectual effort required in the study of Torah is beyond the capacity of a number of people. They speak with compassion of those "who come to Bible and Mishnah and have no understanding", including them among "the sad who nevertheless are to be presumed upright" (בחזקת כשרין);[183] and we have seen that they make certain provisions for the *'am ha-areẓ* so as not to deny him the reward of Torah.[184]

But indeed mental ability at best is no sure guarantee in the study of Torah. The study of Torah is a gift from God, and "Pray thou (lit., plead for the mercy) that the words of the Torah enter and become part of thee".[185] Prayer for knowledge of Torah can come with good grace only if certain other, moral, efforts have been made.[186] Because such prayer can only rise out of deep longing and long and earnest effort at study, there must of necessity be the type of man who himself is bound to feel that he "has not merited to pray that the words of the Torah enter and become part of himself."[187] Such an attitude toward the study of Torah prevents its becoming either the sport or the pride of scholars. It is, rather, in harmony with the entire concept of Torah, adding the theme of man's humble longing to that of divine inspiration and the one of human dependence to that of God's beneficence, and as overtones calling up again at once the pure joy and inexorable obligation of the study of Torah.

Since knowledge of Torah is a gift from God, a man must measure up to certain requirements in order to be worthy of it. In the several passages we shall consider we shall notice that the number of these requirements varies, but there is complete agreement as to the kinds of standards enumerated. Besides the technical qualifications and methods of study that are mentioned as necessary, the Rabbis insist upon the highest ethical qualities as prerequisites for the acquisition of Torah. In fact, the impression is left that the ethical and religious qualities required are, if anything, more emphasized by the Rabbis than the methods and aids to study; and this, of course, is what we should expect regarding a study the prime motive of which is not intellectual.

One passage enumerates twelve rules of study: "A man should conduct himself according to twelve rules: A man should be pleasant in entering (the house of study); pious in sitting (at study); 'inventive' (ערום) in fear (of God); wise in Torah; clever (פיקח) in (the doing of) Good Deeds; pleasant and agreeable to people; and acknowledge the truth; and speak the truth in his heart;[188] and 'confess and forsake' (evil ways);[189] and love the Holy One blessed be He with an absolute love whether He do good to him or whether He do evil to him; and grieve over the lack of glory of the Holy One blessed be He and over the lack of glory of Israel, all his days; (and) desire and long and expect that the glory of Jerusalem and the glory of the Temple and the glory of the House of Israel sprout speedily, and (long etc.) for the gathering of the Dispersions. (As to such a man), the Holy Spirit (will be) in his words."[190] The last sentence need not lead us to believe that these qualities were demanded only of the exceptional man, for this passage apparently is followed by a "commentary" which closes with the warning that each of these twelve rules brings with it reward if observed and punishment if not, a warning certainly addressed to the average man. The list by itself, without commentary, is characterized by an almost total absence of technical requirements, being largely an enumeration of ethical and religious qualities.

Apparently a vindication of Ginzberg's theory regarding the composition of our Seder, there follows immediately upon the selection we have quoted what appears to be commentary material.[191] Beginning with the first rule "A man should be pleasant in entering", the commentary adds "— the house of study, that he may be beloved Above and desirable below and in the eyes of people, in order that he may fulfill his days;"[192] and the commentary continues in the same vein to explain the second rule as referring to the house of study, adding again the need to be beloved Above and below.[193] Then there follow injunctions to increase the study of Torah, to ask questions in study and to respond to questions in order both to increase one's wisdom and to keep from drowsing in the house of study which is indeed a most evil trait and which is also brought about by (much) food and drink.[194] The rest of the commentary is in poor condition textually, but according to Ginzberg's reconstruction of it,[195] the student is further urged to pray that his transgressions — eating and drinking to excess — be forgiven him, and only then to pray that the words of the Torah enter and become part of him; and not to be too bashful to ask for the explanation of a biblical verse, if he is a student of Bible, or for the explanation of the *halakah*, if he is an advanced student. If these rules are followed, the commentary adds, the student will both understand and retain his studies.[196] It is worth noting that, in contrast to the

"Baraita" the commentary pays great attention also to technical matters and aids to study. Remembering that angelology and pictorial vividness are also far more characteristic of commentary than "Baraita",[197] and bearing in mind the attention to the more technical rules displayed here, may we not conclude that the commentary reflects the more literal-mindedness of the later generations while the "Baraita", both holding the concepts more abstractly and the ethical ideals more clearly, reflects the temper of the earlier generations?

Another list sets the number of requirements necessary to acquire the knowledge of Torah at forty-eight. Fixing a number was probably a way of intimating that the requirements demanded were rigorous and that Torah could not be acquired in easy-going, slipshod manner, as the very comparisons in the introductory statement would indicate: "Torah is greater than the priesthood or kingship, for kingship demands thirty qualifications and priesthood twenty-four, but Torah is acquired through forty-eight."[198] The passage continues: "And they are: By study, by the listening of the ear, by the ordering of the lips (i. e., by distinct pronunciation) by the understanding of the lips (?),[199] by the discernment of the heart, by intelligence (?),[200] by awe and fear, by humility, by joy, by attendance on the learned, by cleaving to associates, by sitting (at study),[201] by Bible and by Mishnah, by *Derek Ereẓ*, by little sleep, by little pleasure, by little *Derek Ereẓ*,[202] by little business, by long-suffering, by a good heart, by trust in the learned, and by acceptance of chastisements;[203] and (he must be a man) that knows his place,[204] and that rejoices in his portion, and that makes a fence for his words, and that does not claim merit for himself; and (he must) love God (מקום), love mankind, love reproofs, love righteous things, and keep aloof from honor [and not pursue honor],[205] and not grow arrogant because of his study, and delight not in giving decisions;

(and he must be a man) that bears the yoke with his associate,[206] and over-balances him on the side of merit (i. e., in judgment) and establishes him upon truth and upon peace, and that is composed (מתישב) at study, that asks and answers, that learns in order to teach, and that learns in order to practice, and that makes his teacher wise, and that is accurate in transmitting his tradition,[207] and that reports a thing in the name of him who said it."[208]

We cannot help but notice in the passage above differences in style between the various sections, indicating a composite authorship. Yet in all the sections the qualifications given are both ethical and technical, with the ethical dominating in the latter half of the passage. Technical aids to thorough study are, of course, necessary requisites, but all our authors recognize that these must be supplemented by high moral and religious virtues. Indeed, the technical requirements are only so many details calculated to focus the student entirely upon his studies and demanding a devotion so intense as even to lead to a number of ascetic rules. That passionate earnestness common to both the ethical and technical qualifications infuses the latter with the spirit of the former so that in many instances there is no clear distinction between the two. What we gather, in fine, is that the acquisition of Torah is possible only for him who is willing to expend the most strenuous effort upon it, spiritually.

We have observed, however, that in these lists the rules for the study of Torah may be classified largely into ethical, technical and ascetic. When the Rabbis elaborate on the conduct requisite for study their homilies on this subject can also be grouped roughly into the same three large divisions. For greater emphasis, they repeat in different phrases and shadings the same need for moral conduct as a requisite for study: "A man should do Good Deeds, and then ask for Torah from God; a man should do the deeds of the righteous and upright, and then ask for wisdom from God; a man should seize the way of humility, and then ask for understanding from God."[209] "If you want to study and you desire the words of the Torah", take an example from Israel who when they went out of Egypt with but dry crust did not question His ways but were "upright in the way",[210] and who apparently heeded Moses' command to separate themselves from transgression and "an unsightly thing" (i. e., from sin) that they might be pure when they stood at Sinai.[211] In the last homily there is also implied, perhaps, that he who studies Torah now may be compared in that respect to the generation that received it at Sinai.

There is one moral pitfall, lurking in learning itself, against which the scholar must be particularly warned, and that is the tendency to become proud of his learning. "Do not seek greatness and do not covet honor."[212] Prov. 24:30–1, verses which speak of the slothful man, the Rabbis take to refer to him who has become proud of his knowledge of Mishnah, and they declare that in the end he will lose that knowledge.[213] Pride of learning, then, according to this interpretation, is a sin that soon brings with it its own punishment for it is bound to lead a man into slothful habits. A moral weakness, here, entails the loss of a technical requisite, diligent study. Citing the case of Hezekiah, the Rabbis say that one who actually boasts "with (his knowledge of) the words of the Torah" is in danger of being "uprooted from the world".[214] The proper way is to be humble with regard to one's knowledge of Torah and in all one's social relationships.[215] Far from making a display of learning, a man should study Bible and Mishnah in a modest, secret place,[216] and indeed should do all good things — Torah, charity —"in secret".[217]

Technical requirements in addition to those mentioned in the two lists of general rules for study already considered are very few. In still another list which enumerates virtues whereby man may acquire this world and the World to Come, those that have reference to study are the following: attending lectures at an academy, engaging little in business, attendance on the learned (i. e. studying under them), the *pilpul* of the students.[218] The only requirement apparently not mentioned before is "the *pilpul* of the students", but this has been expressed above in the phrase "that asks and answers".[219] To one essential, however, in the study of Torah the Rabbis return with repeated insistence, to the necessity for memorizing carefully what has been studied. This is understandable in view of the fact that so much of Torah consisted in law and in a knowledge of the traditions which had to be at the fingers' tips of the students if the discussions were to prove fruitful. "Happy is the man who possesses the words of the Torah and who keeps them safely (lit., in his hand) and knows (how) to give a proper answer concerning them."[220] "When a man studies, he should seize it in his hand (i. e., make it permanent with him) lest shame and confusion overcome him when they tell him, 'Stand and recite the Bible you have studied; stand and recite the Mishnah you have studied' ".[221] Unless one makes a practice of constantly going over these studies, one is bound to forget them. Rabbi Ishmael the son of Elisha, no doubt as a result of his experience with students, declares, "What a man learns in ten years he can forget in two".[222] That this dictum has bearing upon what he himself taught, the Mishnah, is evident from the amplifying details with which he supports it: "If a man sits ten months without studying Mishnah, he says on what is clean (ritually) that it is unclean and on the unclean that it is clean; twelve months without studying Mishnah, and he confuses the authorities with one another; eighteen months without studying Mishnah, and he forgets the chapter headings; twenty-four months (without studying), and he loses (even) the headings of his tractates. The end (will be) that he will sit and be silent."[223] The prayer the

Rabbis attributed to Jabez—"that I forget not my learning"[224]— we may well imagine to have been frequently on their own lips.

The ascetic life is a favorite topic with the Rabbis, if by asceticism we mean not only the strict limitation of physical needs but the submergence of the whole self in dedication, perhaps even in immolation, to Torah. For in this Midrash, there is no mention of asceticism as such, that is, asceticism is not held up as an ideal for its own sake. The ascetic way of life is praised, indeed advocated, by the Rabbis, but only because it is a requisite to the intensive study of Torah. They do not favor bustling business activity, for example, not because they regard it as evil but for the reason that it is a distraction from study. "Happy is the man that studies much at an academy and troubles much (in study), and lessens (his) business activity, (that) sits and meditates on the words of the Torah every day continually."[225] If they urge a man to leave everything — even if he have one hundred houses and one hundred vineyards and fields — it is only that he may go to the places where Torah is studied and renewed.[226] Observing, most likely, that scholars are not often successful in business, the Rabbis declare that such scholars have been the recipients of divine favor: God does not allow these disciples of the learned to prosper, lest becoming wealthy they will also become remiss in the study of Torah; hence, when a scholar does not acquire wealth it is a sign that "the Holy One blessed be He loves his (study of) Torah."[227] Again, here wealth is not despised as evil in itself but is felt to be undesirable because it tempts men to forsake their studies. That the Rabbis do not advocate a life of poverty as a religious ideal is clear from the proof-text attached to the very homily we last cited —"Two things have I asked of thee . . . . give me neither poverty nor riches . . ." (Prov. 30:7–9).[228] Rabbinic theology, it appears, does not make that great dichotomy between matter and spirit that is so striking a characteristic of Greek thought and that informs the ascetic ideals and practices of the Church. Poverty instead of a desideratum is, in the sane view of the Rabbis, an unmitigated evil if it forces the learned to rely on others for their livelihood.[229] The motive for the ascetic regimen being the study of Torah, the ideal of the Rabbis was probably expressed by R. Judah the Prince on his deathbed: "I have worked only sufficient for my sustenance (כדי חיי), and I engaged in Torah all the days of my life."[230]

To what extent are worldly pursuits incompatible with single-hearted devotion to the study of Torah? One opinion verges on the extreme of asceticism. "This is the way of Torah: A morsel of bread with salt shalt thou eat, and water by measure shalt thou drink and on the ground shalt thou sleep, and a life of hardship shalt thou live, the while thou toilest in the Torah."[231] So averse is Jewish tradition to such extremes of asceticism that a very old commentary declares that the passage teaches that a man even when reduced to this economic level must not let that interfere with his study of Torah.[232] If, unlike the commentary, we do not disregard the mandatory tone in the passage, we ought perhaps to interpret it as meaning that a man should confine himself to the bare necessities of existence so as to devote his energies exclusively to the study of Torah. With this interpretation the statement conforms in spirit to others which enjoin an ascetic regimen in food and drink and sleep. He who eats much and drinks much "impoverishes" himself in Torah, and so, also, he that loves sleep,[233] for "the words of the Torah are devoured only by him who is (physically) weary because of them."[234] Here the Rabbis seem to imply that the indulging of appetites brings with it a loss in that self-control and self-discipline required by the rigid adherence to an intensive program of study; and this sentiment is certainly shared by the homily we described as on the verge of extreme asceticism. Present also is an admonitory undercurrent against the time and attention taken away from study and wasted in excessive eating and sleeping, an admonition made more explicit when we are told that food and drink bring to slumber.[235] Every purpose, then, behind the rabbinic advocacy of ascetic practices relates to Torah, be it in order to avoid distractions, to strengthen self-control or to dedicate all time and attention to Torah.

Asceticism, in the rabbinic view, consists in the dedication of the total personality to the study of Torah to the almost complete exclusion of other interests. Expressed in detail, as we have just learned, it is also compressed often into a principle couched in a picturesque metaphor: "Happy is the man that maketh himself like unto an ox for the yoke and like unto an ass for the burden, and sits and meditates upon the words of the Torah every day continually."[236] Almost immediately there follows a recognition of the tremendous strain and self-denial this principle involves, for the next homily continues in the same vein: "Happy is the man that wears himself down (through laboring) in the words of the Torah, and that sits and plows in them like the cow plowing in the field."[237] It is evident that for men animated by this principle no sacrifice can be too great though it lead even to self-immolation.

And such a sacrifice, such an extreme demonstration of devotion, is in truth demanded of him that would acquire the knowledge of Torah. This knowledge we have seen is a gift, given by grace and not gained only by mere labor. To the student who was not expert in Halakah and who complained that despite his longing, Torah eluded him, one of our authors replied in language reminiscent of that "picturesque metaphor" we have just quoted: "My son, no man merits the word of Torah unless he has offered himself for the glory of Heaven (even) unto death — like unto the ox upon whom they place the yoke and who offers himself for the sake (lit. glory) of his owner, to serve him."[238] "The Torah", another homily says, "is given only to him who suffers over it."[239] The noteworthy and meritorious element in suffering undergone for the sake of Torah consists in its voluntary character. Only those men, according to one opinion, will be revived after death who had "caused themselves and their very flesh to dwell in the dust in order to learn Torah"; and scriptural authority for this opinion is found in Is. 26:19, with שוכני, the active form, taken as indicating voluntary suffering.[240] And, again, it was because Israel alone of all mankind had proved willing to suffer over the Torah that they were given the Mishnah.[241] The extent of voluntary suffering for the sake of acquiring Torah is, as has been observed, to be limited by no consideration, not by that of death itself. Being voluntary, death as the result of the pursuit of Torah the Rabbis view as a kind of martyrdom, as being in a sense in behalf of God. "Even though he die on account of Thee, even though he be slain on account of Thee" refers to the man who "has studied the Torah, the Prophets and the Writings and studied Mishnah, Midrash, Halakot and Agadot and served the learned."[242] Voluntary death as a consequence of unremitting study of Torah is thus self-inflicted — it was David's wish that his portion be "with those who kill themselves over the words of the Torah"; but the proof-text here brings out the martyr-like aspect of such a death by ascribing it to God, and hence linking it, as it were, with death in behalf of God: "From those slain by Thy hand, O Lord, . . . whose belly Thou fillest with Thy treasure", etc. (Ps. 17:14).[243]

From asceticism we were led on to speak of martyrdom in this discussion with hardly a break in the continuity of subject-matter. Martyrdom in this connection is, in fact, only the ultimate form of asceticism. And this helps us to grasp the rabbinic conception of asceticism in the Seder from yet another angle. True martyrdom is never motivated simply by a cheap value placed on life itself; on the contrary, the high value of life is a measure of the still higher value of the thing worth dying for. Martyrdom, then, must point to a purpose immeasurably larger than just a disdain of the flesh; in this case, the purpose is the pursuit of Torah. But what has now been defined is not only martyrdom but the rabbinic conception of asceticism, as well. Asceticism practiced out of disdain for the body involves a doctrine utterly foreign to rabbinic thought. Asceticism practiced because there is a higher value — Torah — to which the body and its demands are subject involves a concept, Torah, integral to rabbinic theology.[244]

We have considered in some detail the requirements the Rabbis lay down for the study of Torah — ethical, technical and ascetic. One more, however, remains to be added, though it, too, has already been mentioned in the list of rules we have quoted above.[245] Not content with specific rules designed to engender the proper attitude toward the study of Torah, the Rabbis attempt also to describe the emotional state, the frame of mind, which is the very core of such an attitude. From what we know of the nature of Torah, of its divine origin and of the mystical aura with which it is surrounded, we have no right to expect a calm, dispassionate and objective attitude when it is studied. When the learned study Torah, they do so "for the sake of Heaven and (with) fear in their hearts."[246] "A man should study Torah with awe and fear, with trembling and shaking (for fear)."[247] Does this suppose that Torah is a weird and fearsome study? If Torah were indeed weird and fearsome it is passing strange that it should have been pursued so eagerly. And Torah was studied eagerly, hungrily. The very statement in which the words "awe" "fear" and "trembling" occur is an *inference* from the homily, "'Hunger' (Amos 8:11) — that refers to the words of the

Torah."[248] The contradiction is intensified when we recollect that the study of the Torah was to the Rabbis the one great source of permanent joy in the world.[249] The whole problem disappears, however, once we grasp what is meant by studying "for the sake of Heaven". The Rabbis, we have learned, felt that God manifested Himself primarily in His justice and loving-kindness.[250] To study Torah "for the sake of Heaven" is to study it with the ever-present consciousness of these two fundamental concepts. The awareness of God's justice is bound to evoke the emotions which are here described as "fear" and "awe", and especially so when studying God's laws and commands. The assurance of God's loving-kindness is no less certain to give rise to a feeling of supreme joy, and particularly so when communing with His authentic thought in study or when carrying out His direct wish in action. If there is a conflict between the two sets of emotions engendered, there is an equally clear logical contradiction between the two fundamental notions which are their conceptual parallels. But we have long ago seen that the unity in rabbinic theology is organic and not logical. A similar unity underlies the emotions the Rabbis felt at study, a unity that is a complex blend of several emotions, resembling in that respect the apparently conflicting emotions with which we react to what may be for us a momentous occasion or undertaking.

Can anyone still contend that the study of Torah was as stultifying as it was exhausting, cramping the spirit and mechanizing the mind of the Rabbis? This claim becomes ridiculous so soon as we discover what the knowledge and study of Torah means to the Rabbis themselves. A precious gift from God, the knowledge of Torah is granted only to them who merit it. The pursuit of Torah thus becomes charged with remarkably stimulating spiritual forces: It is a powerful incentive to measure up to the highest ethical standards; it demands a self-discipline amounting to asceticism; it leads even to martyrdom; it engages the profoundest of human emotions — ineffable joy and religious awe. In a word, the study of Torah was to the Rabbis an inward experience, a nexus of spiritual experiences that moulded their innermost being.

Nor does this tell the whole story. By means of the study of Torah there accrued to the Rabbis all that is ennobling in spiritual experience and but little of the merely eccentric and worse to which such experience is prone. For spiritual experience in most religions is seldom an unmixed blessing. Left to itself, uncontrolled, it may manifest itself in the most absurd of human vagaries and sanctify not only unsocial but anti-social behavior and utterly callous selfishness. If there be any virtue in the inner life, that virtue depends largely on the culture which conditions it, the inner life being the crucial, supremely personal apprehension of that culture. To the inner life of the Rabbis the study of Torah lent two inestimable advantages. A cultural undertaking requiring intense application and intellectual ability, the study of Torah organized and controlled the inner life and so disciplined that life as to exclude from it rank chimeras. And the ethical content of the studies further intensified and directed the spiritual life into positive social channels. In fine, the study of Torah concentrated the spiritual life in an exacting ethical and intellectual culture, instead of allowing it to expend itself in mere turbulence or grossness or sentimentalities. On the other hand, religious experience when not rooted in such an exacting culture may become a definitely anti-cultural force. Asceticism is an excellent case in point. Present in some degree in all forms of the religious life, elementary and advanced, asceticism has oftentimes broken forth in expressions so grotesque as to provoke disgust rather than admiration. The study of Torah, however, has not so much curbed asceticism as transmuted it into a potent cultural aid.

The study of Torah, widespread in Israel, necessitated schools for adults, every town no matter how small, possessing its *bet ha-midrash*.[251] The synagogue also served as a place of study at hours when services were not held, and the *bet ha-midrash* together with the *bet ha-keneset* are therefore spoken of as institutions for the study of Torah.[252] These institutions, however, were not merely buildings erected for the convenience of individuals who wished to study, for their institutional function was far deeper than that of convenience. The study of Torah, the Rabbis maintained, could not be carried on effectively by solitary individuals. It demanded the type of coöperative effort which has lately been described as "coöperative thinking"— in this case, perhaps, more accurately to be described as "coöperative learning". The Rabbis illustrate this coöperative function of the *bet ha-keneset* and *bet ha-midrash* by an analogy of ten men who came together, each bringing a different kind of food, and who, after pooling all the eatables they had brought and then dividing them equally, went away, each man in the possession of ten different kinds of food. Thus, also, there is the same interchange at the institutions of learning, each man coming with a verse from the Bible or an *halakah* or a saying and each man going away with ten verses, ten *halakot*, ten sayings.[253] A person engaged in private study however engrossing or valuable — be it even the study of *Ma'aseh Merkabah* (the mystical lore restricted to solitary study) — ought therefore "to drop all and go to the *bet ha-keneset* and *bet ha-midrash* and to every place where Torah is renewed," for it is there that he will find new joy every day.[254] The Rabbis regard Num. 24: 6 as a verse which refers to Torah since it speaks of "gardens by the river-side", and take it to be in praise of "even two or even three who are engaged in Torah every day continually."[255] Here we note again the high regard for coöperative study confined though that study may be to a minimum of persons.

It seems to have been the experience of the Rabbis that coöperative study — one is almost tempted to say "community study"— resulted in more than just an interchange of learning. The passage containing the analogy of the interchange of foods describes the *bet ha-midrash* also as the place "where Torah is renewed". Now this phrase, which occurs elsewhere in the Seder and usually in connection with the *bet ha-midrash*, we have found above to connote the new interpretations of Torah inspired by the Holy Spirit.[256] The *bet ha-midrash* had, therefore, a creative function. "Viewed from this angle, we can understand why the Rabbis, interpreting Jer. 4:20, say that 'My tent' (i. e., God's) refers to the houses of study:[257] they are the abode of the Holy Spirit".[258] In keeping with this creative function of the *bet ha-midrash* is the rabbinic conception of the great *bet ha-midrash* "of the future" in which God and the righteous will finally decide moot questions of law.[259]

The course of study was in a sense graded. The various divisions of Torah were studied in the order of their historical development, although, to be sure, the Rabbis did not have the notion of historical development we possess today. But they were aware, of course, of the distinction in time between the written and the oral Torah even if they did regard the latter as the unfolding of the former. Probably, also, pedagogic considerations of the increasing intricacy of the material affected the order of the subjects of study. They assigned the Bible to the youthful years and Mishnah, Midrash, Halakot (and Talmud) and Agadot to the mature years, since it is thus, according to the Midrash, that one's youthful and mature periods are made harmonious.[260] The stages of study can best be rendered in the Rabbis' own words: "If one has studied the Torah, let him study the Prophets; if he has studied the Prophets, let him study the Writings; if he has studied the Writings, let him study Halakot."[261] "If one has studied Halakot", continues the next homily after repeating the preceding formula, "let him study the Midrash on the Pentateuch, let him serve (i. e., study) in the academy . . ."[262] The last phrase is similar to that used to describe intensive study under the doctors of the law, "serving (i. e., studying under) the learned," the final stage of formal training in the Torah.[263] No division of Torah can be neglected, no stage of study omitted, without great loss. A measure of blame attaches to the man who has neglected the study of either Bible or Mishnah; even if he has studied both but has not "served the learned", his status is just average; only if he has studied Bible, Mishnah, Midrash, Halakot and Agadot and has "served the learned" has he measured up completely.[264] God, Himself, protects such a man whereas angels guard those whose meed has been less — one angel the man who has studied only the Pentateuch, two angels the man who has studied the Pentateuch, the Prophets and the Writings.[265] Another passage declares that he who has studied Bible but not Mishnah, or vice versa, "stands outside", meaning that he has not penetrated to the inner truth.[266]

Of the methods of study we have already spoken. The need, first of all, for knowing the subject-matter, for such clear knowledge "that no one can upset" your words,[267] called, as we have seen above, for thorough memorization.[268] But coöperative study demanded also much more than that. Because of the method of discussion, of "asking and answering",[269] carried on in the *bet ha-midrash*, the latter as both the symbol and institution of coöperative study was conceived to be indispensable for the spread and further probing of Torah.[270] And we have just learned that the same method and the same institution had a creative function as well. We must add here one more, incidental, fruit of the study of Torah. After a presentation or discussion of Haggadah in the *bet ha-midrash* some of the hearers would recite, "May His great name be blessed forever and ever" (a phrase found in the *Ḳaddish*), and others would respond with "Amen".[271] No doubt it is this doxology, or better, *Ḳaddish*, coming at the end of Agadot, that the Rabbis have in mind when they say, "the Agadot, through which they sanctify (שמקדשין) His great name".[272]

No day should pass without some time devoted to the study of Torah. "A man should not say to himself: I have studied Bible and Mishnah today, I do not need to do this again tomorrow".[273] From several passages, it appears that it was the custom to devote the study hours during the day to the written Torah and those during the night to the oral Torah. " 'Day unto day uttereth speech' (Ps. 19:3) — this refers to the Torah, the Prophets and the Writings",[274] meaning that the study of the written Torah, which goes on in the day-time, is carried on from day to day. That the oral Torah was studied at night can only be inferred from the homilies in Seder Eliahu. God Himself, we have learned, watches over the man who has fully studied both the written and the oral Torah, whereas only angels watch over him who has studied the written Torah alone. This is deduced from the verse "Watchman, what of the night?" (Is. 21:11), and the Watchman is taken to be "the Holy One blessed be He who watches over him in whom there are the words of Torah in truth".[275] The relation of the proof-text to the midrash hinges on the implication that the oral Torah, particularly, was studied at night. The same implication is to be found in another homily: The Rabbis interpret Lam. 1:2 by saying that God established "the night" as the weeping-time for Israel because "the night" symbolizes R. 'Akiba and his comrades whose death by torture is thus made the cause for age-long weeping.[276] The symbol of night for the creators and students of the oral Torah can be understood only on the basis of a prevalent custom of studying the oral Torah at night.[277] In still another homily, however, the implication that the oral Torah was studied at night is more direct. This homily declares that if one of the learned committed a transgression during the day it is likely that "he repented in the night, for it says, 'The Torah of thy mouth is better unto Me than thousands of gold and silver' (Ps. 119:72)".[278] Repentance at night and the study of Torah are considered to be in the case of the learned — the exponents of the oral Torah — one and the same thing; hence, the study of the oral Torah was at night. The division of day and night for the study of the written and the oral Torah, respectively, is not, however, true of the Sabbath. On the Sabbath day it was the custom to study both the Bible and Mishnah.[279] At all times the study of Torah by the Rabbis was never done in snatches but was long and sustained if we may judge from their advice that "Standing (when studying) is better than sitting without support."[280]

The knowledge of Torah imposes the obligation on one of teaching others, a kind of rabbinic version of noblesse oblige. We have already observed that, since the Torah contained the life-principle, he that teaches his fellow-man so much as one verse "it is as though he places life before him";[281] and that when a man studies Torah he must have the purpose in mind of teaching it.[282] The Rabbis consider the teaching of Torah tantamount to acts of charity toward those who are in dire want. To teach Torah is "to deal thy bread to the hungry"[283] and to cover the naked.[284] Analogies aside, however, there must be no discrimination either against the rich or the poor, and he "that teaches Torah in public" ought to teach Bible and Mishnah to both alike.[285] Nor should quarrels or grudges cause anyone "to withhold the words of Torah" from his fellow.[286] Instead, he should imitate God who forgives Israel and "does not withhold the words of Torah from them."[287] Nothing indeed should be allowed to interfere with the teaching of Torah since it satisfies one of the great basic needs of the community.

By the same token, the teacher of Torah is indispensable to every member of the community. "To what may he be compared? To the lower door-sill which all must tread upon, and (to) the beam (across the stream) over which all must pass, and (to) the tree in whose shade all sit, and (he is) like unto the candle which gives light of eyes to the multitudes."[288] In like vein, the teacher — he to whom those things (i. e., questions of law, etc.) are easy that are difficult to others — is one who is "like unto the sun that gives light to the multitudes, and like unto the moon that gives light to the multitudes."[289] The teacher of the community had, of course, to be properly qualified, no man having the right to teach Torah in public who had not studied Bible, Mishnah and Midrash.[290]

If there are inescapable obligations on him who has the capacity to teach, there are also some obligations on all who have the capacity to learn. To study with a teacher who comes to you at stated hours is not enough. Rather, "acquire" a comrade who will be with you and eat with you and teach you Mishnah and Bible and reveal to you "the secrets of Torah and the secrets of *Derek Ereẓ*". You cannot expect to receive all this free: "a comrade is not acquired except by money."[291] You must honor your teacher: "He that learns from his comrade a single chapter or a single *halakah* or a single verse, or even a single letter, must give him (the comrade) honor."[292] More, your reverence of your teacher must be so profound as to take on the aspect of awe: "If thou hast learned two or three chapters from him, fear him as a man fears Heaven".[293]

In a society where the learning of Torah was conceived as the main occupation, it is to be expected that unusual care and attention should be given to the education of children. The community saw to it that teachers were hired for the specific purpose of teaching the children, and these seemed to have had a certain professional standing.[294]

Parents went to all lengths, even denying themselves necessities, to provide for the instruction of their children. "Recall how many blind there are in Israel who have no food and yet give money that their children may study Torah!"[295] From the context of the term "master's house", mentioned several times, it appears that the school was in the teacher's home,[296] where "the little lads . . . engaged in Torah every day continually".[297] The latter phrase indicates that the training was limited to boys; the "yoke of the Torah" was not meant for women. The little boys entered the "master's house" at the age of five, and started with the Bible as soon as they had mastered the alphabet.[298] They began the alphabet itself auspiciously by learning first the letter ב, with which the word "blessed" begins, and then the letter א.[299]

Let us take a final glance at the way in which the ideal of the study of Torah affected rabbinic times. "Just as it is impossible for a man to be without bread and water even one day, so is it impossible for a man to be without words of the Torah even one hour".[300] R. Joḥanan, the son of BagBag, conveying the same idea without metaphors, adds to it a mandatory tone: "With it (i. e., the Torah) shalt thou be concerned, and from it shalt thou not stir, for there is no better way."[301] And indeed there seems to be hardly a situation in life where the ideal of the study of Torah had not penetrated. It persisted despite poverty and misfortune. We have observed how the poor and needy in Israel, flayed by the Nations, clung to the study of Torah, and how even the blind and lame went without bread that their children be taught Torah.[302] Wealth but provided the better opportunity for the sacrifice of worldly possessions to the ideal of the study of Torah. In a story which tells of how a certain rich man was judged by his employee "on the side of merit", that rich man, we are told quite incidentally, had vowed all his property to the Temple with the hope that there be instilled in his son the desire to engage in the Torah.[303] The ideal of the study of Torah determined for the learned where they would make their home. One of our authors, who came from Jabne, "a place of scholars and Rabbis", met a Ḳasdir who offered him wheat and barley and beans and linseed and vegetables of all kinds on condition that the scholar would dwell where he, the Ḳasdir, would show him. This was during a year of famine, but the scholar replied, "My son, even if you will give me a thousand thousand thousands of golden dinarii, I will not leave a place of Torah and go to a place where there is no Torah."[304] The study of Torah prepared a man for prayer: "Let no man stand in prayer (בתפילה) until he has studied (at least) one *halakah* or one verse (of the Bible)."[305] It imparted a cultured grace even to points of etiquette: "A man should never part from his comrade except with some word of Halakah, so that he may say, 'Remember so-and-so for good, for this *halakah* was firmly fixed by him.' "[306] On a lonely journey the study of Torah acts in the place of companions.[307] And after a man's death, his name survives, particularly if he had been poor, when his son reads the Torah in the synagogue or asks an *halakah* in the house of study, people saying, "Whose son is this man?"[308] The very variety of occasions in which there enters the ideal of the study of Torah is sufficient evidence of its wide-spread, far-reaching sway.

In this section we have learned that the Rabbis regarded the study of Torah as one of man's primary duties, and as a means of supreme joy, and the knowledge of Torah as a divine gift. Being a gift from God, the knowledge of Torah comes only to him who can measure up to certain requirements, both technical and ethical, with the latter predominant. Since the Rabbis also laid down certain ascetic requirements, there followed a discussion of the rabbinic view of asceticism. This view, we ascertained, has little in common with that asceticism which rises out of the conception of the dichotomy of mind and body. The Rabbis advocate asceticism only if it favors, and to the extent that it favors, the dedication of the total personality to the study of Torah, an utter devotion to the study of Torah that may even lead to martyrdom. We found that the Rabbis' description of the emotional state induced by the study of Torah — ineffable joy and religious awe — is consistent with the type of intellectual unity which is not logical but organic. After evaluating the inward spiritual experience and cultural discipline engendered by the study of Torah, we went on to discuss the institutions which this study necessitated. We learned also of the stress the Rabbis placed on coöperative study; of the course of study and methods of study; of the time of study for the written and oral Torah; of the obligations of teacher and students; and of the provisions for the training of children. Finally, we noticed the great variety of occasions in which the ideal of the study of Torah entered, indicating that there was hardly a situation in life into which it had not penetrated. "With it shalt thou be concerned, and from it shalt thou not stir, for there is no better way."

IV. The Efficacy of Torah

The knowledge of Torah, according to the Rabbis, directly influences man's behavior and conduct. Torah possesses, then, an immediate practical efficacy. Therein lies the explanation for the tremendous significance Torah assumes in rabbinic theology, that organic complex of concepts distilled from *experience*. Indeed, the great pragmatic value assigned to Torah in rabbinic theology is not only in harmony with the organic, experiential character of rabbinic thinking, but, for that very reason, offers another illustration of the difference between organic and logical thought. We have pointed out before that, in marked contrast to rabbinic theology, medieval Jewish philosophy negated the concepts of God's love and justice.[309] Medieval Jewish philosophy, if we take Maimonides' views as typical, also tends *in a measure* to negate the pragmatic efficacy of Torah. The primary function of the Torah, says Maimonides, is to inculcate right ideas, ideas having to do neither with "deeds nor with qualities of character, being purely ideas"; the Torah's function of promoting right conduct is secondary.[310] The Rabbis, of course, know of no such distinction. Maimonides' whole discussion and the concepts involved in it are utterly foreign to their way of thinking. Without recourse to philosophic niceties, they simply teach that Torah has practical efficacy in the affairs of life.

In the first place, a knowledge of Torah means a knowledge of the *mizwot* — commandments and laws — contained in the Torah. If your knowledge of Torah is sound "your very bones will be alert for *mizwot*," that is, you will seek opportunities for performing them.[311] Even the man who is taught but one verse of the Bible or but one *halakah* is, apparently, made alert for *mizwot*.[312] The knowledge of Torah, which means the knowledge of the *mizwot*, stimulates the individual to perform the laws and commandments he has learned.

From Torah man also learns to do Good Deeds. Later, when we come to consider in detail the two categories of *mizwot* and Good Deeds, we shall see what, if anything, distinguishes one from the other. Here it is sufficient to recognize that Good Deeds certainly refers to actions regarded as necessary to good conduct. And these actions, as we have said, result from a knowledge of Torah —"since a man comes to Bible and Mishnah and learns from them the fear of Heaven and Good Deeds."[313] "The end of all things," according to our Seder, "(should be) fear of Heaven and Good Deeds." From the context we see that by "the end of all things" is meant the purpose of study, and that "Good Deeds" here refers to respect for elders and parents.[314] The knowledge of Torah, moreover, is doubly effective. It not only influences a man to do *miẓwot* and Good Deeds, but prevents him from committing sins, as well. "If there is Torah in a man he takes care that he come not to transgression and sin,"[315] says one midrash. And another puts it thus: "If there are the words of Torah in a man he well knows that he must not come to transgression and to any unsightly thing."[316]

Further, from Torah Israel learns *Derek Ereẓ*. This term has a number of meanings but, again to anticipate a later chapter, in this connection *Derek Ereẓ* always means ethical conduct. "Blessed be the Omnipresent, blessed be He, who gave the words of the Torah to Israel that they may learn from them *Derek Ereẓ* in order that their sins should not multiply in the world."[317] Another midrash states the same thing with explicit reference to the story of "the concubine in Gibeah," thus equating a violation of *Derek Ereẓ* to sexual licentiousness. "At that time the Holy One blessed be He thought to destroy the entire world. He said: I gave My Torah to these only in order that they study (the Bible) and study (the Mishnah) and that they might learn from it (i. e., the Torah) *Derek Ereẓ*." In this instance, however, the Sanhedrin, whose duty it was to teach Torah, was derelict, thus allowing the people to remain ignorant of Torah which, in turn, made them capable of committing a heinous crime.[318] But knowledge of Torah is efficacious in producing individuals who act according to *Derek Ereẓ*.

Besides instilling in a man a general spirit that renders him alert for *miẓwot*, anxious to do Good Deeds, and heedful of *Derek Ereẓ*, the knowledge of Torah is efficacious in strengthening him against specific evil inclinations. "Happy are Israel! When they are engaged in Torah and in Deeds of Loving-kindness, their (*Evil*) *Yeẓer* is controlled by them and not they by their *Yeẓer*."[319] In this homily, the study of Torah is linked with Deeds of Loving-kindness, an implication that the study of Torah has already been efficacious. A similar implication is to be found in the statement that every one of the learned who studies Bible and Mishnah and is engaged in the Torah and repents and does Good Deeds, is saved from "ten powerful ones."[320] Since the chief characteristic of the learned is their knowledge of Torah — in fact, it accounts for the term which designates them — we must infer that both repentance and Good Deeds follow from it. Indeed, no inference is necessary: we have learned above that the study of Torah implies repentance,[321] and we have also just seen that it is productive of Good Deeds. But now to return to our homily. The "ten powerful ones," it goes on to say, are the various members of the body by means of which man is tempted and sins;[322] and he is made safe from these definite temptations and sins by the study of Torah. Immediately following this passage is another by the same authority, R. Simon the son of Joḥai, also enumerating temptations from which a man is saved by the study of Torah. Here, however, he "who (continually) has words of Torah in his mind" is said to be free not only of temptations but also of fear in any form; not only are thoughts of sin, of folly, of the *Evil Yeẓer*, of adultery, of a wicked woman, of idolatry, and of vanities "removed from him", but also thoughts (i. e., fears) of the sword (i. e., government — Friedmann, note #10) and of the yoke of flesh and blood.[323] The study of Torah is efficacious, then, in removing from the mind of a man both evil and harmful thoughts, in dispelling both temptations and fears.

Finally, the study of Torah has the power to purify a man of the sins he has committed: The houses of study have a cleansing effect analogous to the effect of rivers, for men enter into the houses of study "full of sins, mayhap, but go out of them clean."[324] We have met with this idea before when we found that Torah was a means to repentance or of reconciliation with God.[325]

We are now in a position to clarify several matters hitherto left obscure or else unexplained. One of these matters is the ambiguous use of the term "Torah." Friedmann, as we have observed above, erred in taking the term "Torah" to refer only to study since there are a number of passages in the book where it is employed unequivocally in the sense of "practice."[326] We concluded, after an analysis of these and other passages, that "although 'Torah' can convey the ideas of both study and practice, in the vast bulk of the statements where the term occurs it does have reference to the study of Torah."[327] Nevertheless, in all these statements, what definitely decides the meaning of the term is the context in which it is placed; where the context throws no light, the term "Torah" certainly appears ambiguous to us. And now we can account for its apparent ambiguity. The study of Torah is inseparable from the efficacy of Torah; in other words, the study or knowledge of Torah immediately implicates action, behavior, practice — the practice of *mizwot*, Good Deeds and *Derek Erez*. It was entirely natural, therefore, for the Rabbis to use the term "Torah" in a double connotation, the term standing both for the study of Torah and for the immediate pragmatic efficacy of that study. If this appears confusing or ambiguous to us, it is because the concept does not possess for us the same rounded and inclusive significance it had for the Rabbis.

But it is extremely important to grasp this inclusive meaning of the concept, and several passages in Seder Eliahu may help us to do so. In these passages both connotations of "Torah" are present at once, the study or knowledge of Torah being equated, in one way or another, with practice or conduct. Thus in one midrash, the contrast to the learned man who knows Torah — who "has in his mind a hundred thoughts of Bible, a hundred thoughts of Mishnah, a hundred sorts of answers on Talmud" and who can therefore be compared to Moses and Aaron — the contrast to such a man is one who "has in his mind a hundred thoughts of robbery and a hundred thoughts of incest and a hundred thoughts of murder," being like "Dathan and Abiram the wicked", the fomenters of strife.[328] Evidently, then, to the Rabbis the reverse of the knowledge of Torah is a bad character and evil conduct. Again, the generation or individual that "did Torah", an expression referring to the study of Torah,[329] are placed in contrast with the generation or individual that "did evil."[330] The Rabbis identify David with Adino the Eznite, who prevailed "against eight hundred, whom he slew at one time" (II Sam. 23:8). "He (God) said to him: David, My son, did I not write thus in My Torah that even if there are in you (i. e., Israel) no words of Torah but only *Derek Ereẓ* and Bible alone, then 'five of you shall chase a hundred', etc. (Lev. 26:8)? But if you do the Torah, and you do the Torah extensively (ותעדיפון את התורה), then one of you shall chase one thousand. But thou hast done My will, yet hast not done all My will — only in the matter of Uriah the Hittite (I Kings 15:5). Therefore there are lacking two hundred."[331] Notice that in this selection, "the words of the Torah" are apparently more inclusive than just "*Derek Ereẓ* and Bible"; that "doing the Torah" extensively (i. e., extensive study of Torah) is tantamount to doing the will of God; and that an evil act is not doing God's will—the underlying assumption throughout being that the value of the study of Torah and the value of practice and conduct are, so to speak, interchangeable. If we still need proof that to the Rabbis "Torah" spelt study and conduct simultaneously, the following homily ought to be convincing: "The Holy One says to him (that is, to the man who brings a meal-offering), 'My son, why didst thou not mingle thy deeds with words of Torah?' For 'oil' (one of the ingredients in the offering) refers to Torah and 'oil' refers to Good Deeds. For it says, 'Thine oils have a goodly fragrance' (Song of Songs 1:3) — (i. e.,) thy deeds have a goodly fragrance; 'Thy name is as oil poured forth' (*ibid.*) — . . . Thou hast poured forth for us words of Torah . . ."[332] Here the Rabbis seem to state in so many words that Torah and Good Deeds are equivalents. The way in which they derive this is interesting. The oil in the meal-offering is given a dual symbolic meaning, representing at the same time both Torah and Good Deeds, with biblical warrant consisting of successive phrases from the *same* proof-text. The double connotation conveyed by "Torah" simultaneously, of which all these homilies are instances, indicates the inclusiveness of the concept. We ought to remember, then, that not only are practice and conduct the effect of study but that, in this case, effect and cause are also almost identical, the efficacy of Torah being implicit in the study of Torah.

We must take care, however, lest in our attempt to comprehend the inclusiveness of the rabbinic concept of Torah we obliterate entirely the demarcations that do exist between study and practice. Torah and *mizwot*, we have learned above, are to be taken as two distinct categories when they are found together, and the same holds true for Torah and Good Deeds.[333] The Rabbis, of course, cannot help but recognize that study is one thing and practice, another. The study of Torah is, indeed, accounted as of infinitely greater worth than all the *mizwot* a single human being can accomplish in this world: "For all (the) *mizwot* that a man does in this world have power to give light as much as the light of a candle only, but Torah lights the world from end to end."[334] Now the fact that Torah and *mizwot* are thus contrasted, (and the fact also that these categories are so often found together), suggests that the contrast lies in a ground, a quality, common to both Torah and *miẓwot*, but in which quality Torah is far richer than *miẓwot*. The pragmatic efficacy of Torah, the quality by which practice is already implicit in study, is this common ground of contrast. The Torah is limitless in that quality because new derivations are always possible.[335] Moreover, it is never possible for one man to perform all the *miẓwot* already derived from the Torah, whereas he can absorb them, so to speak, by study. The Torah, then, is infinitely superior to *miẓwot* in the very quality that characterizes the latter, namely, conduct. Conduct, however, as we have learned in this section, is not summarized by *miẓwot* alone; *Derek Ereẓ* is also ethical conduct. And *Derek Ereẓ*, too, the Rabbis imply, is vastly inferior to the study of Torah, again apparently for the same reason that *miẓwot* are inferior. In a homily recently considered wherein the study of Torah was contrasted with *Derek Ereẓ* because of the quality common to both — conduct — the Rabbis speak of the study of Torah as of far greater consequence than *Derek Ereẓ*: "If there are in you (i. e., Israel) no words of Torah but only *Derek Ereẓ* and Bible alone, then 'five of you shall chase a hundred' etc. (Lev. 26:8). But if you do the Torah, and you do the Torah extensively, then one of you shall chase a thousand."[336] There are, then, demarcations between study and practice, one of them being that the study of Torah is greatly superior, because of its pragmatic efficacy, in just the very quality that characterizes practice itself.[337]

We can understand the Rabbis' view that the study of Torah implicates conduct if we realize that to the Rabbis Torah was *the* character-forming agency. By means of the study of Torah, as we have seen, a man not only learns to do what is right but becomes so tempered as to find it natural to do good and to avoid evil. Torah, then, renders good conduct and fine deeds implicit, so to speak, in a man's very personality, in other words, it ennobles and spiritualizes his character. Hence, that which is responsible for man's spiritual powers, the constant source of that spiritual energy so readily manifested on diverse occasions, is accounted as of greater worth than the manifestations themselves, latent as it is with infinite power yet to be evoked.

On the basis of the efficacy of Torah, we have accounted for the apparent ambiguity of the term "Torah". In the light of the same principle a few other matters stand more clearly revealed. We learned before that one of the means of repentance was the study of Torah, another illustration of the organic interdependence of the four fundamental concepts.[338] And now, when we know that conduct is already implicit in the study of Torah, the latter as a means of repentance is entirely understandable. By studying Torah the one who repents thereby demonstrates a complete change of heart and character, since he has, as it were, thus embarked on a new career of good conduct. Perhaps a particular instance of this type of repentance will give point to what we have just said. "If thou hast seen one of the learned commit a transgression during the day, on the morrow thou must not think evil of him, for he may have repented during the night (Torah is studied at night)."[339] Only if we recollect that the study of Torah implicates conduct can this homily be intelligible to us: The commission of a transgression is an act, and it is only by action of an opposite kind, righteous action, that the repentant sinner can demonstrate the change of heart and conduct that repentance involves.

This principle enables us also better to understand the relation between Torah and chastisement. In order to avoid chastisement one should study Torah.[340] Now chastisements are sent by God "to cause the sinner to change his ways."[341] But if it is true that conduct is implicit in the study of Torah then by engaging in the latter, the sinner has already demonstrated a change for good in his conduct, and has thus made chastisement unnecessary.

Rabbinic theology, it is now almost needless to repeat, is the result of the experience of the Rabbis, the integration and interpretation of that experience in the form of an organic complex of concepts. Of the vital dependence of rabbinic theology upon actual human experience we can have no finer example than the aspect of the efficacy of Torah which we shall now discuss. That the Rabbis believed in the pragmatic efficacy of Torah has been made abundantly clear; they even go so far as to believe that the study of Torah itself implicates behavior. And yet, ordinary human experience made it equally plain to them that this pragmatic efficacy of Torah is not inevitable. It is not impossible, even, for a man to be learned in the Torah and act the scoundrel. The Rabbis are aware of "the learned who study Bible and Mishnah" and who are not honest in their business dealings;[342] of the learned who quarrel with one another;[343] and of the hate engendered by scholastic jealousy, even those who know Mishnah hating sometimes those knowing Talmud.[344] In fine, the Rabbis realize that there are "men who come to Bible and Mishnah and are sullied with ugly ways and unseemly things," a euphemism for sins.[345]

The Rabbis certainly do not blink all these facts of experience which stubbornly arise to contradict the principle of the efficacy of Torah. Nor do they attempt in any wise to explain the contradiction away. As we have so often observed, the Rabbis are completely indifferent to logical contradictions if their conclusions square with the facts of experience. Here, as elsewhere, the contradiction seems to be rooted in human nature. No spiritual principle, that of the efficacy of Torah included, can ever function with the absolute inevitability of a physical law. Human nature has about it little of that logical predictability which characterizes physical nature.

The fact that spiritual principles do not function with absolute inevitability, instead of confounding or dismaying the Rabbis, is the ground of their moral concepts. It rests with man, for example, whether Torah shall or shall not possess efficacy. When a scholar is honest in his business dealings with men, he proves that the Torah has efficacy, and so sanctifies the Name; when a scholar deals dishonestly, he proves, as it were, that the Torah has no efficacy, and so profanes the Name.[346] Since the efficacy of Torah is not inevitable, and the onus is placed on man, knowledge of Torah simply means greater opportunity, greater impetus for right conduct; hence, "everyone who knows the words of Torah and transgresses them is an absolutely wicked (man)."[347] The rabbinic concepts of *Ḳiddush Hashem* and *Ḥillul Hashem*, and of the righteous and the wicked, themselves derive, in part, from the fact that the efficacy of Torah is not inevitable.

There is no absolute guarantee that knowledge of Torah will result in right conduct. But the Rabbis' experience was sound enough to teach them also that it is quite possible for men to be upright and to keep from sin whilst being ignorant of Torah. For the Rabbis know of the ignorant "in whom there are *Derek Ereẓ* and the rest of the *miẓwot*, who keep themselves far from transgression and from every unsightly thing;"[348] and ignorant men with these qualities they designate as upright.[349] A man may know neither Bible nor Mishnah, and be able to pray only the main prayers, and yet guard himself from sin.[350] When the Rabbis wish to illustrate an important ethical trait the hero of the story is a man ignorant of Torah —"even though he had not studied Bible and not studied Mishnah he was (nevertheless) of the men of Good Deeds (מאנשי מעשה)."[351] To say that it is possible for men to be upright without knowing Torah is not to deny, of course, that the Torah may have influenced their conduct, albeit indirectly. A community's traditions and the examples and standards set by the learned are certainly not without their effect upon the community at large. But, again, the Rabbis are not concerned with supplying rationalizations for their concepts. Their concern is with deepening and broadening the concepts proper, with finding additional situations to which these concepts apply. In this case, the upright conduct of many of the *'ame haareẓ* (the ignorant) furnishes material for the concept of justice.

In contrast to rabbinic theology, classic philosophy taught that the efficacy of knowledge was absolute and inevitable. It taught that knowledge was conduct, invariably. From the dogmatism which this principle fostered when it was adopted by the Church,[352] rabbinic theology was saved. For dogmatism is the necessary product of a religion committed to logical consistency, and is not a characteristic of a religion grounded in human experience.

V. Integration of the Other Fundamental Concepts with Torah

"No fundamental concept is found in complete isolation from the others. As a matter of fact, the (fundamental) concepts display a marked tendency to go in pairs, God's love and justice often interlacing with one another, as we might expect, but so also do Torah and Israel."[353] Torah and Israel are so integrally related that it is very difficult, actually impossible, to deal with them separately. In our endeavor to describe the concept of Torah, we were compelled throughout to make use of homilies in which Israel figures. The Torah was created one thousand generations before Moses for the sake of Israel; it was destined for them long before the world was created.[354] Both the written and the oral Torah were revealed to Israel at Sinai,[355] the oral Torah being only implicit in the written Torah for the sake of Israel.[356] The oral Torah is not closed for the learned in Israel, divinely inspired, continually add to it.[357] The Torah having been revealed to Israel, the study of Torah becomes Israel's main occupation and chief source of joy.[358] In turn, the Torah rejoices in them forever.[359] Being fundamental concepts, Torah and Israel may be subordinated to one another, as the occasion demands, without damage to the organic harmony of rabbinic theology.[360] It is not surprising, then, that, supported by specific midrashim, we could have said: "Between Torah and Israel the Rabbis see an exclusive, inherent relationship, the exclusiveness of which is broken only at some detriment to Torah."[361]

Simply to reënforce our contention that Torah and Israel are inseparable, let us adduce two more homilies as illustrations. According to the Rabbis, Israel's very existence depends on Torah. "Just as water is (the source of) life for all who enter the world and for all the work of His hands that He created in the world, so the House of Israel... exist only through the words of the Torah."[362] By the same token, when Israel's loyalty to the Torah is challenged by some Rabbis, R. Simon the son of Joḥai exclaims, "God forbid that the Torah should be forgotten by Israel! For it says 'for it shall not be forgotten out of the mouths of their seed' (Deut. 31:21)."[363]

We have by no means, however, come to the end of our search of the ways in which Torah and Israel are inextricably linked. We should find many more instances of this inherently organic relationship were we to consider the concept of Israel proper. But as we turn now to the concept of God's loving-kindness in order to see how it, too, is integrated with Torah, we discover an integration not of two concepts but of three, the third being Israel. God loves the words of the Torah more than all the things He created. Why? "Because they weigh Israel over to the side of merit, and train them in *mizwot*, and bring them to the life of the World to Come."[364] Here the *Torah* is the object of God's love and Israel the cause of that love. In other midrashim, *Israel* is the object of God's love and Torah the *manifestation* of that love. Conceiving Israel as the heroine of the Song of Songs and God as the hero, the Rabbis take Song of Songs 1:4 to have been uttered by Israel and to be an avowal of how precious to her is God's love. "We will recollect Thy love more than wine" (Song of Songs 1:4) means to the Rabbis that the recollection of the words of the Torah is to be preferred above the best of old wines,[365] with "Thy love" interpreted as "the words of the Torah." In this interpretation, therefore, Israel is the recipient of God's love which is manifested in Torah. The same idea is conveyed more simply by another homily: " 'Hatred stirreth up strife, but love covereth all transgressions' (Prov.10:12) —'love' refers to Torah."[366] That this homily intends to teach that Israel is the recipient of God's love as manifested in Torah becomes evident from another proof-text (Koh. 11:3) given here but interpreted elsewhere.[367] The great manifestation of that love took place when God gave Israel the Torah at Sinai, God saying of that occasion, according to the Rabbis, "I spread My skirt over thee" (Ezek. 16:8), one of the phrases in Ezekiel's magnificent description of God's espousal of Israel.[368] The copiousness of the Torah as given by God is itself an additional manifestation of His love for Israel: God wished to make Israel the more worthy, "wherefore He gave them a copious Torah and many *mizwot*."[369] With the concepts of God's love, Torah and Israel so inextricably intertwined we have another proof that we are dealing here with an organic complex, "a mental organism which functioned always as a *whole* organism."[370]

The attempt to make Judaism out to be a religion of salvation renders the discussion on which we now enter, the interrelation between the concepts of Torah and God's justice, particularly pertinent. The notion that the Rabbis believed that the point of gravity in God's justice is not in this world but in the World to Come is, as we have already pointed out, utterly erroneous. On the contrary, the Rabbis go to all lengths to teach that God's justice is infallible in this world, both in the lives of individuals and in the history of nations, and to this end they are even forced to employ a principle with which they have great difficulty, namely, corporate justice.[371] We tried to account in some way for the prevalence of that "erroneous notion", all the more surprising because of the mass of evidence which refutes it.[372] But its basic cause seems to be the view that Judaism, like those religions which sprang from it, is a religion of other-worldliness, a means of salvation. Those who hold this view look upon Torah as the central element in rabbinic Judaism, and not, of course, as but one of the four fundamental concepts in an organic complex. Citing such homilies as the one recently quoted here in which Torah has the rôle of bringing individuals "to the life of the World to Come,"[373] they claim thereby to have proved that the Rabbis regarded Torah as the means of salvation. The term "salvation", however, has around it a penumbra of meanings for which it would be impossible to find counterparts in rabbinic theology. Such as are by this time familiar with the method of organic thinking will probably realize that the conception of Torah as the means of salvation involves the assumption that rabbinic theology possesses a logical order rather than an organic harmony.

To be sure, the Rabbis attach great importance to the life in the World to Come as we can judge from many homilies, including the one we have last cited. But to say that they attached great importance to the future and to say that they regarded the present as of no consequence in itself is to say two entirely different things. That the Rabbis were deeply absorbed in this world, striving to demonstrate that it contains an infallible moral order which can be discerned here and now, we learned in our earlier study in the chapter on God's justice.[374] The following analysis of the interrelation of God's justice with Torah will corroborate these conclusions.

In the first place, it is wrong to attribute to the Rabbis the belief that Torah brings one to the life of the World to Come and leave the impression that this, according to rabbinic theology, is the prime function of Torah. The Rabbis teach that he who studies the Torah and practices it not only merits life in the World to Come but that he receives, as his just reward, life here and now, in this world. "And in what shall a man glory in this world? Let him glory in the crown of the Torah. For she (the Torah) enriches him and gives him life *in this world* and in the World to Come."[375] And again: "The Torah gives life to those that do it (i. e., study it) and to those that keep it — *in this world*, in the World to Come and in the days of our Messiah." The large number of proof-texts from Proverbs supporting this statement cannot but add to the conviction that the Rabbis did not lose the healthy concern for the life of this world which characterizes that biblical book. These texts are plain enough: "It shall be health to thy navel and marrow to thy bones" (Prov. 3:8); "Length of days is in her right hand" (*ibid.* 16); "For by me thy days shall be multiplied" (Prov. 9:11); etc. etc.[376] As reward for "Good Deeds and the study of Torah" God causes man "to acquire *this world* and the World to Come and the days of the Messiah."[377] He who fulfills certain ascetic requirements for the study of Torah is told, "Happy art thou in *this world*, and it will be well with thee in the World to Come."[378] He who has studied all the branches of Torah is assured by God, "*This world* and the World to Come are Mine and yours . . ."[379] Because of their Good Deeds and the study of Torah, Abraham, Isaac and Jacob "acquired *this world* and the World to Come."[380] In a midrash showing the superiority of him that both fears and loves God to him that but fears Him, this world and the World to Come are spoken of as *two* portions, this world going to him that only fears God whereas both portions go to him who also loves God. He "with whom there is Torah" acquires both *this world* and the World to Come.[381] All the homilies above teach, true enough, that Torah brings man to the life of the World to Come; but they also teach that Torah assures him of the very important matter of life in this world. To claim, therefore, that the Torah is primarily an instrument of salvation is to ignore half of its function, even perhaps, to misunderstand all of it.[382]

Before we leave this phase of our topic we must mention one midrash of a kind subject to misinterpretation. "He who does the Torah (i. e., studies it) in suffering (בצער) and does the *miẓwot* in suffering," says one of our authors, "the reward of *Derek Ereẓ* is given him and the principal (קרן) is kept for him."[383] Obviously, "the reward of *Derek Ereẓ*"— of righteous conduct — refers to reward in this world and "the principal is kept for him" to reward in the World to Come. Does not this, then, prove that, since the reward in this world compared to reward in the World to Come is but as interest to the principal, the major function of Torah is to ensure life in the World to Come? Moreover, according to Ginzberg's analysis of the text,[384] our author answered here one who questioned God's justice in this world by assuring him that there is reward in the future, "the principal is kept for him" in the World to Come; does not this definitely indicate what the Rabbis conceived the prime function of Torah to be? The effort thus to give to Torah a salvationary rôle again overlooks the fact that, minor or major, Torah's function extends to ensuring reward in this world, also. In his very answer to the doubter, our author, according to Ginzberg, speaks of a "double reward", meaning reward both in this world and the next, and hence recognizing them, apparently, as of equal value. The Rabbis believed life in the World to Come to be everlasting, and that alone would account for the analogy of interest and principal. We certainly have no grounds, however, for stating that Torah's function in bringing life and happiness in this world was regarded by the Rabbis as a minor matter.

Far from being a minor matter, material and immediate rewards for engaging in Torah are the theme of many a homily. This by itself should be sufficient proof that, like the justice of God in general, the specific rewards for Torah have "no single point of gravity".[385] No evil thing can befall two men walking in the way who are at the same time "engaged in the words of the Torah."[386] For the Rabbis felt that the study and knowledge of Torah are the only means of ensuring safety in this world: One angel guards him who possesses *Derek Ereẓ* and *miẓwot*(?); two angels guard him who has studied the Torah, the Prophets and the Writings; God Himself guards him who has pursued the whole course of study.[387] Even the unworthy, those who are sullied with sins but who have studied Bible and Mishnah, are almost entitled, because of the Torah they possess, safely to live in this world, "and it comes hard for the Father of Mercy to destroy them from the world."[388] To reward the learned in this world for their zealous concentration on the study of Torah would be nothing more than "measure for measure", a rule applied in visiting divine justice in this world; hence, "if a man (among the learned) were, so to speak, to ask for the entire world in one hour that would be granted him immediately."[389] From another midrash, closely akin to the last, it appears that the learned and the righteous do not desire this reward, mourning as they are throughout the night of the exile; nevertheless, "observing toward them (the rule of) 'the measure that a man metes out is meted out to him'... the Holy One blessed be He, so to speak, gives the righteous joy against their will."[390] With complete assurance the Rabbis declare that every generation and every individual are rewarded here for whatever of Torah they may have "done".[391]

They also describe these mundane, contemporary rewards for Torah concretely. Bible and Mishnah having taught a man the fear of Heaven and the doing of good, these things actually supply him with food and sustenance until he dies. As though to underline the contemporary and material character of God's justice in connection with Torah, a parable introduces this midrash which tells of a king who supplied food to his servants on condition that the latter read a scroll that had been hung up, and the parable concludes with this phrase, "To this may be compared the House of Israel in this world with (regard to) the words of the Torah."[392] In order to gain vividness for their teachings the Rabbis often use the old device of illustration by story. They tell of a certain child who had been captured by the soldiers of an emperor that had just conquered the land. Now the child had kept, through all his vicissitudes, the Book of Genesis, which was all that his father had had the opportunity to teach him; and one time when the emperor was in a black mood and demanded a book of chronicles, this very book was brought to him, and the only one who could read from it was, of course, the Jewish child. The emperor heard but the first chapter of Genesis when he rose from his throne and kissed the child, and then set him free and gave him silver and gold and precious stones and pearls, male servants and female servants and sent him back home with great honor. "And are not these things *a fortiori*?" says the lesson at the end of the story, "If this one who learned only the Book of Genesis had all this happen to him, all the more he that learns the entire Torah."[393] Thus, daily sustenance and even wealth are the rightful portion in this world of those who know the Torah. The respect of one's neighbors, so essential to the maintenance of one's own self-respect, is also the reward for Torah. That small Jewish community consisting of but ten families in the midst of a city inhabited by Gentiles will find the Gentiles "honoring and fearing them" when they — the Jews — honor the Torah "every day continually".[394] "Fear" in this midrash is associated with "honor" and therefore no doubt conveys the idea of deep respect rather than actual fear. This rendering of the word "fear" is borne out by another homily in which we are told that "when there are Torah and Good Deeds in a man his wife fears him and his children fear him and the members of his household fear him, his neighbors fear him, his relatives fear him and even the Nations of the World fear him".[395] Prestige and position are the reward of Torah: He that labors in the Torah is raised on high.[396] The Torah gives a man the ability to govern and to rule and to judge cases.[397] Food and affluence, the respect of one's fellows and the prestige of high position, all are the just deserts of him who is engaged in Torah. For the observance of every single rule in the twelve prerequisite requirements for the study of Torah there is reward;[398] and for temporarily leaving wealth and possessions and withdrawing from business in order to study Torah, instead of losing anything, a man, on the contrary, is entitled to ("merits") everything.[399] Need we wonder, then, that in the view of our author the study of Torah under the fearful circumstances of the nations' oppression constitutes a claim on God's justice, a claim expressed in an anguished prayer for help?[400] Small comfort would he have found in the idea that Torah is primarily an instrument of salvation, designed mainly to bring reward in another world, and he apparently does not entertain that notion.[401]

Were it the purpose here to present a brief against the notion that rabbinic theology is mainly concerned with other-worldliness, with salvation, contrary proof from the many midrashim dealing with corporate justice in this world in connection with Torah would be in place now. But our argument against the "erroneous notion" is only incidental to the description of the interrelation of the concept of Torah with the concept of justice; and this aspect of corporate justice we have referred to belongs rather to the concept of the righteous and the wicked where it can be seen in its proper setting. Even in the presentation of the material, the organic complex of rabbinic theology blocks our attempt to behold a single concept in isolation if we wish at the same time to view it in its proper perspective.

So far we have spoken only of the material rewards in this world given for Torah. The Rabbis know also, however, of rewards given for Torah that may be described as "spiritual", satisfactions that are not conditioned by material things. And these spiritual satisfactions are not other-worldly but this-worldly. One of the great spiritual satisfactions gained from the study of Torah is the intellectual joy we have mentioned above.[402] But since that joy rises out of the study of Torah it has spiritual concomitants deeper than those produced by any ordinary cultural study. "The words of the Torah give satisfaction (קורת רוח) to him that labors at them, and revive his soul, and give light to his eyes; for it says 'The law of the Lord is perfect, restoring the soul . . . The precepts of the Lord are right, rejoicing the heart' (Ps. 19:8–9)".[403] The "satisfaction" mentioned here is, apparently, of an entirely different order from those satisfactions which are brought about by material things, as the supplementary phrases in the midrash and the proof-text testify. It is again associated with knowledge of Torah in the blessing of God which the Rabbis take the meal-offering to symbolize: "My son, blessed be thou, and mayest thou find satisfaction in the world and may the words of the Torah be hidden in thy mouth forever."[404] That the term קורת רוח possesses a purely spiritual connotation in Seder Eliahu can also be adduced from its use in other contexts — in the prayer that God may have "satisfaction from Israel,"[405] and in the statement that he who refrains from swearing falsely gives "satisfaction" to God.[406]

The tremendous significance of Torah in the eyes of the Rabbis[407] leads them also to regard the acquisition of Torah as such as sufficient reward for all the effort expended on it. "As our reward for having come to learn Thy Torah, Thou hast poured forth for us the words of the Torah."[408] Naturally, the only knowledge of Torah worthy of the name is correct knowledge; and the discussion in the academy is an acid test of the soundness of one's knowledge of Torah. Hence, in reward for the daily, continuous study of Torah, God promises such a thorough knowledge of Torah as cannot be upset by the discussion.[409] In the same way, the phrase, "That will be easy for you which is difficult for your fellow", immediately preceding the homily just considered and united to it by the same proof-text — that phrase, too, contains a promise that your knowledge will be sound in reward for having "done His will in His Torah every day continually", and that such clear knowledge will come to you with far less difficulty than to your fellow who has not properly earned it.[410] Knowledge of this sort renders you not prideful but a source of light to others: "And thou wilt be like unto the sun that gives light to the multitudes," etc.[411] Instructing others in Torah is, as we know, a paramount duty. The reward therefor presents a particularly apt application of the rule of "measure for measure": To him who "provides others" with Torah is given added knowledge of it.[412]

Spiritual rewards in this world given for the pursuit of Torah consist, then, of those deep spiritual satisfactions we have mentioned and profounder knowledge of the content of Torah itself. There is one more reward that can only be classified as spiritual. The religious individual longs for nothing so much as a sense of nearness to God; and that nearness to *Shekinah*, the Rabbis declare, is the reward of him who has engaged in the study of Torah and in Good Deeds.[413] This midrash, which is rather long, seeks especially to impress on those striving to be upright the virtues of modesty and humility. And if a man has done all good things, including charity and Torah literally "in secret", then "all the more will he be beloved before his Father who is in heaven."[414]

We must not suppose that the classification of the rewards in this world for Torah into material and spiritual is one made by the Rabbis themselves, or even that the material brought forward altogether imposes such a classification. Most of the homilies cited in this connection are limited, true enough, to what we have designated as spiritual rewards. But there are other homilies speaking of rewards in which there is a mixture of both kinds, material and spiritual, without any distinction between the two. Thus a statement partly quoted above reads: "A man should be pleasant in entering — the house of study — that he may be beloved Above and desirable below and in the eyes of people, in order that he may fulfill his days; a man should be pious in sitting — in his sitting in the house of study — that he may be beloved Above, etc. . . A man should study much the words of the Torah for there is no reward greater than (because) of them."[415] In another statement listing a larger number of rewards for Torah, the mixing of spiritual and material rewards is even more evident, and this statement is that of a single authority, R. Eliezer: "Everyone who labors in the Torah for its own sake merits many things. And not only that, but the whole world is (regarded as) worthwhile for him (alone). He is called 'beloved friend'. He loves God (מקום); he loves mankind; he gives joy to God; he gives joy to men. It (the Torah) clothes him with humility and fear; and it makes him fit to be pious, righteous and faithful; and it removes him far from sin, and brings him toward virtue (זכות). And (men) profit from him in counsel, wisdom, understanding and strength. And it (the Torah) gives him (the ability) to govern (מלכות) and to rule and judging ability. And (the) secret (i. e., of true judgment?) is revealed to him from heaven, and the secrets of the Torah; and he is made like unto a living fountain that does not cease and like unto an ever-renewed river. And (he?) (is?) modest and long-suffering and forgives an insult. And it (the Torah) raises him and exalts him above all created things."[416] This is really not merely a list of the rewards of Torah but a summary by R. Eliezer of the effect in general of the study of Torah, and includes, therefore, matters that belong under the efficacy of Torah as well as rewards. Yet the impression received from the quotation as a whole is that man's reward for studying Torah is manifold and of all degrees, material and spiritual. And material or spiritual, now and later, it may be counted on with absolute confidence: "He that employs you is faithful to pay you the reward of your labor."[417]

Accustomed as we are to the method of organic thinking, we need not look upon this mixing of spiritual and material rewards as harboring an inconsistency. The very division of rewards into spiritual and physical is of our own, not of the Rabbis', making, for as the result of the philosophic tradition we have come to prefer the abstract, intellectual and intangible — which we call the spiritual — to the concretely material, and this preference caused us to divide the "higher" reward, the spiritual, from the "lesser", the material. Now this tendency to regard the abstract as being "purer" and "higher" than the concrete does not play the great rôle in rabbinic theology that it does in classic philosophy. Although it may be discerned here and there in various homilies and locutions, it never becomes strong enough to assume the dignity of a stated principle. Rabbis who possess such a tendency will couch their views accordingly, as we have observed before.[418] Here, especially, where the discussion concerned the rewards for an intellectual matter like Torah, homilies evincing the tendency toward the abstract were much in evidence. And the organic complex of rabbinic theology is elastic enough to give room for this tendency as for other preferences and moods of individuals. What must be noted, however, is that these abstract, spiritual rewards no less than the concrete, material rewards for Torah are regarded by the Rabbis as taking place in this world. Nothing else is to be expected from those who believe the justice of God to be absolute and infallible at all times.

But it cannot escape anyone that the concrete descriptions of rewards for Torah are in the great majority, in accordance with our observation made above that the Rabbis have a positive predilection for the concrete. And the reason is quite obvious. Rabbinic theology is "a complex of concepts which constituted the mind of the Rabbis itself, mental habits so deeply ingrained as to be inseparable from the daily, hourly facts of life they interpreted."[419] Those "daily, hourly facts" are the concrete occasions of life, and it is these concrete occasions that the fundamental concepts (among them the concept of justice we are discussing) interpret. Conversely, the fundamental concepts, including the concept of justice and its relation to Torah, can be illustrated at their relevant best by these concrete occasions.

We cannot close our discussion of the interrelation of the concepts of Torah and justice until we have spoken also of the punishments in this world for the neglect of Torah. "Great and grievous," says our author to the Ḳasdir who asks him to leave the learned and the Rabbis of Jabne and to dwell in a place where there is no Torah, "Great and grievous is (accounted) before the Holy One blessed be He the neglecting of (or, faithlessness towards) Torah."[420] When men cease from the (study of) Torah, "the Holy One blessed be He wishes to destroy the whole world".[421] "R. Joshua, the son of Levi said: Every day a *Bat-Ḳol* goes out from Mt. Horeb and calls out and says: 'Woe to men for the contempt of the Torah.' For he that does not engage in Torah is under (divine) censure."[422] The period from the fifteenth of Ab and onward, when the heat of the sun begins to diminish, was regarded as an especially favorable time for the study of Torah; and he that adds then to his Torah, says an authority, gains merit whilst he that does not, "his mother will bury him."[423] For the infraction of each of the twelve requisites for the study of Torah a man is punished.[424] The Rabbis warn particularly against boasting "with the words of Torah", and declare that he who does so "will be uprooted (from the world)."[425] Punishment for pride of learning is the theme of another homily: He that has become proud of his learning, "the end will be that he will seek for something in the Mishnah he learned and will not find it; . . . in the end he will never see a sign of blessing (i. e., success)."[426] Punishments in this world, we may note here, are also both spiritual and material and both may be found together in one homily, just as was true of rewards. And just as he who teaches others receives the spiritual reward of additional knowledge so he who possesses the words of the Torah and yet refrains from teaching others receives his punishment, spiritually, by a lessening of his wisdom.[427]

In this section we have discussed the interrelation between Torah and the other fundamental concepts. We have found that the concepts of Torah and Israel are integrally related, and also that God's loving-kindness is intertwined with both. We saw that, as with God's justice in general, rewards or punishments for Torah infallibly take place in this world, as well, thereby negating the notion that Torah is primarily an instrument of salvation which rewards those who possess it mainly by causing them to inherit the World to Come. We also touched upon the distinction between abstract or "spiritual" and concrete or material rewards, and decided that, while both kinds are to be found in the various homilies, this division is not rabbinic, and that the tendency toward abstraction never becomes a stated principle with the Rabbis. Finally, we had occasion to mention some of the punishments in this world for the neglect of Torah.[428]

CHAPTER III

TORAH AS LAW AND ETHICS

I. Miẓwot

The study of Torah leads, according to the Rabbis, to the practice of the *miẓwot* contained in the Torah.[1] The Torah being of divine authorship, the commandments and laws of the Torah — the *miẓwot* — are divine behests. "Thy great name has been called . . . on the Seventh Day and on the other *miẓwot*."[2]

We have learned, also, in the last chapter, that the Rabbis taught that the divine authorship is not limited to the laws and commandments of the Bible. The unwritten Torah, containing laws derived from the Bible by means of the various hermeneutic rules, they likewise regarded as of divine origin. Supported by a clever analogy, this rabbinic doctrine is admirably presented by one of our authors to a man who seems to have belonged to an heretical sect which disputed the divine authorship of the oral Torah.[3] Another such argument, again with a man "in whom there was Bible but no Mishnah", deals not with the general doctrine but with specific laws which the sectarian takes to be purely rabbinic and therefore, apparently, not valid for him. Our author, however, proves by means of rabbinic dialectic that these laws — commandments regarding the washing of the hands[4] and the slaughtering of animals at the neck;[5] and the prohibitions of human blood[6] and the fat of all animals (whether sacrificial or not) for food[7]— are biblical in the sense that they are legitimately derived from the Bible. He also uses the same method to invoke biblical authority for regarding the property of Gentiles (according to Ginzberg) as in the category of things that may not be taken illegitimately (גזל),[8] and for placing a daughter and a daughter's daughter on an equal plane, as far as the law of prohibited marriages is concerned.[9] The final question asked by the sectarian seems to indicate that his group also employed the rabbinic method of interpretation. In case of failure to take the ritual immersion prescribed for the woman after menstruation and for the man who has had gonorrhea, is the sin graver, he asks, with the former or with the latter, and then remarks that, after all, it is from the latter that we derive the obligation for the former. Our author, however, proves by an *a fortiori* argument that the sin is graver in the case of the woman.[10] The entire passage illustrates the Rabbis' contention that divine authorship extends beyond the laws of the Bible to the laws derived by them from the Bible, and that both kinds are equally to be regarded as *miẓwot*, commandments of God.

Being commands of God, man's plain duty is to practice the *miẓwot*. We have already observed that the study of Torah itself, important as it is, must lead to practice. One's very purpose in studying Torah must be "in order to practice".[11] Nay, "more than you study, you must practice".[12] There is no inherent contradiction between this statement and those midrashim which seem to exalt study above practice, as in that comparison, for example, wherein all the *miẓwot* a man may do "have power to give light as much as the light of a candle only but Torah lights the world from end to end."[13] We need only recall that the comparison itself is possible because the Rabbis believed the study of Torah to be of immediate practical efficacy, that study implicates conduct, forms character. Conduct is thus the standard of comparison. That the study of

Torah never supersedes conduct, the practice of the *miẓwot*, is surely evident from the fact that he who is learned in the Torah but transgresses its commandments is guilty of profaning the Name.[14]

The practice of the *miẓwot* of the Torah, like the study of Torah, should be accomplished with joy. Practiced with joy, the *miẓwot* are not burdensome commands imposed from without but partake of the nature of voluntary actions, done freely and generously. Both *terumah* (the priest's portion of grain, etc.) and tithes, for example, are obligatory by law. Yet, "a man should set aside his *terumah* with joy, and it will be counted to him as though it were charity; a man should give his tithes with joy, and it will be counted to him as though it were charity"[15]— that is to say, as though he gave both obligatory gifts with spontaneous generosity. Only when joy enters into the performance of a *miẓwah*, apparently, is it done out of the fullness of heart. We shall speak further of the inward aspect of the *miẓwot* later on.

Let us return now to the description of *miẓwot*. Regarded as commands of God, whether found in the written or the oral Torah, what is the character of these laws? Does the term *miẓwah* apply only to ritual acts or does it include ethical regulations also? If the same term is employed for both, should we infer from that that the Rabbis did not distinguish between them, in other words, that the Rabbis had no awareness of the ethical as such?

Ethical and ritual laws and regulations are alike commands of God, according to the Rabbis. On that score they make no distinction between the two. We need only recall the passage cited at the beginning of this section in which a ritualistic matter like the washing of the hands and an ethical one like the definition of what constitutes theft or robbery are alike placed in the same category of divine law. In this regard, the rabbinic tradition is at one with the Pentateuch wherein ritual and ethical laws are intermingled. The Ten Commandments, themselves, include the injunction to keep the Sabbath, an injunction violated by "the gatherer of sticks" (Num 15:32) who was one of the ten men, say the Rabbis, each of whom broke one of the Ten Commandments and thereby rejected God.[16]

From the point of view of *miẓwot*, commandments of God, the Rabbis, as we have said, do not distinguish the ethical from the ritualistic. Virtue consists in the practice of both. Both are woven out of the same texture: From the single ritualistic practice of circumcision current among those who later went out from Egypt, the latter were able "to multiply from it one hundred *miẓwot*", among which was the practice of loving-kindness with one another.[17] When the Rabbis ascribe virtuous conduct to biblical characters, that virtuous conduct, in consonance with the implicit rabbinic definition of virtue, is described in both ethical and ritualistic terms. The great moral heroes who carried out the Ten Commandments even before these were given on Sinai also observed ritual practices before these were promulgated. Joseph, for instance, not only acted according to the Fifth, Sixth, Seventh and Eighth Commandments but also observed certain ritualistic regulations regarding the slaughtering of animals.[18] In the same spirit the Rabbis interpret the Song of Deborah as an apostrophe to the Sanhedrin of her day, those men who were free from any taint of taking things illegitimately, who were careful in their dispensation of justice, but who were also careful in their decisions as to what was ritually pure or impure.[19] Just as the Rabbis often describe the virtuous as practicing alike the ethical and ritualistic *miẓwot*, they sometimes depict the wicked as having an equal disregard for both. Thus they speak of the householders (בעלי בתים) who are not averse to taking things illegitimately and who fail to adhere to prescribed sex ritual,[20] and of the woman who does not observe the law regarding the first of the dough and, among other things, makes vows and does not keep them.[21] The ethical and the ritualistic *miẓwot*, in short, are equally the commandments of God; the good practice, and the wicked break, both.

In the preceding paragraph it was not the intention, of course, to say that the term *miẓwah* always denotes, whenever it is used, at once both the ethical and the ritualistic laws. The term may be applied to both or either. To specify what is meant by "a matter involving a *miẓwah*" the Rabbis adduce, on one occasion, the ritualistic law regarding the unclean reptile which touched a loaf of bread.[22]

There are other occasions, not at all infrequent in the Seder, when ritualistic laws alone are mentioned, among them food laws — concerning animals slaughtered not according to law or otherwise declared unfit and the law forbidding reptiles and certain insects for food[23]— and the laws of ritual uncleanness at death.[24] Other ritualistic laws mentioned rather frequently are those of circumcision,[25] sex,[26] and the law concerning men and women afflicted with gonorrhea.[27]

The term *miẓwah* is employed at times to denote ethical matters only. In the statement, "There is no favoritism before Me: Whether Gentile or Israelite, whether man or woman, whether male-slave or female-slave, he that has done a *miẓwah*, the reward thereof is at hand,"[28] the term *miẓwah* can only refer to ethical matters since a Gentile certainly was not expected to conform to the ritual laws.

The Rabbis naturally stress those ethical laws which are most commonly broken in the daily struggle to secure an advantage. For that reason, no doubt, they inveigh against the men who break the Third Commandment and swear falsely;[29] and for that reason, too, they admonish in every way to be careful not to take anything illegitimately (גזל).[30] On the other hand, they are also concerned with laws having to do with the more delicate relationships of man to man, clothing with their own wisdom and social experience the bare, if lofty, biblical injunctions. "Thou shalt surely rebuke thy friend" (Lev.19:17),[31] for example, needs further elaboration if the commandment is to be followed seriously by the ordinary man. Hence the Rabbis explain the phrase "thy friend" to include everybody except those whom thou knowest to be thine enemy, thus extending the sphere of the commandment to a larger group than that of your well-wishers; but, recognizing that you cannot be effective "with the wicked that hate thee", they also limit "thy friend" who may be reproved to him "that is with thee in *miẓwot*."[32] R. Eleazar, the son of Matya, offers the sage interpretation that the whole verse (Lev. 19:17) refers to matters that have come up between you and your neighbor about which you are commanded to speak out openly rather than harbor a grudge in your heart.[33] R. Eleazar, it would appear, disapproves of that indiscriminate fault-finding which literal obedience to the biblical command might easily become.

An interesting illustration of how rabbinic interpretation reënforces a biblical commandment, bringing out to the full its ethical implications, is the manner in which the Fifth Commandment is treated in the Seder. The Fifth Commandment is mainly reënforced by bringing five other Commandments to bear upon it; at the same time its ethical implications are drawn forth by means of instances of how it may be violated. The section is introduced by coupling the Fourth and the Fifth Commandment and, aided by an interpretation of Is. 56:2, drawing therefrom the lesson that if a man honors his father and mother he will not violate the Sabbath.[34] A man should not misconstrue, moreover, the respective positions God and the two parents have in the Ten Commandments: Despite the fact that God is placed first (in the First Commandment), a man must not think that by doing God's will he is absolved from doing his parents' will, nor because "father" precedes "mother" in the Fifth Commandment is he absolved from doing his mother's will when he has done his father's.[35] When a man curses his father and mother and smites them, making a bruise, God, Himself, the midrash continues, is strongly affected, for the three of them (i. e. God and the two parents) are alike in the honor due them.[36] In each of the remaining interpretations where the Fifth is always coupled with another Commandment, the lesson that results is couched in terms of concrete family-life. Coupled with the Sixth Commandment, the lesson is that if a man has much sustenance in his house and does not give of it to his father and mother when they are old, "it is as though he were a murderer all his days, as though he were killing people before God"; with the Seventh, the lesson is that "if a man marries a woman and she herself does not honor his father and mother when they are old, it is as though he committed adultery all his days"; with the Eighth, the lesson is that if a man's children do not honor his father and his mother when they are old, "it is as though he stole all his days, as though he stole people before God"; with the Ninth, the lesson is that if a man has much property in his house and gives none of it to his father and mother when they are old, "it is as though he were testifying false testimony all his days before God."[37] But a man who honors his father and mother when they are old will have "satisfaction (קורת רוח) in the world" for he has honored the King's friends.[38] The lessons in the foregoing interpretations teach that a man must share his property and sustenance with his parents. A passage somewhat farther on, separated from these interpretations by a few midrashim on other themes, goes much further. A man should not only not turn away when his father and mother are clothed raggedly, but should clothe them in garments far costlier than he himself wears—"the Holy One blessed be He has made the honor due one's father and mother equal to the honor due Him".[39] "And even though the spittle of his father run down on the beard, he should obey him immediately," that is, even when the father because of old age becomes senile and demented.[40]

We began our description of *miẓwot* by demonstrating that the term includes both what we call ritual matters and what we call ethical matters, and that it may be applied to either, as well. We went on to give some instances showing how the Rabbis were attentive to both categories, the ethical instances showing how rabbinic interpretation enlarged and reënforced biblical commandments and how the ethical implications of the latter were minutely drawn forth by this process. Now, if the Rabbis were so sensitive to ethical matters, why do they place them, apparently, on a par with ritual laws by regarding both as *miẓwot*, commandments of God? This question is, of course, similar to the one asked above and as yet not answered: "If the same term (*miẓwah*) is employed for both, should we infer from that that the Rabbis did not distinguish between them, in other words, that the Rabbis had no awareness of the ethical as such?"

First of all, it is necessary to challenge the assumption current today upon which this question rests. The simple dichotomy of the ritualistic and the ethical into which we are prone to divide all religious behaviour is far too simple, too easy. Actually, if we set about to examine the *miẓwot* and attempt, after some analysis, to state categorically that this one is ethical or that one ritualistic, we soon find that many *miẓwot* defy this sort of treatment. It is often impossible to assign a *miẓwah* to either category unequivocally, unless, indeed, we assume that that only is ethical which springs spontaneously from the human heart, and that anything defined or enjoined by law is *ipso facto* non-ethical. In that case, of course, not only would the *miẓwot* not be ethical but all our modern laws as well. Unless we forego all human development, we cannot dismiss any law as not ethical simply on the ground that it is law.

Granted, then, that a particular *miẓwah*, as a law or commandment, may very well be included in the sphere of the ethical, depending on its quality or character. But what is to determine its character so conclusively as to enable us to decide whether that is ethical or ritualistic? Take, for example, the Third Commandment, the law against false swearing. The Rabbis couple the first three Commandments together, after the method we noticed above, drawing therefrom the lesson that "everyone that is accustomed to vain oaths and false swearing worships idols, and he that is not accustomed to vain oaths and false swearing 'gives satisfaction' to Him who spake and the world came into being."[41] With their usual insight, the Rabbis recognized that to swear falsely is tantamount to a denial of God, since thus not only is God's name invoked falsely but there is also an implicit denial of God's power. For that reason, no doubt, the habitual breaking of the Third Commandment is taken, of all the laws, as an indication that the sovereignty of God is not accepted.[42] Are we, therefore, dealing here with a ritualistic matter involving a man's relation to God or with an ethical matter involving a man's relation to other men? Obviously both are involved at once and neither can be separated from the other.

A number of other *miẓwot* mentioned in Seder Eliahu likewise escape simple classification into ritualistic and ethical. *Terumah*,[43] and the various tithes and the law regarding the produce of the seventh year[44] undoubtedly had a ritualistic background but they certainly had also the elemental ethical function of providing the priests and the poor with food. With polygamy legitimate under rabbinic law — actually, however, not practiced — laws forbidding a man to marry two sisters[45] and to marry *ẓarat ha-bat*,[46] prohibitions perhaps originating in "taboos", made for an improvement in the institution of the family. The minutiae of the laws of *sheḥitah*,[47] of slaughtering of animals, while ritualistic, were consciously an attempt to minimize the suffering of the animals.

More pertinent to this discussion even than the demonstration that *miẓwot* cannot by their content or effect be readily classified into ritualistic and ethical is the mental and emotional state they engender, the mood in which they are performed. It is because we tend to associate the ritualistic with the formal, with the habitual and mechanical, that we look upon it as antithetical to the ethical. If we recall, however, that the Rabbis urged the need to perform the obligatory *miẓwot* with joy, and the strong implication that this transformed an obligatory into a voluntary act,[48] we shall begin to appreciate the rôle of the ritualistic *miẓwot* in developing the inward life. *Miẓwot*, ritualistic as they may be, which call forth and engage the profoundest as well as the most subtle emotions and sentiments, cannot but have the most far-reaching effects on a man and thus on his ethical behaviour. Joy is but one indication that a *miẓwah* is heart-felt, inward. There are other indications. In a midrash attributing certain virtues to Israel when they dwelt in Egypt, the Rabbis say that the Israelites circumcized their children even though taunted by the Egyptians that the children would be shortly thrown into the river. "We shall circumcize them. After, do as ye will with them."[49] The utter loyalty which the *miẓwah* of circumcision called forth cannot be lightly dismissed as merely a matter of ritual. It was the same loyalty, say the Rabbis, that made Israel in Egypt cling to Hebrew, "the language of the house of Jacob their father," a matter which they identified with worshipping their "Father who is in heaven" and with the opposite of idol-worship.[50] Of course, these views are the Rabbis' own rather than those of Israel in Egypt and, as Friedmann suggests, may even reflect the conditions under which the former lived. All the better, therefore, can we perceive what these *miẓwot* meant to the Rabbis and the tremendous implications which the *miẓwot* had for them.

The ritualistic *miẓwot* became, for the Rabbis, the means whereby the inward life, with all its fine sensibilities and aspirations, was cultivated. The ritualistic *miẓwot* both quickened their sense for the holy and stimulated the aspiration to embody that holiness in their daily lives. "Not to the priests alone was holiness given," say the Rabbis, "but to all — to the priests and to the Levites and to the Israelites." How was this to be demonstrated in daily life? By the practice of the washing of the hands, a ritualistic *miẓwah*. According to the Rabbis, this biblical law — as given in the Bible (Exod. 30:19–20) it is to be observed by the priests when entering the tent of meeting or when approaching the altar — is to be observed by all Israel in keeping with the injunction, "Sanctify yourselves, therefore, and be ye holy" (Lev. 11:44).[51] The ethical consequences of this ideal of holiness incorporated in daily life are incalculable.

Two groups of ritualistic *miẓwot* by their very nature are the chief means of fostering the inward, spiritual life and at the same time the most potent aids to social and personal morality. One group consists of the laws concerning the Sabbath and the holidays. On the Sabbath, regarded as equal to God and Israel in holiness,[52] the dominant note is to be one of joy, a characteristic of the spiritual life as expressed in *miẓwot* by now familiar to us. Indeed the very manner of rendering the Sabbath holy is through joy: "With what do you render it (i. e., the Sabbath) holy? With Bible, with Mishnah, with food and with drink and with rest; for he who makes the Sabbath joyous is as though he made joyous Him who spake and the world came into being."[53] The same elements of physical and spiritual pleasures which, as we noticed here, combine to make the joy of the Sabbath are contained in a regimen of the Sabbath given in another midrash: "A man should always rise early on the Sabbath and study Mishnah, and then go to the synagogue or *bet ha-midrash*, should study the Torah and the Prophets, and then return to his home and eat and drink."[54] An ideal blending of spiritual striving and physical relaxation, the Sabbath thus became a day of moral re-creation. On the festivals there was the additional stimulus of the great pilgrimages to Jerusalem;[55] and the Rabbis felt keenly the absence of this stimulus in the Diaspora after the destruction, for they complain that when in Palestine Israel observed one day and that properly, and now two days but not one properly.[56] The loftiest spiritual experience, however, exalting the individual and greatest in its moral consequences, is occasioned by the Ten Days of Repentance the last of which is the Day of Atonement.[57]

We learned in our previous study that the prescribed prayers are referred to as *miẓwot*, are prescribed by authority,[58] that they are, in other words, ritualistic *miẓwot*. In our discussion there of the prescribed prayers,[59] we saw that the Rabbis recognized the danger of formalism inherent in prescribed prayer and that they attempted to obviate it. But we saw also the great need that the prescribed prayers filled in supplying "expression to the devotional moods of all Israel alike" and in arousing "these devotional attitudes in the hearts of those men who might otherwise be insensible to them". The prescribed prayers, then, are indispensable to the spiritual — including the moral — development of Israel at large. As a matter of fact, were it not that these prayers are fixed, and the times for prayer stated as well, it is extremely doubtful whether most men would have acquired the aptitude for prayer at all. By thus institutionalizing prayer, it was especially adapted for public worship, and hence its effect was intensified through community factors.[60]

The division of the *miẓwot* into the two simple categories of the ritualistic and the ethical is inadmissable. For we have shown, first, that a number of *miẓwot* by their content would have to fall into both categories at once; second, that many ritualistic *miẓwot* foster and develop the inward life and so are indispensable to the development of moral and ethical attitudes. Now we do not mean to impute this line of reasoning to the Rabbis: much of the terminology used in the analysis is our own. But at least we can now appreciate that the ethical and ritualistic *miẓwot* are all, intrinsically, of one piece, and it is no longer strange to us that the Rabbis should put both ethical and ritualistic matters into the one category of *miẓwot*, commandments of God. This is, indeed, what we should expect of a theology that is organic, the elements of which are always so integrally interrelated as to permit of no hard-and-fast classifications.

And yet, granted that there can be no clear-cut distinction in the *miẓwot* between the ethical and the ritualistic, is it not possible to tell whether "the Rabbis had any awareness of the ethical as such?" If today we are inclined to make such a distinction it is precisely because we are deeply aware of the category of the ethical. That the Rabbis, too, possessed this category cannot be doubted for there are rabbinic concepts that embody and express it, concepts that we shall soon consider. But that the Rabbis were aware of the ethical as such we can also glean without going beyond the consideration of the concept now under discussion, that of *miẓwot*. We are not referring now to the way in which they draw forth all the ethical implications in biblical commandments, of which some illustrations were given above, though that too is an important indication of their sensitiveness to matters ethical. We refer, rather, to an almost rationalistic tendency on the part of the Rabbis to assign functions to *mizwot*, and to another tendency actually to make gradations in *mizwot*. Either tendency is logically in conflict with the basic belief that all *mizwot* are alike the commands of God. By now, however, we have come to recognize that rabbinic theology is a complex of experiential values rather than a system of logically consistent truths. The unity of religious behaviour is one value; the ethical aspect of life is another value; both find expression in rabbinic theology. And from the standpoint of organic thinking there is no contradiction, of course, between the two values. The awareness of the unity of religious behaviour is nothing other than the recognition that all the details of the Torah are divine; it is the stressing of the concept of Torah. The awareness of the ethical aspect of life crystallizes itself in the new concepts we shall soon consider, a characteristic method for resolving "contradictions" in rabbinic theology we have already had occasion to observe.[61] But traces of the awareness of the ethical as such can also be discerned in the two tendencies we shall now describe.

There is a tendency, not very pronounced but still revealed in a few midrashim, to assign ethical functions to ritualistic *mizwot*. To be sure, we noticed above that many of the latter had ethical bearings, that there was no clear demarcation between the ethical and the ritualistic in the *mizwot*. But this is not to be confused with the tendency we are discussing here. When the Rabbis assign an ethical purpose to a ritualistic *mizwah* by saying that the latter was given by God in order to serve certain ends of social and personal betterment, the ritualistic is definitely subordinated to the ethical. The *tefillin* on the head and on the arm have, according to the Rabbis, an ethical purpose: They serve to remind a man to scrutinize (or to repent of) his actions. The *zizit* perform the same function on the holy days and Sabbath, reminding a man to strive to be perfect, not to take anything illegitimately, not to transgress.[62] R. Meir states that there is a social purpose in the law declaring a woman to be ritually unclean for the seven days after menstruation: her husband is thus made more desirous of her.[63] The Sabbath is also given a large social function: "A man works all the six days and rests on the Sabbath; he then becomes companionable with the children and with the members of his household. Again, a man works in the face of his enemies all the six days and rests on the Sabbath; he forgets all the trouble he had."[64] It is not unlikely that the Rabbis had in mind "reasons" of this kind, ethical explanations for ritualistic *miẓwot*, when they said that in the World to Come God "will reveal the reasons of Torah (טעמי תורה)",[65] this expression reflecting, perhaps, a belief that all ritualistic *miẓwot* have "a reason", an ethical purpose, ultimately to be made known.

There is also the tendency to make gradations in *miẓwot* by designating some as "grave" and others as "light", *miẓwot*. Both kinds are equally obligatory, to be sure, as the Rabbis are careful to point out. "For the lightest *miẓwah* is like the grave one, and the grave one like the light one: both are healing for Israel whether in this world or in the days of the Messiah or in the World to Come."[66] The *miẓwah* of *ẓiẓit* is placed near the grave one of *Malkut Shamayim* (in the prayers)—"Thus you learn that the lightest *miẓwah* is like the grave one, and the grave one like the light one."[67] Nevertheless, the designations of "grave" and "light" certainly do indicate an awareness that *miẓwot* differ in significance. Now what *miẓwot* did the Rabbis deem "grave", or as possessing the highest significance? We have just learned that *Malkut Shamayim* — the acknowledgement of the sovereignty of God, with all its manifold implications — is a grave *miẓwah*.[68] The love of God, associated with *Malkut Shamayim* in the prayers, is also a grave *miẓwah*.[69] These *miẓwot*, basic as they are to rabbinic theology because they epitomize the four fundamental concepts, the Rabbis naturally regarded as of the highest significance. The only other *miẓwah* mentioned in our Seder as being "grave" is charity (in contrast to the law found in Deut. 22:6–7, a "light" *miẓwah*),[70] which the Rabbis also say is equal to the Torah in importance.[71] Placing such high significance upon the *miẓwah* of charity argues not only that the Rabbis were deeply aware of the ethical aspect of life but that this awareness was among the dominant factors making for gradations in *miẓwot*, a dominance shared only by basic theological attitudes.[72]

After having taken account of these tendencies, it should be obvious that the ethical has the right of way with the Rabbis. In the face of human need, the ritualistic *miẓwah* is subordinated to that need. *Terumah*, for instance, may be eaten by all men, not only by the priests, in time of famine.[73] The Rabbis abhor nothing so much as the performance of ritualistic acts which is coupled with the neglect of ethical duties. To those who brought turtle-doves and young doves and other sacrifices but who did not do their parents' will, they apply the verse, "O, priests that despise My name" (Mal. 1:6).[74] But even in the performance of the ethical laws, when there is a conflict of laws precedence must be given to that which is of larger social significance: When a father commands his son to transgress, to take things illegitimately, it is the son's duty to disobey his father despite the great stress upon filial obedience.[75]

The *miẓwot*, being an aspect of Torah, are integrated with the other three fundamental concepts. As is true of Torah in general, they intertwine inseparably with God's love and Israel. We noticed above that God deliberately left many important *miẓwot* only implicit in the Bible because of His love for Israel so that the latter by making the *miẓwot* explicit might receive greater reward;[76] and, again, that God gave Israel "a copious Torah and many *mizwot*" in order to make Israel the more worthy.[77] The Day of Atonement, on which the sins of Israel are forgiven, is a source of great joy to God "for He gave it with great love" to Israel.[78]

The justice of God follows inevitably upon each *miẓwah* done or every transgression committed. "From the day the world was created until this hour everyone who does a *miẓwah* is given his reward; everyone who commits a transgression is given his punishment."[79] In the previous chapter we demonstrated that the point of gravity with God's justice is not in the World to Come, just as we pointed this out before in the chapter on God's justice. And for emphasis' sake we shall demonstrate this again now. In most of the passages where reward in the World to Come is assured for the *miẓwot* performed, the formula includes an assurance of reward here and now. We mentioned above, in connection with Torah, two such passages — one saying that the Torah gives life *in this world*, in the World to Come and in the days of the Messiah to those who study the Torah and to those who practice it,[80] and the other stating that reward for him, who does Torah and *miẓwot* through suffering, is given in this world and the principal kept for him (in the World to Come).[81] Two other passages having reference to *miẓwot* alone likewise have a similar formula. Both the "light" and the "grave" *miẓwot*, as we learned, "are healing for Israel whether *in this world* or in the days of the Messiah or in the World to Come;"[82] and "everyone that wishes days and years and riches and goods and life *in this world*, and long life in the World to Come without end", let him do God's will and his parents' will.[83] The last passage given ought to be particularly convincing that the Rabbis are concerned with definite reward in this world.

For the sake of completeness let us mention again several other aspects of justice in connection with *miẓwot* discussed before under the former concept. The justice of God is universal in scope: Jew or Gentile, man or woman, slave or free — everyone receives reward for a *mizwah* performed.[84] The reward is greater the more self-control the performance of the *mizwah* exacts.[85] And, in accordance with the rabbinic conception of corporate justice, the reward for doing a *mizwah* extends to the fourth generation, as witness the fortunes of the kingly line of Jehu.[86] Indeed, the reward for a *mizwah*, as we learn from another midrash, is not limited to any set number of generations, for he who refrains from taking things illegitimately and from illicit sexual intercourse — both matters involving great self-control — stores merit not only for himself but for his generations after him "until the end of all generations."[87]

The justice of God manifests itself also in punishment, again in this world, for the transgression of *mizwot*. The sectarian who questioned the biblical grounds for certain laws,[88] was told, among other things, that those who disregard the laws concerning a woman ritually unclean "will never have satisfaction in the world",[89] and that those who treat lightly the law concerning the washing of the hands will be punished.[90] If a man does not honor his father and mother severe decrees (i.e., punishments) will come upon him.[91] The wicked, who swear falsely, fooling people, are punished both by having their wealth destroyed and by themselves being consumed.[92] Previously we noticed how the Rabbis apply the principle of "measure for measure" in various cases, among them that of the priest whose wealth was destroyed by fire because he did not burn unused *terumah*, and that of the slaughterer who commits *hagramah*.[93] We learned also that they employ the same principle to supply the grounds for the afflictions mentioned in Leviticus, accounting for the plague on clothes by saying that their owner had been fond of taking things illegitimately, and for gonorrhea by stating that the afflicted men and women failed to adhere to prescribed sex ritual.[94]

The spiritual life demands vigor and earnest zeal on the part of those who are committed to it. They who are weak and vacillating in the performance of the *miẓwot* do quite as much harm as they who deliberately transgress them. It is for this reason that the Rabbis are so severe in their condemnation of him "who does a *miẓwah* but does not complete it." Such a man, they say, forfeits his own life and that of his wife and sons[95]— a stern application of the always difficult principle of corporate justice.

In this section, we learned that the *miẓwot*, being divine commands, are all obligatory, although to be accomplished with joy; and that from this point of view the Rabbis do not distinguish between the ethical and the ritualistic *miẓwot*. But we challenged this easy dichotomy by analyzing the content of the *miẓwot* and especially by a description of how the ritualistic *miẓwot* contributed to the inward, and hence the moral, life. We saw, moreover, that the Rabbis were aware of the ethical as such, and found traces of this awareness in the tendency to assign functions to *miẓwot* and in the tendency to make gradations in *miẓwot*, coming finally to definite instances where the ethical had the right of way. We concluded the section by describing how the *miẓwot*, an aspect of Torah, were integrated with the other fundamental concepts.

II. Good Deeds[96]

"From Torah man also learns to do Good Deeds", the latter, indeed, being "the end of all things" or the purpose of study.[97] Man's entire function on earth, according to the Rabbis, is to do Good Deeds and to engage in the study of Torah and to avoid transgression.[98] Injunctions urging both the doing of Good Deeds and the study of Torah are scattered throughout the Midrash, confirming the impression that this formula summarizes the whole of man's function.[99] When the Rabbis reinterpret the Temple sacrifices by making them symbolic of the conditions for the good life, these conditions consist, outside of repentance, of Good Deeds and the study of Torah.[100] Many times again does this formula —"Good Deeds and the study of Torah"— summarize, apparently, all that is required of man. It constitutes the standard by which God judges a man's life from the age of thirteen until his death;[101] the reason for which a man is held in universal respect;[102] the source of strength shielding a man from ten powerful evil influences.[103] It epitomizes the virtuous life of Abraham, Isaac and Jacob,[104] and the virtues of Israel that caused God to come and manifest His sovereignty.[105] The use of the formula in these instances, and in other midrashim where the term "Good Deeds" is employed in conjunction with "the study of Torah",[106] cannot but lead to the conclusion that by "Good Deeds and the study of Torah" the Rabbis summed up all of man's duties.

If this conclusion is sound, then the concept of Good Deeds must be the equivalent of the concept of *miẓwot*, with, perhaps, a special connotation of its own. For, if "Good Deeds and the study of Torah" summarizes the whole of man's function on earth, a conclusion just drawn not from one or two but from many homilies, then Good Deeds must obviously refer to the practice of the commandments contained in the Torah, and these commandments are the *miẓwot*. We are obliged to resort to inferences because, with one exception, our Seder unfortunately never specifies just what are Good Deeds.

Although equivalent, by and large, to *miẓwot*, the concept of Good Deeds seems to possess, as we have said, a special connotation of its own. This connotation apparently lies in the direction of the ethical bearings of the *miẓwot*, being a kind of trend toward finer behaviour, a mindfulness of the effect of one's actions upon others. Thus, in that midrash where the phrase "Good Deeds" is equated to a definite virtue, the virtue is respect for elders and parents: "The end of all things (should be) fear of Heaven and Good Deeds. And a man should not study Bible and Mishnah and object (lit. 'kick') to one who is older than he is; and a man should not study Bible and Mishnah and not honor those who begat him; and a man should not study Bible and Mishnah and not have the fear of Heaven."[107] If the concrete instances in this midrash are explanatory of the introductory sentence, respect for elders and parents is explanatory of "Good Deeds". In some midrashim, the mention of Good Deeds is accompanied by certain ethical exhortations. "A man should always be humble in Torah and in Good Deeds . . .";[108] "Happy is the man in whom there is no transgression, and in whom there is no deliberate trespass or sin, in whom there are Good Deeds and the study of Torah, lowly and humble . . .".[109] These homilies and the one earlier cited, describing the function of man on earth,[110] leave the impression that Good Deeds mean deeds done whilst being particularly regardful of social and ethical relationships.

The capacity for the doing of Good Deeds is a gift from God, a bounty of His grace, just as is the capacity for studying Torah. Hence the Midrash often states that it is God, who, in His mercy, gives the learned their "Good Deeds and study of Torah."[111] The Rabbis thought of this capacity as being the quality of a man's nature or character. Interpreting Ezek. 36:26 in terms of the World to Come, they say, "'A new heart also will I give you'— that refers to the *Good Yeẓer*; 'and a new spirit will I put within you'— that refers to Good Deeds."[112] Of course, that quality of character can be brought forth, nurtured and developed only by the study of Torah, as we have already learned.[113] Among the twelve rules, or goals, set up for the study of Torah is, therefore, the one urging a man to be "clever" in the doing of Good Deeds.[114] And it is also not fortuitous that in that peculiar rendering of Ps. 133:1 where the periods of one's youth and one's maturity are taken to be the "brothers" mentioned in the Psalm, one interpretation assigns the study of various divisions of Torah to these periods of life and another interpretation teaches that the verse refers to a man who "did a good deed in his youth and became old and doubled his deeds for good."[115] The youthful period and the mature period are made harmonious or "brothers", in other words, through constant growth either in the study of Torah or in the doing of Good Deeds, for the former makes for the latter. This close association between the doing of Good Deeds and the study of Torah extends also to the similar emotion engendered by both. The learned long for Good Deeds and the study of Torah, says one homily which finds the joy of Good Deeds and the study of Torah symbolized in physical terms, in the "wine" and "milk" of Song of Songs 5:1.[116]

The other fundamental concepts are, of course, integrated with Good Deeds which, like *miẓwot*, is Torah viewed as conduct or practice. It is Israel's duty and privilege to do Good Deeds and to study Torah, and thus to follow the example of Abraham, Isaac and Jacob;[117] and Israel ought to do these things because God has manifested His love to them, collectively and individually.[118] As to God's justice, since Good Deeds are so often linked with the study of Torah we have already dealt with that aspect in the previous chapter, and need, therefore, but give it the barest mention here. God judges a man, from the age of thirteen onward, in accordance with what he has achieved in the doing of Good Deeds and in the study of Torah.[119] He who possesses Torah and Good Deeds is rewarded by being respected by all — by his family, neighbors and by the Nations of the World.[120] He who has come to know Bible and Mishnah, and has learned from them fear of Heaven and the doing of good will be provided, as reward, with food and sustenance until his death.[121] And, finally, the highest spiritual reward is granted him who is engaged in the study of Torah and in Good Deeds — nearness to *Shekinah*.[122] These rewards, it is hardly necessary to add, refer to this world.

III. Derek Ereẓ[123]

The concept of *Derek Ereẓ* enables us to conclude that the Rabbis possessed the category of the ethical as such. No rabbinic concept better exhibits the experiential character of rabbinic theology. And for that reason, as we shall discover immediately, no rabbinic concept is more confusing, at first sight, than that of *Derek Ereẓ*.

The literal translation of *Derek Ereẓ* is "the way of the world". What the Rabbis meant by this phrase will become apparent only after an examination of some of the matters which it includes. When Lot remonstrated with the men of Sodom (Gen. 19:8–9), say the Rabbis, he spoke to them at first of things in accordance with *Derek Ereẓ* and then went on to speak of things not in accordance with *Derek Ereẓ*.[124] Here the phrase can only mean "normal or natural sex behaviour," for what Lot proposed at first was to hand over his daughters to the men of Sodom and at the end he pleaded that they molest not the strangers, refusing to permit his guests to fall victims to the homo-sexuality of the men of Sodom.[125] Another matter called *Derek Ereẓ* consists in the observation that when a learned man dies or is exiled, his sons will be learned if their mother was the daughter of a learned man and will be ignorant if she was the daughter of an ignorant man.[126] *Derek Ereẓ*, then, is also the powerful, if indirect, influence of the maternal grandfather, or perhaps, more generally, of the early training given the mother, on one's character and interests. The contrast between a man's state of contentment while he is unmarried and without children and the state of sorrow later brought about by bad children is also *Derek Ereẓ*.[127] Normal sexual relations, hereditary or environmental influences, the sorrows of having bad children are all *Derek Ereẓ*. It would seem, therefore, that the term summarizes the commonly observed facts of human experience and is thus elastic enough to include everything typical or characteristic of man.

We have been led to conclude that *Derek Ereẓ* is the term applied to whatever is typical or characteristic of man. A very broad concept, it joins together human interests at the farthest remove from one another. The refined taste for the aesthetic is *Derek Ereẓ*, the Rabbis employing the term when describing the aesthetic quality of the stars as they are hung pendant-like yet separate in the firmament.[128] But man's purposeful direction of his daily activities toward practical and useful ends is also *Derek Ereẓ*, as when he builds a house in order to store in it fruit, furniture and other things and not, of course, just to destroy it by fire,[129] or when he plants a vineyard in order to have grapes and wine and not, of course, just to fill it with weeds.[130] Man's effort to make a livelihood for himself is thus *Derek Ereẓ*: "Is it not *Derek Ereẓ* for a man to do it (i. e., provide for himself) with his own hand, and the Holy One blessed be He (then) blesses all his handiwork?"[131] The Rabbis draw a contrast between him who dedicates himself to Torah and him who dedicates himself to *Derek Ereẓ*, comparing the latter to a skin-bag filled with water which may soon be spilled, leaving the skin-bag empty, and the former to all manner of things of which man makes constant and grateful use.[132] *Derek Ereẓ* here no doubt again refers to business activity, for the lesson seems to be the familiar one that the man whose entire energy goes to the making of wealth has nothing left once that wealth has been lost whereas the man who devotes his energy to Torah and learning always retains that which makes him endeared and useful to his fellow-men.[133] On the other hand, the Rabbis recognize that a business career also requires training and ability and speak of those who pursue it not without approval, apparently. In a parable they tell of a king who had grown sons, of whom there were some who knew Torah, some who knew Mishnah, some who were business men. The parable goes on to say that the king married again and had more sons whom he sent to study Bible and Mishnah and *Derek Ereẓ* but to his chagrin later found that they had learned nothing of Bible or Mishnah or *Derek Ereẓ*.[134] Obviously, the sons by the second wife are compared unfavorably with those by the first, in this parable, and in order for the comparison to hold *Derek Ereẓ* must refer to business capacity and knowledge. Moreover, linking those who know *Derek Ereẓ* to those who know Bible and Mishnah argues that the Rabbis approve of and respect the former.

Varied as are the instances of *Derek Ereẓ* thus far brought forward, they are all matters that common observation finds typical or characteristic of man. True enough, the very breadth of the concept renders the connection between the concrete instances it subsumes of the loosest possible kind, a connection so tenuous that at first sight only a confused mass of instances is apparent. But the broad, amorphous quality of the concept is inevitable. For the concept of *Derek Ereẓ* points precisely to the wide-flung, universal character of a great number of human experiences. *Derek Ereẓ*, in other words, refers to what is universally human, that is to say, to human traits. As such it is the perfect frame for the category of the ethical.

It is the perfect frame for the category of the ethical because every human trait or action is *potentially* of ethical import. The Rabbis indicate their awareness of this by calling all ethical traits *Derek Ereẓ* despite the fact that that term is also used for every action or experience typically human. Indeed, the Rabbis employ the term in this wise not despite its wider meaning but because of it, *Derek Ereẓ* pointing to actions, traits, that are good and at the same time universally human in character. This ethical *Derek Ereẓ* can be identified as such and is not likely to be confused with the larger meaning of the term particularly when it is made specific by some concrete instance involving God's justice, an indication that the matter is *actually* of ethical import. The people of Israel who dwelt in the days of the First Temple, though idol-worshippers, nevertheless had *Derek Ereẓ* in them. "And what was that *Derek Ereẓ* that was in them? Charity and Deeds of Loving-kindness." As reward, the period of exile following the destruction of the First Temple was fixed while no period was fixed for the exile following upon the destruction of the Last Temple.[135] Scripture speaks of "the priests and diviners" of the Philistines (I Sam. 6:2): They are called "priests", even though they were idol-worshippers, because "there was *Derek Ereẓ* in them" for they advised not to send away the Ark of the Lord empty (*ibid.*, 6:3).[136] *Derek Ereẓ* here describes the reverence the priests of the Philistines felt for the Ark, and that reverence entitled them to be called priests. In contrast to the action of the priests was the behaviour of the men of Beth-Shemesh who, instead of prostrating themselves before the Ark in reverence, laughed and remained upright and even spoke unseemly words, so that as punishment fifty thousand men, including the Great Sanhedrin fell in Israel.[137] The behaviour of the men of Beth-Shemesh is summarized later by the phrase "there was no *Derek Ereẓ* in them", with *Derek Ereẓ* again referring to reverence or respect.[138] Above we learned that the Rabbis looked upon the mistreatment of "the concubine in Gibeah" as a violation of *Derek Ereẓ*, and hence *Derek Ereẓ* refers also to *proper* sex behaviour.[139] In this instance, the violation of *Derek*

Ereẓ involved Israel in a civil war in which seventy thousand men were slain, although the Rabbis place the ultimate blame on the Great Sanhedrin which failed to teach Torah to the populace.[140] The reward of *Derek Ereẓ* is given in this world, says another midrash, and "the principal remains for him for the World to Come"; and the midrash goes on to attribute each miracle whereby God protected and nourished Israel in the wilderness to a corresponding act of hospitality on Abraham's part when the angels visited him.[141] Here *Derek Ereẓ* summarizes acts of hospitality, and the reward is an aspect of corporate justice, the descendants benefiting from the *Derek Ereẓ* practiced by their progenitor. All of the instances mentioned in this paragraph are examples of ethical *Derek Ereẓ*, easily identified as such by the element of reward or punishment connected with each.[142]

Ethical *Derek Ereẓ* is not confined to overt acts. It consists of certain attitudes, as well, attitudes or viewpoints as essential to the good life as are good deeds. Just as the single motive behind a course of conduct may or may not be ethical, as with the motive in marrying,[143] so one's whole outlook may be ethical, "proper", or the reverse. To Mordecai's plea that Esther intercede with the king in behalf of the Jews, Esther first replies that to enter the king's inner court without being called was to risk one's life. "And I have not been called" (Esther 4:11). The Rabbis say that when Esther spoke thus she said "words that were not proper" and therefore merited Mordecai's wrath. But when later "she spoke with him properly he consented to her words. And these are the words that she spoke with *Derek Ereẓ* — when she said, 'Go, gather together all the Jews . . .' (*ibid.* 16)."[144] Notice that the Rabbis characterize as "proper" and as spoken "with *Derek Ereẓ*" those words in which she bids the Jews to gather for a fast; on the other hand, when she expresses her fears they say she spoke "words that were not proper". To be afraid of the outcome when engaged in a righteous cause is to lack faith in God, and hence "improper" or wrong. But to call upon God in trouble is to rely on Him and hence "proper" or right — in other words, in accordance with *Derek Ereẓ*. The Rabbis also apparently characterize another attitude as being not in accordance with *Derek Ereẓ*. They condemn the man who wearies of life — of "the good life in this world", as they put it — and they say that he who takes such an attitude will be punished. Enlarging on the theme with a parable of a subject who was invited by his king to a feast for thirty days and who declared at the end of fifteen that he didn't want to stay for the remainder, the Rabbis stigmatise such behaviour as not being *Derek Ereẓ*.[145] Attitudes, then, as well as conduct, are included in ethical *Derek Ereẓ*.

It is advisable now to survey somewhat more critically the concept we have been studying. Without indulging in formal definitions that aim to classify acts or motives as ethical, the Rabbis nonetheless possessed a concept reflecting their complete awareness of the category of the ethical. This concept is *Derek Ereẓ*. It denotes at once universal human traits and those human traits that are "proper", good. Such a double use of the term reveals in a single phrase the assumptions which together constitute the rabbinic "definition" of the ethical: Good actions, motives and outlooks have their ground in human nature; good actions, therefore, can and should be universal human traits. But this is not all that is implied in the rabbinic conception of the ethical. By insisting that divine justice follows upon the practice of ethical *Derek Ereẓ*, the Rabbis strongly imply that good actions not only ought to be but *must* be universal traits, that otherwise human beings and groups cannot exist, an implication that is made very explicit, as we shall see later on. Finally, there is the corollary that by good actions, by ethical *Derek Ereẓ*, the Rabbis do not mean all those deeds and attitudes which the Torah enjoins only upon Israel but those deeds which all nations and individuals must do in common with Israel. Striking illustrations of this corollary are the instances which the Rabbis give of idol-worshippers practicing *Derek Ereẓ* and receiving reward therefor.

Now it may appear to us, with our modern historical approach, that this corollary does not have the force of a consistent principle. Certain traits, notably attitudes involving a belief in God, the Rabbis characterize as *Derek Ereẓ* whereas by the very circumstances of history these traits could be characteristic only of Israel. Thus, of the four motives in marrying, all of them spoken of as types of *Derek Ereẓ*, the motives of marrying for fornication, for money and for social position are common human traits but the motive of marrying for the sake of Heaven can only be prevalent where there is a conception of Heaven (i. e., God), namely, amongst Israel. Notice also that he that marries from this high motive is rewarded by children who will save Israel in time of distress, certainly an acknowledgement by the Rabbis themselves of the milieu favorable to the motive.[146] Again, when Esther indicates that she places her reliance upon God, the Rabbis describe her words as being in accordance with *Derek Ereẓ*; yet could this kind of reliance upon God be a characteristic of peoples other than Israel? But we must not commit the error, in our turn, of convicting the Rabbis of inconsistency after we have invested them with an historical outlook wholly foreign to their theology. The Rabbis did include certain attitudes involving a belief in God as being among the ethical essentials that no part of mankind dare violate, even though in rabbinic times such attitudes were characteristic of Israel alone. *Ḥillul Hashem* is one of the eight things that bring destruction upon the world, according to the Rabbis, "the world" here referring to all nations and individuals as can be seen from the examples cited.[147] We are dealing, then, with matters which the Rabbis regarded not as peculiar to Israel but as applying to the whole world and which, therefore, must be included in their conception of ethical *Derek Ereẓ*.

In the discussion thus far we have attempted to arrive at the rabbinic view of the ethical by analyzing all that is contained and implied in the category of ethical *Derek Ereẓ*. But have we established as yet, beyond any doubt, the existence of such a category? Have we not, perhaps, arbitrarily segmented one phase of the large, amorphous concept of *Derek Ereẓ* and, by attaching to it the name of "ethical *Derek Ereẓ*", speciously given it the character of a category? That the category of ethical *Derek Ereẓ* is a genuine one, however, has already been partially demonstrated. Divine justice, we learned above, follows inevitably upon some matters designated as *Derek Ereẓ* and not upon others so designated; the former, consisting of deeds or attitudes for which man is held responsible, must, therefore, constitute a distinct category, the category of the ethical. Two other considerations, moreover, completely establish the genuineness of the concept of ethical *Derek Ereẓ*.

For one thing, the Rabbis conceive of *Derek Ereẓ* itself as being part of the category of *miẓwot*. They speak, in several places, of "*Derek Ereẓ* and the rest of the *miẓwot*."[148] Obviously, when they speak thus they cannot have in mind that large concept of *Derek Ereẓ* that takes in such things as natural but not proper sexual relations and the effect of the children's bad behaviour on the father's peace of mind, things that are certainly not *miẓwot*. Hence, the Rabbis must have in mind only a certain aspect of *Derek Ereẓ*, those matters that are in keeping with their conception of *miẓwot* which we have called "ethical *Derek Ereẓ*". And, by the same token, since ethical *Derek Ereẓ* is part and parcel of the *miẓwot*, the commands of God, it follows that the practice of ethical *Derek Ereẓ* is rewarded, and its infraction punished, by God, something we have already noted.

There is one important distinction between ethical *Derek Ereẓ* and the other *miẓwot.* The *miẓwot* consist of disparate commandments, each of which is distinctly enumerated either in the written or the oral Torah. *Derek Ereẓ,* on the other hand, is the equivalent of our term "ethics" and, like the latter, does not have reference to a fixed list of actions or attitudes but designates a general quality common to an indefinite number of occasions. These occasions, moreover, are so richly varied that the term covering them in rabbinic theology is the same as that used to describe anything characteristic of human beings. The distinction just made is adumbrated, perhaps, by the difference in the grammatical forms of the two concepts: *miẓwot* is the plural of *miẓwah,* the plural standing thus for an aggregation of individual instances, whereas *Derek Ereẓ* is a singular noun. Since *Derek Ereẓ* is the quality of being ethical it is to be expected that some *miẓwot* will also be referred to, occasionally, as *Derek Ereẓ.* We have learned that charity, for example, is a "grave *miẓwah*",[149] but we have seen, too, that elsewhere the Rabbis deliberately state that charity is *Derek Ereẓ.*[150] Again, when the Rabbis say that he who studies the Torah and performs the *miẓwot* through suffering can be assured that "the reward of *Derek Ereẓ* is given him and the principal kept for him,"[151] they undoubtedly imply that a portion, at least, of the *miẓwot* is to be characterized as *Derek Ereẓ.*[152] Since many *miẓwot* are thus included in the category of *Derek Ereẓ,* the gradations in *miẓwot*[153] will make for corresponding gradations in *Derek Ereẓ,* so that since charity, to take the example cited above, is a "grave *miẓwah*" it will also be a grave matter in *Derek Ereẓ.* The wide variety of occasions which ethical *Derek Ereẓ* covers makes it but natural that some of these occasions will possess greater ethical significance than others.

We said above that there are several considerations that completely establish the genuineness of the concept of ethical

Derek Ereẓ, and we just now dealt with one, namely, the relation betwen *Derek Ereẓ* and *miẓwot*. Another substantiation of its genuineness is its relation with Torah. In the previous chapter we saw that from Torah Israel learns *Derek Ereẓ*,[154] that the study of Torah implicates action, *Derek Ereẓ*,[155] and that Torah is, therefore, superior to *Derek Ereẓ*.[156] Obviously, when the Rabbis speak of *Derek Ereẓ* in connection with Torah they refer to that phase which we have called "ethical *Derek Ereẓ*", not to anything and everything characteristic of man. Only ethical *Derek Ereẓ* can have that in common with *miẓwot* and Good Deeds which permits all three to be aspects of the practical efficacy of Torah.[157]

Torah teaches, and is bound up with, ethical *Derek Ereẓ*. The study of Torah involves, therefore, the study of ethical *Derek Ereẓ*. A man should acquire a comrade who will "teach him Mishnah and Bible and reveal to him the secrets of Torah and the secrets of *Derek Ereẓ*."[158] Torah implicates ethical *Derek Ereẓ*. The Rabbis argue that because Torah is to be found in Israel ethical *Derek Ereẓ* must also be in them: "There is twice Torah — all the more must there be *Derek Ereẓ* in you."[159] Yet despite this close relationship between Torah and ethical *Derek Ereẓ* there is a demarcation between them, as we pointed out in the section on "The Efficacy of Torah" in the previous chapter. Because of its pragmatic efficacy, Torah is infinitely superior to *Derek Ereẓ* in the very quality that characterizes the latter, namely, conduct.[160] Hence, when our author calls on the people to pray for the householders "because of the *Derek Ereẓ* in them"— that is, for the business men who lead an ethical life but who do not occupy themselves with the Torah — he affirms that they ought to pray all the more for the children of these householders who are engaged in the study of Torah.[161]

We also saw in the section just mentioned that the Rabbis

were completely aware that the efficacy of Torah is by no means inevitable and that good conduct is not always dependent on the knowledge of Torah. *Derek Ereẓ* bears out this observation especially well. At the basis of this concept lies the recognition that ethical traits are universal, that they are not confined to Israel, therefore, and do not necessarily flow out of Torah. The Rabbis say this in so many words. Commenting on Gen. 3:24, they interpret the word "way" as referring to "the way of the world", *Derek Ereẓ*, and the phrase "the tree of life" as referring to Torah, and draw the conclusion "that *Derek Ereẓ* preceded everything", that is, came before Torah.[162] In a parallel passage elsewhere the same verse is the warrant for the explicit statement that *Derek Ereẓ* preceded the Torah by twenty-six generations,[163] meaning that the world practiced *Derek Ereẓ* throughout the generations which had elapsed before the Torah was given on Sinai. The Rabbis recognize also that it is possible for a man to practice *Derek Ereẓ* now, although possessing no knowledge of Torah. Reward is promised first to him who possesses only *Derek Ereẓ* and the Pentateuch alone, "provided only that he guard himself from transgression", and then to him who knows no Torah at all but who recites the *Ḳeri'at Shem'a* and prays the *Tefillah*, "provided only that he guard himself from transgression."[164] Evidently, the latter man is in the class of the ignorant who practice "*Derek Ereẓ* and the rest of the *miẓwot*, keeping themselves far from transgression and from every unsightly thing",[165] again an acknowledgement by the Rabbis that the practice of *Derek Ereẓ* does not always depend on the knowledge of Torah. That this contradicts the principle that Torah implicates *Derek Ereẓ* is obvious. In the section on "The Efficacy of Torah", however, we learned that the Rabbis met this logical contradiction in a way characteristic of the experiential, organic nature of rabbinic theology.

Ethical *Derek Ereẓ*, we have surely noticed, is integrated with the fundamental concepts. It is an aspect of Torah. Obligatory upon all of mankind, the Rabbis feel certain that Israel practices *Derek Ereẓ* because the latter is implicated in Torah. God's justice is associated with ethical *Derek Ereẓ*, for its practice brings reward and its infraction, punishment; and it was just this, indeed, that enabled us to distinguish ethical *Derek Ereẓ* from *Derek Ereẓ* in general. Now the numerous instances of God's justice connected with *Derek Ereẓ* which have been given thus far are all of them concerned with justice in this world. That is to be expected of rabbinic theology, devoted as it is to guiding man's life here and now. But God's full justice, we have learned, extends both to this world and to the next. God gives the reward, say the Rabbis, for "*Derek Ereẓ in this world* and the principal remains for him in the World to Come."[166] Again we must note, as we have so frequently before, that even when the Rabbis speak of reward in the World to Come they often say in the same breath that there is reward in this world. Nevertheless, they sometimes do promise, of course, also, reward in the World to Come independent of reward in this world: "Even though a man possess only *Derek Ereẓ* and the Pentateuch alone, his reward is deposited with Me (מונח לפני) — provided only that he guard himself from transgression."[167] Misfortunes of various kinds the Rabbis attribute to infringements of ethical *Derek Ereẓ*, regarding them not, however, only as visitations of God's distributive justice but as chastisements calculated "to save them (i. e., men) from the day that comes to meet them", that is, from the day of final reckoning, apparently.[168]

We began this section by remarking that the concept of *Derek Ereẓ* exhibiting as it does to the full the experiential nature of rabbinic theology is, for that very reason, at first sight confusing. We have established, however, that *Derek*

Ereẓ has both a general and a specific meaning. Denoting everything that is characteristic of human beings, *Derek Ereẓ* is also the rabbinic term for that aspect of human behaviour which we categorize as ethical. The latter is to be distinguished within the former by being included in the category of *miẓwot*, subject thus to God's justice, and by being implicated with Torah. Hence we are now enabled to determine the meaning of *Derek Ereẓ* in passages which formerly would have left us puzzled. In a passage quoted above,[169] for example, the Rabbis say that the knowledge of Torah is acquired "By study . . . by Bible and by Mishnah, by *Derek Ereẓ*, by little sleep, by little pleasure, by little *Derek Ereẓ*, by little business . . ." It is unnecessary to assume that the passage contradicts itself or else that it is corrupt textually. *Derek Ereẓ* is used here first in its special and then in its general sense: Associated with Bible and Mishnah, it refers to ethical behaviour; associated later with pleasure and business, it refers to "worldly" pursuits.[170] Again, a passage enumerating virtues whereby man may acquire this world and the World to Come concludes with these words: ". . . through labor, through *Derek Ereẓ*".[171] In a variant of this passage, "labor" is not mentioned and *Derek Ereẓ* is placed not at the end but among other virtues and refers there without doubt to ethical behaviour.[172] Whatever the phrase "through labor, through *Derek Ereẓ*" means, there can be no question that *Derek Ereẓ*, being among the virtues that bring reward in this world and the World to Come, can only mean ethical behaviour.[173]

A term that possesses two meanings cannot be otherwise than ambiguous occasionally. A later variant of a powerful prayer to which we have referred before proves this. In that prayer, the author cries out against the grinding poverty and oppression of Israel who nevertheless give unyielding devotion to Torah.[174] In the variant found a little below, there is added, "God forbid! If Israel should disappear (or perish) from the world, Thy Torah would disappear (or perish) from the world: The learned have taught in the Mishnah (Abot 3:17), 'If there is no Torah there is no *Derek Ereẓ*; if there is no *Derek Ereẓ* there is no Torah.' "[175] If the mishnah quoted is to have any bearing upon the statement, or rather plea, introducing it, *Derek Ereẓ* in this mishnah must have been taken to refer to business, work, or means of sustenance, the author reënforcing his own daring words with earlier authority. The Torah, he says, will disappear unless Israel occupy themselves with it, and Israel cannot continue to endure in their terrible state. And have not the learned also stated in the mishnah, he goes on to say, that if there is no Torah there is no sustenance, that is, that God gives sustenance to those that study Torah; and that without sustenance there can be no Torah? The mishnah, however, is sufficiently ambiguous to have caused the commentators to differ as to its meaning, one authority taking *Derek Ereẓ* here to mean ethical *Derek Ereẓ*.[176]

The Rabbis, we can conclude, certainly had an awareness of the ethical as such. And the strength of their category of the ethical lies in its experiential character. They offered no formal definition which, at best, can only constrict and harden a warm human conviction. Instead, their experience of the ethical found expression in a concept, *Derek Ereẓ*. Besides the three factors which distinguish ethical *Derek Ereẓ* within the general concept, the rabbinic concept of the ethical has three other characteristics. Far from being confined to Israel, ethics, according to the Rabbis, are obligatory on all of mankind, being universal in scope as well as in their mandatory nature. Further, there can be no fixed list of ethical actions; the ethical quality may be present in innumerable situations. Finally, there are gradations in ethical significance.[177]

IV. Derek Ereẓ (cont.):

Charity and Deeds of Loving-Kindness[178]

Charity and Deeds of Loving-kindness are ethical *Derek Ereẓ*, as we have learned.[179] Charity is also a *miẓwah*[180] and so, too, is the doing of Deeds of Loving-kindness.[181] Frequently associated, and even occurring together as a stereotype phrase,[182] the sub-concepts of charity and Deeds of Loving-kindness are closely related to each other. We shall best arrive at this relationship, however, after having analyzed first each sub-concept separately.

The scope of charity is determined for the Rabbis by two main considerations. One elemental purpose behind the giving of charity is to save the life of a fellow human-being. "A man gives charity to his fellow in this world, intending thus that he (i. e. his fellow) should live and not die."[183] No doubt the Rabbis had this elemental function of charity in mind when they classed charity as "a grave *miẓwah*,"[184] for they declare that he "that saves one life is accounted as though he had saved an entire world."[185] A sub-concept under ethical *Derek Ereẓ*, charity, too, is a quality inherent in a number of different deeds, depending on the needs of the one whose life is to be saved. We find, therefore, that the Rabbis use the word *ẓedaḳah*, an abstract noun,[186] when they speak of charity in general and *ẓedaḳot*, the plural, when they speak of specific acts of charity, e. g., "(If a man) has done *ẓedaḳot* (acts of charity) all his days and has been feeding the hungry and giving drink to the thirsty and clothing the naked and redeeming the captives . . ."[187] Since the most pressing needs have to do with physical sustenance, *ẓedaḳah* ordinarily refers to alms-giving intended to satisfy those needs. The Rabbis ask, for instance, why God commanded that we give *ẓedaḳah* to the poor when He Himself feeds and provides for and sustains all who enter this world.[188] Not only the helpless or those in dire want because of misfortune are the proper subjects of charity, however. It is also an act of charity to provide for the wants of the scholar of the neighborhood who has dedicated himself entirely to the study of Torah "for the sake of Heaven", and for the wants of the scholar's family and of those who study with him.[189] This extension of the scope of charity to include students devoted to Torah is in line with the Rabbis' emphasis upon, and preoccupation with, Torah, and made it possible, materially, to maintain academic institutions.

For the connotations of the word *ẓedaḳah* in rabbinic literature, it is not very helpful to go back to the derivation of the word or to its usage in the Bible, a procedure not apt to give reliable results with respect to any rabbinic concept. It has been often remarked, for example, that, since *ẓedaḳah* in the Bible means "righteousness", Jewish tradition has looked upon the giving of charity as restoring justice to the poor. But the Rabbis, it is pertinent to notice, never use the word *ẓedaḳah* in the sense of "righteousness" even when it occurs in the biblical verses they quote; to them it still means charity.[190] The best way to discover the connotations of *ẓedaḳah* in rabbinic usage is to note the manner in which the Rabbis employ the word in settings other than those strictly of the giving of charity. We have learned that God's providence in supplying food to all His creatures is termed *ẓedaḳah*, and we recognized His providence to be a manifestation of His loving-kindness.[191] In the measure a man or a generation have "done Torah", say the Rabbis, God acts "with *ẓedaḳah*" toward them, an expression that again must refer to His loving-kindness.[192] Further, among the three men whose great worth makes comparison with them laudatory, the first is Aaron, the High Priest, "who intended and increased peace between Israel and their Father who is in heaven", and the second is David "who intended and increased *ẓedaḳah* between

Israel and their Father who is in heaven,"[193] *ẓedaḳah*, as we can see by the context, epitomizing here all the qualities of tender relationship. Hence, while *ẓedaḳah* ordinarily means the giving of charity, it also connotes love and tenderness. The rabbinic concept of *ẓedaḳah* is thus conveyed remarkably well by the word "charity": Denoting help to the needy, *ẓedaḳah* possesses also all the warm connotations of the literal meaning of the word "charity".[194] Acts of charity, it would appear, should not be prompted merely by a sense of duty, an uninspired desire to fulfill a *miẓwah*, but should well out of love and tenderness and compassion for those in need. The Rabbis declare that man must imitate God who is compassionate toward Israel, toward the poor, the fallen, the needy, the orphan and the widow, and then go on to speak in praise of charity.[195] Because charity is associated with acts that are heartfelt, obligatory gifts when given with joy assume the high status of charity.[196] Once more we find that a *miẓwah*, far from being an act performed coldly out of a sense of duty, engages, on the contrary, the warmest and tenderest emotions of man.

In consonance with their predilection for the concrete, whether expressed in the details of law or theology, the Rabbis are not content with expounding in a general way on the importance of charity. They set forth also specific rules indicating those to whom priority should be given in charity and those who have special claims upon one's consideration. He who "has much sustenance" and wishes to do charity that he may support others should act in this wise: First, he must provide for his father and mother; then, out of the surplus which may be left over in each case, for the following who come in the order of priority — his brother and sister, the members of his household (i. e., the poor who work for him, according to Friedmann), the (poor) members of his family, the poor of his neighborhood, the poor of his street; "and from then on let him do much charity in (all) Israel".[197] The principles employed here are relationship and propinquity, but it is worth noting that in one instance the latter takes precedence over the former, a man's responsibility being greater, apparently, for those who work for him than for the more distant members of his family. Others who have a special claim are a divorced wife who has become poor and the scholar living in the neighborhood who studies "for the sake of Heaven", in reference to both of whom the Rabbis apply the verse, "Hide not thyself from thine own flesh" (Is. 58:7).[198] From the law that one must help the wicked who are poor can be judged how great is the duty to help "the righteous of the world who do His will every day continually."[199]

The Rabbis made of modesty a principle, as we have learned above, and this principle has special force with regard to charity. Charity, like all good things, must be done in secret,[200] thus both sparing the feelings of the recipient and preventing the glorifying of the giver.

Charity is integrated with the four fundamental concepts; it is, therefore, of the very warp and woof of rabbinic theology, not just an isolated teaching. Torah has already entered into our discussion of the concept of charity, for we have learned that charity is a grave *miẓwah* of the Torah, that it is an aspect of *Derek Ereẓ*, and that the scope of charity extends to those who study Torah "for the sake of Heaven". But the Rabbis integrate Torah with charity in all literalness. They declare that charity has been made equal to Torah and that Torah has been likened to it, called, indeed, by the name "charity".[201] Israel has been marked from the very beginning by the practice of charity, according to the Rabbis. "Our early ancestors" practiced charity, "charity" being the term that designates and distinguishes the lives of Abraham, Isaac and Jacob, Moses and Aaron, David and Solomon.[202] And the redemption of *Shekinah* (from exile) and that of Israel from "among the

Nations of the World" is to be achieved only by such as "practice justice and charity and save many lives."[203] "Great is charity for it hastens the coming of the days of the Messiah and the days of the Redemption."[204] Incidentally, in all the biblical proof-texts bearing on charity the word *ẓedaḳah* is, perforce, taken as "charity".[205]

We have noticed above, in our attempt to discover the connotations of charity, how intertwined with the concept of charity is that of God's love. The giving of charity is a manifestation merely of tenderness and compassion, components of God's attitude toward man that the Rabbis epitomize as *ẓedaḳah.* It is in this relationship of God to man, summarized by *ẓedaḳah*, that the Rabbis see God's most distinctive attribute. "The Holy One blessed be He is 'praised' by *ẓedaḳah*," and so is the throne of glory — just as "our early ancestors" were "praised", or distinguished, by *ẓedaḳah.*[206] To account for the prevalence of poverty, the Rabbis make use of the principle of corporate justice;[207] but God's concern for the poor is, nevertheless, expressed in the parable of the king's anxious love for the son he had banished from his table: "To what may he be compared (i. e., the poor man who formerly possessed wealth)? To a king of flesh and blood who decreed against his son that he be not admitted to his table. And the king knew that his son was hungry and thirsty. And he said, 'Happy is he who will bring my son into his house and will give him bread that he may eat and drink, for (then) all that is mine is his'. For it says, 'He that is gracious unto the poor lendeth unto the Lord' (Prov. 19:17)."[208]

God's justice follows inevitably upon the doing of charity. The world as a whole grows and develops only because of the charity within it;[209] and one of the four things that establish civilization is charity.[210] For the individual, there can be no greater reward than that which comes as the result of the doing of charity. "Great is charity": "It saves man from the way of death"; "it lengthens man's days and years."[211] Charity, accordingly, is the one potion of life that can counteract the Angel of Death.[212] When two priestly families, in which the males died at an early age, came to R. Joḥanan the son of Zakkai for help, he told them that they were no doubt descendants of the High Priest Eli upon whom such a curse had been pronounced, and advised them to redeem each male upon puberty with money to be devoted to charity. The advice was followed, and the men were saved.[213] "Great is charity, for from the day the world was created and until the present, everyone that gives it is 'praised' and saves himself from the judgment of Gehenna."[214] "Great is charity, for it brings man to the life of the World to Come;"[215] it was because they practiced charity that "our early ancestors" merited "this world, the days of the Messiah and the World to Come".[216] Finally, "great is charity, for it raises up and seats its giver opposite the throne of glory."[217] Spiritual reward here and now is assured him who does charity in secret: he is all the more beloved by his Father in heaven.[218]

Just as God rewards with life those who practice charity, so He also punishes with death those who have wherewith to give but refrain. The Rabbis regard Nabal's death as an example of such punishment. His life was taken because he would not save life, an instance of the principle of "measure for measure".[219] Indeed, since the purpose of charity is to save human life, the reward of life to the giver of charity is also but an aspect of the principle of "measure for measure,"[220] a principle generally employed to illustrate God's justice in *this* world.[221]

Like charity, the practice of Loving-kindness, as we have stated, is both an aspect of *Derek Ereẓ* and a *miẓwah*. There are other points of similarity. The word *ḥesed* which is the singular of *ḥasadim* in the phrase *gemilut ḥasadim* — that is, the practice of Deeds of Loving-kindness — means a deed done out of love and kind friendship. How rich are the connotations and how deep the emotions that cluster about the phrase *gemilut ḥasadim* is revealed by the rabbinic interpretations of the word "man" in Lev. 1:2 and Ezek. 2:1. According to the Rabbis, the word "man" in Lev. 1:2 is "a term of brotherhood, a term of entreaty, a term of friendship", whilst to call Ezekiel "the son of man" (Ezek. 2:1) is tantamount to calling him "the son of upright people, the son of righteous people, the son of those who do Deeds of Loving-kindness, the son of such as suffer for (the lack of) My glory and for (the lack of) the glory of Israel."[222] The practice of Deeds of Loving-kindness, the Rabbis thus imply, goes with uprightness, righteousness, devotion to God and Israel, connoted as these things all are by the word "man"; it is associated, by the same token, with feelings of brotherhood and friendship. The emotions and sentiments called into play in the practice of Deeds of Loving-kindness are, then, very similar to those that inspire the giving of charity.

What are Deeds of Loving-kindness? They are, apparently, deeds in behalf of his fellow-man that an individual may do which are not specifically set down in any list of commands or duties but which are prompted solely by kindness of heart. One of our authors explains the longevity of the First Generations by saying that God tested them thus, to see whether they would practice Deeds of Loving-kindness with one another. Only Noah, however, met the test. When they told Enosh, for example, to serve his father, he fed him and supported him and provided for him; but when they told Enosh to serve his grandfather, he replied, "I am not bound to (i. e., by law — איני חייב בו)." All of the succeeding generations acted likewise excepting Noah, who, besides providing for his father, supported not only his grandfather but also all his ancestors then living.[223] Deeds of Loving-kindness, then, are not prescribed in detail by law but are deeds necessary for the welfare of others that are done out of love and kindness. Another characteristic, as is suggested by the word "serve", seems to be that while such deeds often involve an expenditure of money they may also, at times, be in the nature of personal service. In passing, we may remark that Noah's deeds could also be regarded as acts of charity.

This concept also is integrated with the four fundamental concepts. Being a *miẓwah* as well as an element in ethical *Derek Ereẓ*, it is an aspect of Torah as conduct, and hence may well stand for the latter occasionally, which it does in the phrase "When they (Israel) are engaged in Torah and in Deeds of Loving-kindness . . ."[224] Like charity, the practice of Deeds of Loving-kindness is rooted deep in Israel's history, for it was one of the virtues that marked the generation that went out of Egypt.[225] The practice of Deeds of Loving-kindness, according to a prayer ascribed by the Rabbis to David, is made possible by God, an expression of His loving-kindness.[226] And, as we can see from the fate of the First Generations who, because they failed to meet the test, perished in the Deluge, refusing to do such deeds results in punishment, an expression of God's justice.

Impelled by similar feelings and sentiments and possessing the same dual status under Torah, charity and the practice of Deeds of Loving-kindness are closely akin to one another.[227] We have even observed that some deeds may be classed either as one or the other. In fact, so closely akin are these concepts that they may, apparently, even be substituted for each other. Commenting on the verse, "Happy are ye that sow beside all waters" (Is. 32:20), the Rabbis say, "Happy are Israel! When they are engaged in Torah and in Deeds of Loving-kindness, their (*Evil*) *Yeẓer* is controlled by them (מסור בידן) and not they by their (*Evil*) *Yeẓer*. 'Sowing' here refers to *ẓedaḳah*, for it says,

'Sow to yourselves according to *ẓedaḳah* (charity)' (Hos. 10:12)."[228] By employing a proof-text concerning charity in order to give warrant to what they say regarding Deeds of Loving-kindness, the Rabbis reveal that the two concepts are so alike as to allow the substitution of one for the other, at times.

Related so strongly, the two concepts may, on occasion, be joined and act almost in the capacity of a single concept. It is in this fashion, and not as two distinct and separate concepts, that they are integrated with the fundamental concepts in several midrashim. Thus, they are treated as a unit with respect to God's justice. Why was the time fixed for the end of the first and not for the end of the last, exile? Because in the days of the First Temple, Israel, though they worshipped idols, practiced "charity and Deeds of Loving-kindness."[229] For even a little Torah which a man does, God stores for him a reward a thousand thousand times as great, "and not a single creature knoweth of it;" for even "a little charity and Deeds of Loving-kindness" which a man does, God gives him reward a thousand thousand times as great, "and not a single creature knoweth of it."[230] This statement with regard to God's justice illustrates also how the two concepts as a unit are integrated with Torah. The first part of the statement deals with the "doing of Torah", that is, the study of Torah; the second part deals, therefore, with Torah as conduct, for the whole statement has to do with the elements of the good life. Hence, just as, above, we noticed that the practice of Deeds of Loving-kindness alone stands for Torah as conduct, of which it is an aspect, so here, too, we see that the two concepts as a unit have that rôle. Charity and the practice of Deeds of Loving-kindness, as a unit, again stand for Torah as conduct in the following contemplation: "A man should not say to himself: I have studied Bible and Mishnah today, I do not need to do this again tomorrow; I have done acts of charity today, I need not do this again tomorrow; I have done Deeds of Loving-kindness today, I need not do this again tomorrow. But he should look searchingly into himself" etc.[231] In this contemplation, the good things that one ought to do are enumerated; and they consist of the study of Bible and Mishnah, that is, of the study of Torah, and of charity and Deeds of Loving-kindness, that is, of Torah as projected into conduct.

Finally, reverting to God's justice, there is one more way in which that is associated with the two concepts as a unit — in a solution of the problem of evil. On the basis of the principle of corporate justice, the Rabbis account for four successive generations of poor men by saying that the great-grandfather did evil. But, asks Moses of God, according to the Rabbis, what if all the four generations were upright? And the answer given is that poverty, in that case, is not a punishment but a stimulant to the good life: Poverty is that condition which God found most conducive to Israel's spiritual welfare, for out of poverty they come to fear God and pray to Him, and are led to engage in charity and in Deeds of Loving-kindness.[232]

V. Derek Ereẓ (cont.):

Ethical Dicta

In an earlier section, we analyzed all the statements in our text in which the term *Derek Ereẓ* occurs and came to the conclusion that *Derek Ereẓ* has both a general and a specific meaning. "Denoting everything that is characteristic of human beings, *Derek Ereẓ* is also the rabbinic term for that aspect of human behaviour which we categorize as ethical."[233] We cannot expect the Rabbis, however, meticulously to designate as ethical every concrete instance they may happen to discuss which belongs to that category.

Such meticulous use of rubrics and classifying terms in homilies or exhortations was as far from the Rabbis as it is from our ordinary usage today. Hence, our Seder deals with a large number of ethical matters without designating them specifically as *Derek Ereẓ*. But these matters do fall into this category, nonetheless, for they conform to the characteristics of ethical *Derek Ereẓ*. Details of universal human behaviour, they are, as we shall see, subject to God's justice and bound up with the other fundamental concepts, as well. Moreover, many of these very dicta are to be found also in the tractate Derek Ereẓ or in other tractates of a similar ethical nature.[234] We are justified, then, in regarding them as belonging to the concept of *Derek Ereẓ*.

Nevertheless, the omission on the part of the Rabbis to designate these ethical dicta as referring to *Derek Ereẓ* reveals something of deep significance. All of the ethical dicta are haggadic statements, all of them, that is, are Torah. This broad classification is, apparently, sufficient in itself. Evidently, therefore, to the Rabbis Torah meant not only definite commandments and laws but also guidance in those varied and innumerable situations in life calling for ethical discrimination. Indeed, a statement summing up the significance of the five books of the Pentateuch, and given at the close of a parable, reads: "The King (God) loves truth, loves peace, loves justice and righteousness".[235] In other words, Torah spelled not only disparate *miẓwot* but general ethics.[236]

True to the organic cast of rabbinic theology, these ethical dicta are not systematized, present no neatly arranged classifications. They are not classified with respect to subject-matter. The subjects of the dicta are human traits or occasions for ethical action, but the dicta themselves, the comments, the teachings, are given from the point of view of the fundamental concepts. (The concept of Israel, to be sure, figures but little because the human traits and occasions involved in the statements are universal). Now it is possible, of course, to arrange the dicta in accordance with the subjects considered, to classify the statements on the basis of the traits or occasions referred to; this, however, the Rabbis seldom do, since their main concern is with the fundamental concepts. We do not imply that there is never any grouping of the ethical material; it is only natural that a number of ethical traits should sometimes be grouped together. But it is highly significant that such grouping is rarely a real classification, but merely a loose aggregate or collection of traits or occasions. The aggregating principle is usually a fundamental concept, or several fundamental concepts in combination, and the material aggregated consists of a number of different human traits or occasions for ethical conduct in regard to which a fundamental concept has been evoked.

Thus, the concept of God's loving-kindness is such an aggregating principle. From various aspects of God's loving-kindness, the Rabbis derive corresponding ethical attitudes incumbent upon man. " 'And thou shalt walk in His ways' (Deut. 28:9) — in the ways of Heaven." Man must imitate God, i. e., imitate aspects of God's loving-kindness: Just as Heaven is merciful and compassionate toward the wicked and receives them in repentance, so ought ye to be compassionate toward one another; just as Heaven is gracious, giving free gifts both to those that know Him and to those that do not know Him, so ought ye to give gifts to one another; just as Heaven is long-suffering, patiently biding with the wicked and receiving them in repentance, so ought ye to bide patiently with one another in (a spirit of) kindliness and not bide patiently with one another in (a spirit of) retaliation; just as Heaven is abundant in loving-kindness, leaning toward loving-kindness, so ought you to lean toward the good to do it more than to the bad.[237] Here, true enough, the traits are very closely related to each other, all being aspects, as we have said, of loving-kindness. But such close relationship between aggregated traits is rare. In another passage the Rabbis also dwell upon the imitation of God, but in this case the concept of God's loving-kindness serves in a looser manner as the aggregating principle: God pleads that Israel imitate His qualities on the ground of His love for them. God, according to the Rabbis, investigated within Himself and found eleven qualities, those mentioned in Ps. 15:2 ff—"He that walketh uprightly, and worketh righteousness," etc. And He asks of Israel nothing but that they imitate these eleven qualities, basing His request on the ground that "ye are My children and I am your Father, ye are My brothers and I am your Brother, ye are My friends and I am your Friend, ye are My beloved and I am your Beloved."[238]

The justice of God is an aggregating principle in rabbinic ethics. Those who strike in secret, or profane the Name in public, or make light of the many (?), or cause strife—their end will be like that of Korah and his congregation.[239] Gamblers, informers, apostates, sectarians, hypocrites, those that lend money on interest, or that profane the Name, the priests and Levites that borrow (from an Israelite) on their share (of the tithes he will give later), and those that raise small cattle do not leave inheritance to their children, and most certainly not to their grandchildren.[240] Good deeds are also gathered together with the promise of reward: He that marries the daughter of his sister, and that loves his neighbors, and that draws his relatives near to him, and that lends to a poor man in need—of him Scripture says, "Then shalt thou call and the Lord will answer," etc. (Is. 58:9).[241]

The concept of Torah is likewise an aggregating principle in rabbinic ethics, though as such it usually acts in combination with other fundamental concepts, most often with that of God's justice. In proving that God's justice extends to the whole world, to Gentiles as well as Israel, we cited the midrash which lists eight things causing destruction to those who practice them and four things which cause civilization to be established.[242] This midrash is in the nature of a deduction — it is introduced by מיכן אמרו ("From this they taught") — from the general statement, "Because of (violating) the words of the Torah are (people) punished, and because of (obeying) the words of the Torah are (people) healed."[243] The eight evil and the four good things are, then, grouped together under the concepts of Torah and justice at once. The concept of Torah groups rabbinic ethics in another way, too, again in combination with God's justice. Torah includes both the ethical and the ritualistic; violations of either bring punishment by God. Hence, there are several lists in which ethical and ritualistic matters are, without discrimination, equally made subject to God's punitive justice: The wicked wife who causes punishment to descend on her children is not only a gadabout, ogling men, cursing her husband's forbears, and regarding herself as superior to him but also does not observe the law regarding the first of the dough and makes vows but does not keep them;[244] they will cry "Woe" (Prov. 23:29) not only who are smooth-tongued or boastful, or who are insolent and haughty with all men, or who do not refrain from taking things illegitimately, but also those who do not remove themselves from a woman ritually unclean.[245] Thus, Torah and justice combine again to group ethical, if also ritualistic, matters, together. And there is still one more way in which a number of ethical qualities and attitudes are collected by means of the concept of Torah. In order to acquire a knowledge of the Torah, a man must measure up to certain requirements; and of these, as we saw above, only a few are technical, the majority by far being ethical prerequisites.[246] We continued there by giving several technical requirements from another list of virtues whereby man may acquire this world and the World to Come.[247] But that list also enumerates, in addition, a much larger number of ethical matters: Love (and fear) (of God), comradeship, friendship, truth, peace, lowliness and humility, a good heart, ethical *Derek Ereẓ*, the letting of nay be nay and of yea be yea, (and mercy).[248] A list of qualifications which entitle a man to this world and the World to Come is manifestly an aggregation of qualities subsumed by God's justice; yet, since this list contains also technical prerequisites for learning Torah, and since, by and large, the whole list is similar in nature to the collections of ethical and technical qualifications for the acquiring of Torah, the qualities are aggregated not only by the concept of justice but also by that of Torah. We see from the last example, and, more clearly, from the collections of ethical and technical prerequisites for the acquisition of Torah, that the idea of the study of Torah draws in its wake a great number of ethical qualities and constitutes, therefore, in itself, an aggregating principle in rabbinic ethics.

The ethical dicta, as we have said, are not put into any systematic form. Even mere aggregates of ethical traits or occasions are not the rule. Strikingly indicative of the non-systematic character of rabbinic ethics are both the casual way in which the ethical dicta are scattered throughout the entire Seder and the fact that most of these widely-scattered dicta are concerned with single virtues and a few only with several closely related traits. On the other hand, we become aware of the organic character of rabbinic ethics when we notice that the aggregating principle in such groupings of traits as do occur is a fundamental concept, and that the dicta concerning single or several closely related traits usually embody a fundamental concept — a fact we shall shortly establish. Like the concept of *Derek Ereẓ* itself, under which they are subsumed, and like the sub-concepts of charity and the practice of Deeds of Loving-kindness, to which they are cognate, the ethical dicta are integrated with the fundamental concepts.

We have now to establish the fact "that the dicta concerning single or several closely related traits usually embody a fundamental concept." In doing so, we shall be obliged, in order not to be confusing or unduly repetitive, to classify the traits or occasions according to subject-matter. In this work, we have been employing, of course, logical procedures to demonstrate the organic unity of rabbinic theology.

Honesty and fair practice in business are the themes of a number of midrashim. Those who know Torah can either sanctify or profane the Name when, as the result of their business practices, they cause Torah to be prized or else held in small repute by men;[249] the fundamental concept embodied here is Torah, of course. Every one of the learned who is not absolutely honest in his business dealings is, according to the Rabbis, among those that destroy the world;[250] here the fundamental concept is God's justice. Those who store up crops and withhold them from market (for purposes of speculation), who lend money on interest, who give short measure, or who cause prices to rise (suddenly) — of them Scripture says "Surely I will never forget any of their works" (Amos 8:7).[251] The laborer who has undertaken a task is duty-bound to do it as the owner wishes it done; if he fails to do it thus, it is of him Scripture says, "Cursed be he that doeth the work of the Lord with a slack hand" (Jer. 48:10).[252] The last two midrashim cited involve God's justice in a punitive sense. But God also rewards those who deal with integrity: Men of trust, and those who return that which is deposited with them, and who return lost articles, and who keep secrets — of them Scripture says, "Mine eyes are upon the faithful of the land" (Ps. 101:6).[253] In all these ethical dicta having as their theme honesty and uprightness in business, a fundamental concept is involved.

The possession of the virtue of "acknowledging the truth and speaking the truth in his heart", a virtue akin to honesty, is the reason the Rabbis give for God's love for Jacob.[254] He that often engages in falsehood, however, be it in his relations with the members of his family or in his relations with his teacher or, indeed, in his relations with any man, is, in accordance with God's justice, punished by the plagues mentioned in Leviticus.[255]

Arrogance, which the Rabbis place on the same level with idol-worship as an "abomination",[256] is a trait for which men are sure to be punished. The Holy One blessed be He cannot bear the arrogant.[257] Anyone that is arrogant is uprooted from the world.[258] Because of Ahitophel's arrogance, he was uprooted from the world;[259] and because the people of the Deluge, and the people of the Tower (of Babel), and the people of Sodom, and Sennacharib, and Nebuchadnezzar, and Pharaoh were arrogant, all of them were uprooted from the world.[260] God punished the arrogant of Israel, as well: Because the people of the Wilderness were arrogant, they died and did not enter the Promised Land; because Saul, king of Israel, was arrogant, he was slain and "the kingship was uprooted from him"; because the House of Israel — "may I be their atonement in all the places of their habitation"— were arrogant, they were exiled from their land.[261] In the examples of arrogance just cited, the supporting proof-texts, together with the rabbinic interpretation, make clear just what the Rabbis meant by "arrogance". According to the Rabbis, arrogance consists in the defiance of God. The biblical texts alone suffice to prove the charge of defiance of God in most cases, though Job 21:14 is applied to the people of the Deluge. There is need for rabbinic elaboration on the texts, however, to prove the charge against Saul and especially against "the House of Israel" and Ahitophel. With arrogance construed as defiance of God, we can understand now why arrogance and idol-worship are placed on the same level by the Rabbis. But another thing, also, is implied by the proof-texts and their rabbinic elaborations. If the defiance of God is arrogance, then, conversely, any exhibition of arrogance is tantamount to a defiance of God. Insolence, or as the Rabbis put it "strength of face" (עזות פנים), goes hand-in-hand with arrogance, is but an aspect of it, for in either case there is extreme self-assertion, the essence of wickedness. All who display such wickedness are punished. Those who cause fear (?), those who are haughty, and those who are insolent (or brazen) — of them Scripture says, "For the arms of the wicked shall be broken" (Ps. 37:17).[262] He that conducts himself with arrogance towards his father, mother, wife and children, toward his teacher, and, indeed towards any man, or that is insolent to his father and mother and elders, is punished by the plagues mentioned in Leviticus.[263] Thus far we have considered dicta concerning arrogance which embody the concept of God's justice. But in a contemplation where our author bids his people not to come to arrogance of spirit, and to behold God's love in giving all His creatures food and in restoring one's soul every morning,[264] the concept involved is God's love.

Humility is the opposite of arrogance. To the Rabbis, the virtue of humility, like the fault of arrogance, is much more than just a simple human trait. It is both a laudable trait in social life and one that has great religious implications. As a trait in social life, humility manifests itself in divers situations and, therefore, in a number of attitudes. There are various terms and phrases that have reference to this trait in rabbinic theology, among them *'anaw* (meek),[265] and *'alub*. "Be *'alub* to every man, and to the members of your family (even) more than to all the people", say the Rabbis; and they add that this is to be derived from God's attitude toward His people, for "He was meek (*'anaw*) with His people" on a number of occasions and did not punish them for their sins, as was proved especially during the hundred and twenty days that elapsed from the giving of the Torah until the (first) Day of Atonement.[266] "To be '*alub*" must mean here, because of the example invoked, to be ready to forgive trespasses. But since '*alub* and '*anaw* are used interchangeably in this midrash, it is evident that the Rabbis regarded this quality as but an aspect of humility. This dictum on humility involves a fundamental concept, God's love.[267] Another passage, in which the type of humility depicted conforms more to the popular notion of it, embodies the concept of God's justice. "A man should not say in his heart, 'Since there is in me no transgression, and there is in me no deliberate trespass or sin, I can count myself higher than other people and can hold myself greater than they' ". Such a man ought to be told, "Do not so, that you may fulfill your days;" and he is to be informed that a lowly spirit and an humble soul are more preferred than all the sacrifices mentioned in the Torah. For he that offers up any sacrifice, no matter what it be, has only the reward for that sacrifice, but he that has an humble opinion of himself, Scripture accounts it to him as though he had offerred up *all* the sacrifices mentioned in the Torah; for it says, "The sacrifices of God are a broken spirit" (Ps. 51:19).[268] Here the midrash condemns the arrogance of "the holier than thou" attitude, in the popular mind also the antithesis of humility, whilst it promises infinite reward for humility. From the two midrashim brought forward thus far, we can see, then, that, according to the Rabbis, humility expresses itself in more than one attitude.

Humility is the ethical trait with the highest religious significance. Just as arrogance is tantamount to defiance of God, so humility spells obedience to God and His will. "Thus did the Holy One blessed be He say to Israel: My children, have I caused you expense in the worship of Me? What do I desire of you? I desire only that ye love one another, and honor one another, and respect one another, and that there be found in you neither transgression nor anything taken illegitimately nor any unsightly thing... For it says, 'It hath been told thee, O man, what is good... to walk humbly with thy God' (Micah 6:8) — Read not 'to walk humbly with thy God', but 'walk humbly and with thee (will be) thy God': when thou actest with humility toward Him, He will act with humility toward thee."[269] Humility toward God, as can be told from this midrash, consists in acting according to His expressed desire. God, in turn, the last statement in the homily tells us, rewards obedience to Him by granting the wishes of such as obey Him. That humility was, to the Rabbis, a sign of complete obedience of God is again evident from the following homily where humility is in apposition to the absence of sin and to the presence of Torah and Good Deeds: "Happy is the man in whom there is no transgression, and in whom there is no deliberate trespass or sin, in whom there are Good Deeds and the study of Torah, lowly and humble." Such a man dwells on high with the Holy One blessed be He; he is near the *Shekinah*.[270] The Rabbis must have had in mind not only humility in social relations but also, as above, that humility which accompanies the study of Torah and the practice of Good Deeds when they declared, "A man should always be humble in Torah and in Good Deeds, with his father and mother and with his master and with his wife, with his children and with the members of his household, with his neighbors ... and even with the Gentile in the market-place, that he may be beloved Above and admirable below."[271] With humility almost symbolic of man's whole relationship to God and his acceptance of divine commands, it is easy to understand the Rabbis' emphasis on modesty, "secrecy", in the performance of all good things. All good things — Torah, charity, things done for one's wife, children and grandchildren — should be done "in secret". And if a man "has done so, all the more will he be beloved before his Father who is in heaven."[272] All the homilies on humility here given, it is hardly necessary to point out, are associated with the fundamental concept of God's justice.

Humility, we have learned in the preceding paragraph, is both a desirable trait in all social relationships and a sign of obedience of, and cleavage to, God. This dual character of humility is not fortuitous. That meekness which, in social life, expresses itself in various attitudes, be it in the readiness to forgive trespasses against oneself or in the utter absence of any taint of arrogance — such meekness is of a piece with a pious acceptance of whatever is meted out by God, and with unshaken loyalty to Him. A midrash tersely but concretely summarizing the dual character of humility, and embodying the concept of God's justice, is the following: "Those who are insulted but do not insult (others), and hear themselves shamed but make no return, and act from love (of God), and rejoice in chastisements — of them Scripture says, 'They that love Him shall be as the sun when he goeth forth in his might' (Judges 5:31)."[273] The passage continues with another statement, also embodying the concept of God's justice, in which truly inward humility is linked with control of the evil impulses in man: "They that are despised in their own eyes, and contemptuous in their own estimation, and cause their spirit to be humble, and control their (*Evil*) *Yeẓer* — of them it says, 'Thus saith the Lord . . . to him that despises himself . . . kings shall see and arise' (Is. 49:7).[274]

The harm done by means of the tongue is incalculable. The Rabbis call calumny or slander by the name of "the evil tongue" (לשון הרע), which, apparently, can vent its venom in two ways. " 'Thou shalt not bear a false report' (Exod. 23:1) — this is a warning to those who listen to 'the evil tongue'."[275] Slander, according to this interpretation — an interpretation, by the way, which renders the injunction against slander a *miẓwah* of the Torah — consists in the uttering and carrying of false reports concerning one's fellow-man. But simply to tell of a wrong deed someone has committed may also be a form of "the evil tongue": God, according to the Rabbis, refused to tell Joshua who had taken "the devoted thing", giving as His reason that He would not speak "the evil tongue."[276] Farther down, the same midrash employs the term "the evil tongue" as we first met it, as referring to a false report or a false imputation. To Joshua's statement, "Ye cannot serve the Lord . . . He will not forgive your transgressions and sins" (Josh. 24:19), the midrash has God uttering a reply in which He rebukes Joshua for slandering Him again —"again the evil tongue"— and in which He points out that, on the contrary, He forgave Israel at Moses' intercession, and that to forgive transgressions is His nature.[277] This midrash is of interest to us not only because it illustrates the meaning of "the evil tongue" but because of the setting in which it places the term, as well. The setting is that of God's forgiveness, an aspect of His loving-kindness. It is more usual, however, as we can see from the following homilies, for the term to be involved in statements having to do with God's justice. The trait of "the evil tongue", say the Rabbis, is so monstrous that even Gehenna has difficulty in containing those who had displayed it.[278] When the Quality of Justice endeavors to accuse Israel, one of her charges is that they slander each other.[279] On the other hand, great reward is given those who refuse to listen to slander: Because Jereboam, the son of Joash, refused to listen to Amaziah's slander of Amos, he, although an idol-worshipper, reigned over territory greater even than David possessed.[280] Slander, of course, is not the only form of evil that may be wrought by the tongue. "Those who plot evil, or distort the words (of others), speak with evil insinuations, or are smooth of tongue — of them Scripture says, 'Let their way be dark and slippery' (Ps. 35:6)."[281] Indeed, the Rabbis regard "smoothness of lip and tongue" as among the greatest sins in the world.[282]

Instead of condemning a man on the basis of his words or overt actions, it is the part of virtue, on the contrary, always to place on them a good interpretation. "Always judge a man on the side of merit, and do not over-balance him on the side of guilt," say the Rabbis. And they add this assurance of God's justice: "He that judges everyone on the side of merit will himself be judged (by God) on the side of merit."[283] There follows a story of how a working-man who placed good interpretations on his employer's repeated refusals to pay him his wage was later proved to be right. Concluding with another story in which the pupils of R. Joshua similarly judged some suspicious actions of their master "on the side of merit", the passage closes with the master's remark, "Just as you have judged me on the side of merit so will the Holy One blessed be He judge you on the side of merit."[284] That these ethical dicta embody a fundamental concept is obvious.

The promotion of peace among men is one of God's activities, according to the Rabbis, an aspect of His loving-kindness.[285] Because Aaron likewise made this his task, promoting peace "between Israel and their Father who is in heaven, between Israel and the learned, between the learned themselves, between a man and his fellow, between husband and wife," he was given lasting reward — "Say ye of the righteous that it shall be well with him" (Is. 3:10). For having promoted peace between Israel and their Father in heaven, God promised Aaron that his sons would atone for Israel every year and that every day they would bless Israel with "Peace" (in the benediction given in Num. 6:24 f.),[286] thus rewarding Aaron "measure for measure". In another passage wherein Aaron's peace-making proclivities are described by exactly the same formula as above, his reward is said to be the intimacy with which the Holy One blessed be He favored him, an intimacy so close as to be characterized by the verse, "Behold how good and how pleasant it is for brethren to dwell together in unity" (Ps. 133:1). The Rabbis consider such intimacy with God as natural for Moses, "the most learned of the learned, the greatest of the great, and the father of the prophets", but, because of Aaron's peace-making, say that it must have been all the more true in Aaron's case, so profound was the Rabbis' attachment to peace.[287] In still another passage wherein peace-making is described by the same formula employed above, Moses and Aaron both are the peace-makers. Their reward consists in the good name established for them "and their children and their children's children until the end of all generations". By the same token, the punishment of Dathan and Abiram, who promoted strife where Moses and Aaron promoted peace, consists in the bad name established for them and their descendants "until the end of all generations".[288] Reward and punishment, in this midrash, alike are examples of corporate justice. When Elisha interfered with Joram's intention to slay the hosts of Aram brought by God to Samaria, the Rabbis say, Elisha accomplished more by the friendly overtures than did Joram, king of Israel, with all his wars.[289] For the God-fearing individual, then, there can be no other way than that of peace. "A man should always be inventive in fear (of God), and (always have) a soft answer in his mouth, and still wrath, and increase peace (in relations) with his father and mother, and with his teacher, and with his fellow, (and) even with the Gentile in the market-place, that he may be beloved Above and beloved below, that he may be acceptable to people and that his days be fulfilled in well-being."[290] The rewards of peace-making are spiritual as well as material in this ethical dictum, which, as usual, embodies a fundamental concept.

In order that harmonious relations may exist between men, it is necessary to exercise forgiveness and generosity, considerateness and gentleness. " 'Pour out thy heart like water' (Lam. 2:19) — Just as water goes down the river and never returns, so ought every one in Israel who has quarreled with his fellow not harbor towards him jealousy or revenge in his heart, nor hold himself superior to him, and he must not withhold the words of the Torah from him."[291] This homily implies that by teaching Torah to his neighbor, with whom he may have quarreled in the past, a man demonstrates that he holds no grudge, and thus again we find an ethical dictum embodying a fundamental concept, that of Torah. Far more frequently, as we may have noticed, is the concept of justice imbedded in the ethical dicta. You should accustom yourself never to refer matters of dispute to the court on High (i. e., to God), for if your deeds chanced to come under scrutiny, you would not be able to bear it.[292] Considerateness and gentleness should mark your relations with your neighbor. Never say to a repentant sinner, "Recall your early deeds"; never say to the son of a proselyte, "Recall what were the deeds of your ancestors."[293] Do not be soft with your mouth and hard in your heart.[294] In any kind of relationship, he that shows himself hard will surely be punished, be it a relationship between father and son, or between brothers, or between scholars, or between partners.[295]

In the section on "Charity and Deeds of Loving-kindness", we discussed a number of ethical dicta on the deeds that are to be done in behalf of one's fellow-man. There are, however, other dicta on this theme that are not specifically designated as belonging to either sub-concept. Just as the Holy One blessed be He, say the Rabbis, is compassionate toward Israel "in all the places of their habitation", toward the poor, toward young orphans and toward widows, so ought a man feel compassion toward them all lest his wife become a widow and his children orphans.[296] Here two fundamental concepts are involved: God's loving-kindness, which man must imitate, and God's justice which descends on him if he does not. He who does not extend his help to anyone in distress is punished. The plague on houses comes as punishment for lying to a poor man who asked for a loan of wheat or barley, for declaring that these are not in the house.[297] Some occasions call not for material aid but for personal service. Such a service was performed by him who accompanied a traveller on a journey, a companion being absolutely necessary in those days of unsafe roads. R. Eliezer declared that a man should be compelled to accompany a fellow-man on a journey, "for the reward for accompanying is without measure". The midrash goes on to describe all the rewards given the man who showed the Israelites the entrance to Beth-el (Judges 1:22–26): The city of Luz that he afterward built was the town which produced the purple thread (תכלת) for all Israel, and so protected is that city by God that Sennacharib did not disturb it and Nebuchadnezzar did not destroy it; even the Angel of Death has no permission to pass through it, but when the old men and women who dwell there are wearied of life, they are taken outside the wall and then they die. "And", concludes the midrash, "if a man who did not have to walk with his feet, nor to speak with his mouth, but only pointed with his finger caused thereby himself and his family to be saved until the end of all generations, all the more (is it certain) that he who accompanies one of the learned from town to town, and from city to city, and from province to province, and walks with his feet and speaks with his mouth, will receive his reward from the Holy One blessed be He."[298] Again we notice how frequently the ethical dicta involve the fundamental concept of justice.

Hospitality was a virtue highly regarded by the Rabbis, and one that was often associated with the concept of justice. We have learned that Israel in the Wilderness was rewarded for Abraham's hospitality to the angels, every kindness of God corresponding to an act of Abraham's when he entertained the angels.[299] The same passage also declares that the slaying of the people of Nob and later that of Saul and Jonathan was due to their having refused bread to David;[300] and that the *Shekinah* rested on the false prophet (I Kings 13:18–20) because he gave food to the true prophet.[301] Whilst it is a duty to be hospitable, the guest, on his part, must be grateful and have only kindly feelings toward his host even if the repast consisted of nothing more than a morsel of bread with salt or of some greens dipped in water or of some dried dates, although the host may have an hundred sumptuous meals a day.[302]

The Rabbis extol the man who eats of his own and does not depend on others for his sustenance. They observe that only "when a man eats of his own" is his heart at rest, but that when he eats of others' his heart is bitter, even if it be of his son's or daughter's, not to speak of strangers'; and they add, "Happy is the man who has much sustenance in his house and his servants and the members of his household come and partake with him at his table." Such a man is likened to Aaron who increased peace "between Israel and their Father who is in heaven", to David who increased "*ẓedaḳah* between Israel and their Father who is in heaven," and to R. Joḥanan, the son of Zakkai, who caused his pupils to rejoice in the Halakah.[303] Even though the Sabbath should be made joyous not only with Torah but also with food and drink, a man ought to hesitate, nevertheless, to apply to public charity for provisions for it. Our author, deprecating R. 'Akiba's statement that a man ought to make the Sabbath "a profane day" (i. e., not have provisions out of the ordinary) rather than to apply to the public, does say, however, that although a man should take meat (from the public) for the Sabbath, he should not take much wine.[304]

The Rabbis insist on moderation in food and drink. We learned above that he who would apply himself to the study of Torah must adopt an ascetic regimen in food and drink.[305] But the Rabbis enjoin even those who cannot hope to master Torah against eating and drinking to excess. "If a man has not merited to pray that the words of the Torah enter his bowels (i. e., become part of himself), he ought (at least) to pray that excess food and drink do not enter his bowels."[306] The same midrash, depicting the uselessness of drinking and eating to excess, likens man's throat to a furnace: Just as the furnace, into which you may put all the wood in the world, will only burn and destroy it, so man's throat, into which you may put all the finest foods in the world, will only swallow and destroy them.[307] Another midrash likens the habitual toper to the Angel of Death, saying that just as it is not in the nature of the Angel of Death to be satisfied even if he be given the entire world, so it is not the nature of the toper who tarries early and late over wine ever to be satisfied. The midrash then continues its characterization of the glutton and toper: Because of his eating and drinking, he comes to desire all the sinful things the Nations of the World engage in and does them himself; "and not only that, but he sits and destroys all the works of the hands of the Holy One blessed be He from the day the world was created and until that time." Such a man will be among those who will cry "Woe" (Prov. 23:29), that is, who will surely be punished.[308] A midrash preceding the last one cited states the punishment of the toper thus: "It is a bad sign for him, and he uproots himself (from the world) with his (own) hand."[309] Of the three passages utilized in this paragraph, the first is associated with Torah, and the other two, as is more usual for ethical dicta, with God's justice.

"Laughter, small-talk and frivolousness" (שחוק שיחה ותיפלות) are linked together in our Seder in a stereotype phrase. "Laughter, small-talk and frivolousness" are, apparently, not compatible with the study of Torah and the doing of Good Deeds. Of the man who engages much in "laughter, small-talk and frivolousness", say the Rabbis, God, after pointing out that he had learned nothing from the regimen of his Father who is in heaven, asks reproachfully, "Thou, from the age of thirteen and onward, what Torah hast thou done, and what Good Deeds hast thou done?"[310] This midrash involves the concept of Torah, of course. We have learned before how he that "engages much in laughter, small-talk and frivolousness" is responsible for the visitation of God's justice on the world in general, on Israel, on the neighborhood he dwells in, on the family of which he is a member.[311] In the midrash which contains this instance of corporate justice, the Rabbis apparently wish to explain why they take such a harsh attitude toward levity. "For everyone that engages much in 'laughter, small-talk and frivolousness' comes to 'lying and killing and stealing and committing adultery' (Hos. 4:2), and swears falsely and lies in court."[312] The Rabbis further warn against engaging much in "laughter, small-talk and frivolousness", and equate these three things with sexual looseness. Continuing, they equate, by means of proof-texts, "laughter" with idol-worship, with murder, with grave transgression and with attempting to change the judgment of Gehenna.[313]

Sexual purity and proper sex-relations between husband and wife are the subjects of a number of homilies, all of them involving, in one way or another, the concept of God's justice. One of the grounds in a plea for justice for Israel is that so many lads and maidens in Israel remain virgin until their marriage.[314] This standard of sex-purity was responsible for early marriages: "He that does the desire of his wife, and trains his children aright, and marries off his son before puberty, before he (the son) comes to sin — of him Scripture says, 'And thou shalt know that thy tent is in peace . . . Thou shalt know also that thy seed shall be great,' etc. (Job 5:24–25)."[315] The first phrase of the homily just quoted teaches the importance of gentleness in marital relations, as well. In those instances, rare in rabbinic times, where polygamy was practiced, "there is great punishment" for a man who has two wives and he supplies to one "her food, her raiment, and her conjugal rights" (Exod. 21:10), but not to the other.[316] Sexual perversions bring death upon those that practice them, according to the Rabbis. Such practices may even result in the visitation of corporate justice. The story is related of the death of a teacher and that of his wife and son and son's son as well as that of his two hundred pupils because of the wicked ways and the practice of masturbation indulged in by the pupils.[317] One of the virtues that renders an Israelite worthy of the function of a priest and "prepared to receive (the presence of) *Shekinah* as are the ministering angels" is freedom from such practice.[318] For the sin of sodomy, the punishment consists of burning in Gehenna, as can be gathered from the story told, according to our Seder, by R. Joḥanan.[319]

The relations of the opposite sexes are carefully regulated by the Rabbis. These proprieties are matters of law, *halakah*.[320] A man should not be alone with two women, nor one woman with two men, but one woman may be alone with three men, for then two of the men could act as witnesses in the court if one of the men sinned with her; even so, the three men must be men of learning and probity.[321] Those men who have business dealings with women must not be alone with them even on such occasions.[322] The Rabbis, apparently, regard poverty as the main cause of prostitution for they declare that under the stress of hunger, a woman will compromise with herself and commit sin and say, "There was nothing (wrong) in that". Hence, the Rabbis instituted the law that if a man dies, leaving sons and daughters, the sons inherit the property and the daughters are provided for — if the property be large; but if there is little inheritance left, the daughters are first provided for, even if the sons have to go begging, literally.[323] This attitude and the proprieties issuing from it were made, then, matters of law, that is, of Torah.

It would not be fair to leave the impression, however, that woman had but slight worth in the eyes of the Rabbis. On the contrary, the Rabbis believed that the woman's influence counts for very much, for good and for ill. True, their conception of what constitutes a good woman was in conformity with the ideal current in antiquity. "An upright woman," they concluded, "is only she who does the will of her husband." This conclusion they drew from the instance of Jael who, according to them, was an "upright woman" and did the will of her husband, and thus merited that she be singled out from all the women to be the instrument of salvation for Israel.[324] On the other hand, they also realized that woman exerts enormous influence in her own right. Deborah caused Barak, say the Rabbis, to be among the upright men and to gain the World to Come. Of every woman like her and who does as she did, Scripture says, "Every wise woman buildeth her house" (Prov. 14:1).[325] Jezebel was the prime example of a wicked woman's influence for evil. She taught Ahab to worship idols, and because of her deeds and her husband's deeds they and their children were destroyed in this world and forfeited also the World to Come. Of every woman like her and who does as she did, Scripture says, "But the foolish woman plucketh it (her house) down with her own hands" (*ibid.*).[326] All the rabbinic statements mentioned in this paragraph involve the concept of God's justice.

Not limited to the relations of one individual with another, the scope of rabbinic ethics extends to the duties the individual owes the group. It is a primary duty to identify oneself with the group, particularly when the group is in trouble. "A man should not see the public in trouble and say, 'I will go and eat and drink, I will enjoy myself, and then I can go from the world.' "[327] Aptly characterizing such a man by Is. 22:13—"And behold joy and gladness . . . 'Let us eat and drink, for tomorrow we shall die' "—the Rabbis add that the verse immediately following (*ibid.*, 14), predicting punishment, applies to him, too. They go on to declare that even the most learned in Israel (חכם שבישראל), be he like Moses, the father of wisdom, the father of prophets, and as pious as Aaron, his brother—even such a man must not say "Since I am within my own home (that is, since nobody can see what I am doing), peace be upon thee, my soul!" Instead, he must go out and identify himself with the community in its trouble. As above, the Rabbis also employ here consecutive verses (Is. 56:12 and *ibid.*, 57:1), the first to describe the attitude of such a man and the second to predict punishment therefor.[328] The Rabbis teach, however, that "everyone who causes himself to suffer with the community merits and sees the consolation of the community," as was the case with Moses, who, watching the battle with the Amalekites, sat on a stone rather than on a cushion or chair in order not to be in comfort while the community was in trouble. The homily continues with a variant of the preceding midrash, certainly appropriate because similar in subject.[329] The learned and the pious have special obligations toward the community. He that knows how to exhort (or reprove) and does exhort the public gives pleasure to God, and causes that "a good blessing shall come" (Prov. 24:25) not only upon himself but also on those whom he exhorts.[330] Likewise, he to whom it is given ought to pray to God for his fellow and for the community. If he does not, he is called a sinner.[331] In this, as in the preceding paragraph, all the homilies embody the concept of God's justice.

The attitude taken toward the world in general comes within the scope of rabbinic ethics, as we noticed above when such an attitude was designated as *Derek Ereẓ*.[332] "A man should not say to himself, 'This world is full of chaos; I will go and eat and drink, I will enjoy myself, and then I can go from the world.'" If a man takes this attitude, then it is of him that Scripture says, "The fool hath said in his heart, 'There is no God' (Ps. 14:1)." If the man (taking this attitude) is one of the learned, then "wisdom and understanding, knowledge and discernment will be withheld from him."[333] It is told that in summarizing his life at his death-bed, R. Judah the Prince said, among other things, "I have never said, 'I will go and eat and drink, I will enjoy myself, and then I can go from the world.'"[334]

Practically all of the ethical dicta in the Seder involve a fundamental concept, the majority involving the concept of justice. This much we have established by the foregoing study. There are, however, some rules of conduct which have no intrinsic connection with rabbinic theology. Purely the result of observation by individuals, and dictated by practical wisdom, these rules of conduct lack the powerful emotional undercurrent characteristic of the ethics developed by the group and integrated with its theology. Thus, several aphorisms in Aramaic are given with Samuel the Small as authority: Fear him who fears not (any thing); weep not with him that weeps; search not with him that searches, etc. — warnings cautioning a man not to imitate blindly someone else for fear the one being imitated may only be witless.[335] Such empiric wisdom may sometimes be in the service of the theologic ethics, as in the case of those men of Jerusalem who made it a rule never to enter a house of feasting unless they knew who entered with them (i. e., who their company would be), and never to sign as witness to a divorce unless they knew who the other signer was.[336] Occasionally, a conclusion drawn from common experience and having no theologic significance is included in a list of matters, the rest of which do have such significance. Among those, for instance, who do not leave inheritance to their children, and most certainly not to their grandchildren, are included such as gain their wealth by traffic with other lands.[337] What prompted the Rabbis to include the latter were practical considerations of safety whilst all the others fall under the rule because of theologic considerations.[338]

In this section, we have enlarged our definition of Torah by concluding that Torah meant not only disparate *miẓwot* but also general ethics. We have demonstrated, moreover, that the ethical dicta of the Rabbis are not systematized or classified, and hence issue from no formal definition. Instead, the ethical standards are organically integrated with rabbinic theology. Ethical traits or occasions for ethical action are sometimes grouped together, but the aggregating principle is always a fundamental concept, or several fundamental concepts in combination; and dicta concerning single or several closely related traits usually embody a fundamental concept. The organic integration of the ethical standards with rabbinic theology is especially apparent in the specific association of many ethical traits with God's loving-kindness: All the finer aspects of human behaviour, those acts and relationships inspired by love for others, are consequences of the imitation by man of the various aspects of God's loving-kindness, according to the Rabbis. Indeed, to imitate God is to exercise all the good qualities. And in the ethical trait of humility, furthermore, the Rabbis see a sign of cleavage to God and His commands, just as in arrogance they see the defiance of God and the denial of His power to act with sure justice. In sum, rabbinic ethics are inextricably interwoven with rabbinic theology.

We cannot conclude our discussion of *Derek Ereẓ* before we have dealt with a problem arising out of the consideration of certain midrashim. The fact that the Rabbis possessed the concept of *Derek Ereẓ* proves, beyond any question, that they were profoundly aware of the ethical as such. More, almost every topic we have taken up testified to the ethical sensitiveness of the Rabbis. The reinterpretation of the sacrifices, the very concepts of God's loving-kindness and God's justice, the ethical requirements for the study of Torah, the efficacy of the Torah, the right of way of the ethical in *miẓwot*, the gradations in *miẓwot*, the imitation of God, the practice of charity and Deeds of Loving-kindness, the integration of the ethical standards with the theology, the inclusion of general ethics under the term "Torah"— these and other things give irrefragible evidence of the Rabbis' absorption with ethics. It is all the more surprising, therefore, that they apparently attach preëminence to laws that are purely ritualistic. In the World to Come, according to the Rabbis, God and the righteous will engage in discussion on all branches of the oral Torah and final decisions will be rendered on what is clean and what is unclean, what is permitted and what is prohibited.[339] It is certainly curious that of all the Halakot, the ritual laws of cleanness and uncleanness and what is ritually permitted and prohibited should be especially taken to await the final decision of God, much as though these laws particularly reflect the divine authority with which all the rest are charged as well. The Rabbis apparently attach the same preëminence to these ritual laws also in other connections: The special characterization of the learned is that they permit the permitted things and prohibit the prohibited things;[340] the one who does not study Mishnah for ten months forgets his learning—"he says on what is clean that it is unclean, and on the unclean that it is clean";[341] at a certain time Israel will not know the oral Torah, for "so-and-so will say that (a thing) is unclean and so-and-so will say that it is clean, so-and-so will prohibit (a thing) and so-and-so will permit it, and a clear statement and a clear mishnah will not be found."[342]

A closer examination of the midrashim in question, however, dispels the impression of the preëminence of the ritual law. What these midrashim are mainly concerned with is the correctness of the knowledge pertaining to ritual law. Declaring a thing to be clean or unclean, permitted or prohibited, effects no change, physically, on the thing thus categorized. Since these ritual laws are confined to Israel, there is really no way of telling whether they are correctly applied except through a sound knowledge of the tradition on these matters. Sound knowledge in such matters is rendered difficult by reason of the infrequency with which these laws are applied—many are suspended, owing to the destruction of the Temple, and the rest also have only occasional application. Hence, the characterization of the learned as those who know what are the permitted things and what are the prohibited things is appropriate enough. Likewise, the knowledge of the ritual laws can easily be made the test of the accuracy of the knowledge of the laws in general, as with the man who did not study for ten months, and with Israel in later times when the confusion of the law will be such that "a clear statement and a clear mishnah will not be found." But there is also no real certainty that the tradition regarding ritual laws is absolutely sound. For that reason, the Rabbis say that God Himself will give the true decisions on these matters in the World to Come, a perfect world-order demanding perfect laws.

On the other hand, there must be no trace of uncertainty concerning what man must do in matters ethical. The necessity for making decisions in such matters confronts man at every step, in all the manifold aspects of life, and whatever be his decision its effects are at once noticeable. Of the ethical traditions the Rabbis felt absolutely certain, for they are *Derek Ereẓ*, universal human traits refined in accordance with the rabbinic outlook. How completely the Rabbis took the correctness of their ethical laws and precepts for granted can be gaged from the fact that these ethical traditions were integrated with their theology, in other words, from the fact that their ethics were habitually authoritative in every situation of life.[343]

VI. Sin

To transgress any of the commands of the Torah, be it a *miẓwah* or an aspect of ethical *Derek Ereẓ*, is to commit a sin. Sin evokes God's punitive justice, according to the Rabbis. When, therefore, in our discussion of the study of Torah, of *miẓwot* and of ethical *Derek Ereẓ*, we enumerated those occasions characterized by God's punitive justice, we were dealing with matters regarded by the Rabbis as sins.

"Transgression" is the literal translation of the rabbinic word *'aberah*;[344] and the verb forms of that word are also employed in the same sense,[345] though they are more often found together with the noun.[346] When the verb is used by itself, that is, not in conjunction with the noun, we can perhaps best grasp the precise meaning of the word and its relation to Torah. The Ten Commandments, say the Rabbis, were at times observed and at other times violated, by Israel; for observing any one of the Commandments they were rewarded, and for violating it, punished. On "I am the Lord thy God", to take the First Commandment as an example, the comment is: "(Because) ye kept that 'ye are god-like beings, and all of you sons of the Most High' (Ps. 82:6); (and because) ye transgressed that 'nevertheless ye shall die like men and fall like one of the princes' (Ps. 82:7)."[347] "To transgress," then, means to over-ride, to violate, any of the commands or injunctions of the Torah, for the term is, of course, not limited to the breaking of the Ten Commandments. The expressions "to transgress any of the *miẓwot* in the Torah"[348] and "everyone that transgresses that which is written in the Torah"[349] indicate in so many words that the violation of any *miẓwah*, indeed of anything enjoined by the Torah, is a transgression.[350]

'Aberah, transgression, is the generic term for all sins. The words for sin are *ḥeṭ*, *'awon* and *pesh'a*; each of these words is equated to *'aberah* in our text. In the passage ". . . a man should not say, 'I will go and commit an *'aberah* and then bring a sin-offering'. . . for the learned have taught in the Mishnah: He that says, 'I will sin (*'eḥeṭa*) and repent'. . . is not given the opportunity to repent,"[351] *'aberah* is equated to a verbal form of *ḥeṭ*. Before the days of Hoshea, the son of Elah, "the transgression —*'aberah*— (i. e., the worship of idols) was bound up with an individual, and it was difficult for the merciful Father to exile a community for the iniquity —*'awon* — of an individual;"[352] here *'aberah* is equated with *'awon*. The same is true of the statement that God gave "the words of the Torah to Israel that they may learn from them *Derek Ereẓ* in order that their sins (the plural of *'awon*) should not multiply in the world, for he who transgresses that which is written in the Torah is punished."[353] And *'aberah* is equated to *pesh'a* in our author's declaration, "Great and grievous is (accounted) before the Holy One blessed be He the neglecting of (or, faithlessness towards) Torah —*pishe'ah shel Torah*— for it is balanced against (i. e., accounted as much as) all the trans-

gressions in the world."[354] In a passage stressing God's love for Israel, "their sinners" (or "their rebellious," "their wicked") — a form of the word *pesh'a* — are assured of forgiveness if they repent, "so that even though a man pile up an hundred *'aberot* . . . I have mercy and receive him in repentance;"[355] here again *'aberah* is equated to *pesh'a*. *'Aberah* seems to be the general term with *'awon* and *ḥeṭ* particulars subsumed under it in the statement, "Happy is the man in whom there is no *'aberah* and in whom there is no *'awon* or *ḥeṭ*,"[356] since *'aberah* is put by itself in one clause and *'awon* and *ḥeṭ* together are put in another. Nor is this merely an accident of style for similar expressions with exactly the same clausal division of the terms occur not only twice again on the same page[357] but also in a passage widely separated from that which we have just considered.[358] Sin of whatever kind is, therefore, *'aberah*, transgression of the Torah.

That there are several words for "sin" doubtless argues a time when each had a shading, a special connotation of its own. In Seder Eliahu, however, the three words *ḥeṭ*, *'awon* and *pesh'a* are usually almost synonymous. Though it may be, for example, that *ḥeṭ*, in earlier sources, sometimes denotes "accidental sin,"[359] in our text a verbal form of the word is used in the phrase "deliberate sinning," a phrase that has reference to the people of Sodom.[360] Indeed another form of the word is already found in that quotation from the Mishnah given above — "I will sin and repent, sin again and again repent"[361] — where the Rabbis wish to convey the attitude of the man who deliberately resolves to sin.[362] *Pesh'a*, on the other hand, still retains its original meaning of "wilfull disobedience" or "rebellion"[363] in the form which the word takes in the stereotype phrases "the sinners (or, rebellious) of Israel"[364] and "their sinners"[365] and perhaps also in the phrase quoted above, *pishe'ah shel Torah*. In another homily, too, where the Rabbis use successively three different words to express forgiveness for *pesh'a*, *'awon* and *ḥeṭ*, respectively, there seems to be a suggestion of the difference in connotation that once characterized these three terms for sin.[366]

In Seder Eliahu there are a number of euphemisms for sin, the Rabbis refraining, at times, from using the plain word out of that delicacy born of true piety. A euphemism that occurs frequently is the phrase "unsightly things and things that are not proper (or, seemly)" as in the statement, "The sins of a man are not only bad enough in themselves but they lead to unsightly things and (to) things that are not proper (or seemly)," where the phrase can refer only to a progression of evil, that is, to other and perhaps graver sins.[367] Besides a doubtful variant of this phrase,[368] a real variant—"corrupt deeds and things that are not seemly"—also is found.[369] Since the phrase as a whole is a euphemism for sin, the terms in it are euphemisms, as well, and it is as such that "unsightly (or, hideous) thing," in the singular, is used, always occurring here in the stereotype phrase "*'aberah* and unsightly thing."[370] Other euphemisms are "superfluous things"[371] and "things that are not proper."[372]

With sin viewed as transgression of the Torah, not only are ritualistic violations regarded as sins but ethical violations, breaches of *Derek Ereẓ*, as well. We need but recall the rabbinic teaching that God's punitive justice follows upon violations of ethical *Derek Ereẓ* to realize that in rabbinic theology ethical infractions certainly do fall under the category of sin. Nevertheless, it might not be amiss to indicate that the actual terms for sin and the rabbinic euphemisms for it are directly applied to violations of ethical standards. According to a midrash already quoted, God gave "the words of the Torah to Israel that they may learn from them *Derek Ereẓ* in order that their sins should not multiply in the world,"[373] the implication being that were Israel not to practice ethical *Derek Ereẓ* they would be committing innumerable sins. We also learned above that to say or do "things that are not proper," a euphemism for sin, is to act contrary to the demands of ethical *Derek Ereẓ*.[374] The Rabbis speak approvingly of the ignorant who practice "*Derek Ereẓ* and the rest of the *miẓwot*, keeping themselves far from transgression and from *gezel* and from (any) unsightly (or, hideous) thing,"[375] "transgression and . . . unsightly thing" being the opposite, apparently, primarily of ethical *Derek Ereẓ*. Specific acts of wrong-doing and failure to measure up to the ethical standards are also designated as sin. "Smoothness of lip and tongue" are among the greatest sins in the world.[376] He to whom it is given ought to pray to God for his fellow and for the community; if he does not, he is called a sinner.[377] We have thus indicated, without, of course, exhausting all the instances in our text, that ethical violations are definitely characterized as sins.

It is man's duty to keep far from sin. "Thus has the Holy One blessed be He said to man: My son, from the day I placed thee on the face of the earth do thou Good Deeds and (engage in) the study of Torah, and save thyself from *gezel* and from transgression and from (any) unsightly thing."[378] Couched in the same stereotype phrase, which seems to summarize for the Rabbis all forms of sin, a similar request is made by God of Israel: "What do I desire of you? I desire only that ye love one another, and honor one another, and respect one another, and that there be found in you neither transgression nor *gezel* nor any unsightly thing."[379] In this midrash there is a suggestion, at least, that love and respect for one's fellow make for the avoidance of sin, still another indication that the Rabbis were in the habit of regarding sin as the violation of ethical standards.

The avoidance of sin is, however, not just incidental to the doing of good. It is something that in itself calls for unceasing vigilance, constant watchfulness. "A man should guard himself and his children and the members of his household lest any of them go forth to transgression or to an unsightly thing."[380] No doubt it is such men, constantly on guard against sin, whom the Rabbis describe as "sin-fearing".[381] But man cannot carry on such a struggle unaided. We learned above that man must look to God for help in the acquisition of Torah and in the doing of Good Deeds;[382] likewise, in the struggle against sin one must pray to God. "A man should pray for himself, his wife, his children and members of his household that none of them go forth to transgression or to an unsightly thing; and a man should not look on whilst his father or his mother speak 'superfluous things' and remain silent, and if he does so neither he nor they will fulfill their days."[383] Both midrashim quoted here, and the last one particularly, teach that it is not enough to endeavor to save oneself from sin. A man's responsibility extends to his especial field of influence, the members of his family and household, whom he must help to keep on their guard by example and admonition. Help in the struggle against sin, then, can come from prayer and from the watchful care exercised by the family circle. In addition, the *tefillin* and *ẓiẓit* act as daily reminders, the Rabbis say, for man to "scrutinize his actions."[384]

There are certain erroneous notions responsible for the commission of sin to which the Rabbis call attention. A man may take the sacrifices to possess propitiatory efficacy and thus feel at liberty to commit sins so long as he resolves to bring an "atoning" offering. The Rabbis take pains to uproot this erroneous notion and to teach, instead, that the true function of the sacrifices lies in their ethical symbolism.[385] Another false notion which they combat is the belief that loving and fearing God are all-sufficient and that a man who avows such love and awe may feel free to transgress any of the *miẓwot*.[386] The great emphasis on filial obedience, the Rabbis also say, should not lead one to imagine that he should obey his father when the latter orders him to transgress a *mizwah.*[387] Finally, the Rabbis denounce the "holier than thou" attitude of the man who regards himself as without sin.[388]

Sin has no boundaries. Once embarked on a career of sin, the sinner cannot limit or confine the extent or magnitude of his wrong-doing. "The sins of a man are not only bad enough in themselves" but they lead to other and even graver sins, as we noticed above.[389] From such small beginnings as excessive eating and drinking, the glutton and toper comes to desire and to do all the sinful things the Nations of the World engage in, "and not only that, but he sits and destroys all the works of the hands of the Holy One blessed be He from the day the world was created and until that time."[390] That sin establishes habits which cannot be controlled is also the argument of those who forbid stealing from a Gentile, or robbing him, or swearing falsely to him, or lying to him, or shedding his blood, on the ground that he who does these things will in the end make an Israelite his victim — an argument, by the way, that we found to be an interpolation in a passage originally having for its theme the sanctification of the Name among the Gentiles through the nobility of Israel's behaviour.[391]

Of all the concepts we have discussed, the concept of sin is least amenable to compact, orderly presentation. It is so organically integrated with the other concepts that we have been obliged, perforce, to incorporate it in almost every discussion, to a greater or less degree. Without the concept of God's love, for example, it is impossible to represent the rabbinic attitude toward sin: God's love in the moral sphere is expressed by the many-sided quality of His mercy;[392] He forgives all sins, no matter how many or how grave, if the sinner repents,[393] and when he prays;[394] the very impulse to sin only serves to supply the wicked with a legitimate excuse when they turn to God in repentance.[395] Thus the rabbinic statements taken up in two entire sections of our earlier study —"The Lord, God, Merciful and Gracious" and "Repentance, Atonement and Reconciliation"[396] — are germane to the concept of sin. Yet, an adequate description of what the Rabbis meant by sin was equally impossible until after we analyzed the concept of Torah and discovered sin to be any transgression of the Torah, with all the ethical implications of that phrase.

And so the concept of sin is inseparable from that of Torah. To study and to observe the Torah is necessarily to keep far from sin. That is why when the Rabbis laud the man "in whom there is no transgression, and in whom there is no deliberate trespass or sin" they add "in whom there are Good Deeds and the study of Torah;"[397] and why when they speak approvingly of the ignorant who practice "*Derek Ereẓ* and the rest of the *miẓwot*," they complete the description with the phrase "keeping themselves far from transgression and from *gezel* and from (any) unsightly thing;"[398] and why they link to the injunction "Do Good Deeds and (engage in) the study of Torah" the warning to keep far from sin.[399] In every instance, the phrase concerning sin elaborates on what was said concerning Torah. Furthermore, having sinned, one of the means of reconciliation with God is the study of Torah;[400] and Good Deeds and the study of Torah together with repentance constitute the symbolic meaning of the sacrifices that may be brought by the individual.[401] This, again, can be more readily understood now that we know that sin is transgression of the Torah: the doing of Good Deeds (i. e., *miẓwot*) and the study of Torah—the latter because of its pragmatic efficacy[402]—are assurance that the erstwhile sinner no longer transgresses but is now on the right path.

The justice of God is interwoven with the concept of sin no less organically than are God's love and Torah. "Everyone that transgresses that which is written in the Torah is punished."[403] The midrash quoted above which told of how the sins of a man lead inevitably to other and graver sins ends with the statement, "and (thus) he uproots himself with his (own) hand from this world and from the World to Come."[404] He that has indulged in "unsightly ways and things that are not seemly" is put at a great remove from the *Shekinah*.[405] If a man remains silent whilst even his father or mother speak "superfluous things", neither he nor they will fulfill their days.[406] Concerning him that avows that he loves and fears God and hence may transgress any of the *miẓwot* of the Torah the Rabbis say, "It is a bad sign for him, and a bad portion (will be) his and severe decrees will come upon him."[407] The proper attitude is to love and fear God and therefore to determine not to transgress any of the *miẓwot*; and as for him who takes this attitude, "it is a good sign for him, and a good portion (will be) his and sin will not occur through him."[408] But we had best cease adding illustrations of how the concept of sin is combined with that of justice if we are not to repeat much of what has already been discussed in earlier chapters. Wherever we gave an account of God's punitive justice—as in the descriptions of individual and corporate justice,[409] and of the punishments in this world for the neglect of Torah,[410] and of the punishments, again in this world, for the transgression of the *miẓwot*[411] and of *Derek Ereẓ*[412] — we dealt at one and the same time with God's punitive justice and with the sins which evoked it. The concepts of sin and justice in rabbinic theology are so interrelated as to be inseparable.

All three concepts of God's love and Torah and justice are woven into a unit by the concept of sin and associated with Israel. "Blessed be the Omnipresent (המקום), blessed be He, who gave the words of the Torah to Israel that they may learn from them *Derek Ereẓ* in order that their sins should not multiply in the world, for everyone that transgresses that which is written in the Torah is punished."[413] God gave

Israel the Torah out of love in order to keep them from sin and thus also from being punished. In another passage God is said to urge Israel to penetrate into the words of the Torah which He has written for them in order to forgive their transgressions, iniquities and sins,[414] a passage which combines the concepts of God's love, Torah, Israel and sin. God also pleads with Israel to love one another and to avoid sin ("transgression . . . unsightly thing"); if they will hearken to Him, He will reward them by acting "with humility" toward them.[415] This homily not only involves the concepts of Israel, sin and justice but God's love is implicit here also. Again, God assures Israel that every-one — even children, even the ignorant — is destined for reward, "provided only that he guard himself from transgression",[416] a statement involving the concepts of Israel, sin and justice. There are also homilies in which the concept of love chiefly figures. "And thus in an hundred places," God says to Israel, "Ye have done before Me unsightly things, things that are not seemly, yet My mercy doth precede you every day continually."[417] God forgives the sins of Israel and does not withhold the words of the Torah from them.[418] Nevertheless, this does not warrant the conclusion that Israel can sin with impunity. We have long ago learned that, in rabbinic theology, it is possible to stress at times one concept and at other times, another. The two preceding homilies emphasized God's love. But God's justice is emphasized in the passage, summarized above, teaching that whilst Israel received reward for observing the Ten Commandments, they were also later severely punished for transgressing them.[419] Indeed, the Rabbis interpret many incidents in Israel's history from the standpoint of God's punitive justice, as has been pointed out in our previous study.[420]

In this section, we have analyzed the concept of sin and found that sin, of whatever kind, is *'aberah*, transgression of the Torah. The various terms for sin, all subsumed under *'aberah*, are usually synonymous in rabbinic theology, although, occasionally, there are traces of earlier connotations. We also noticed that the terms for sin, and the euphemisms for it, are frequently directly applied to violations of ethical standards. We then discussed the duty to keep far from sin, the way to avoid sin, the erroneous notions that make for sin and the progression in evil consequent upon sin. Finally, we demonstrated that the concept of sin is integrated with the four fundamental concepts.

Summary Note

In this and in the earlier study, we have demonstrated that the concepts of rabbinic theology are integrated into one organic complex, that the four fundamental concepts are not only inextricably interwoven with each other but that they also enter organically into every other concept, as well. Every topic discussed revealed the same principle of organic integration — The Independent Attributes, The Anthropomorphisms, *Malkut Shamayim*, *Ḳiddush Hashem* and *Ḥillul Hashem*, The Conception of Nature, Angelology, God's Loving-Kindness, Repentance, Prayer, The Justice of God, The Study of Torah, *Mizwot*, *Derek Ereẓ*, The Ethical Dicta, and Sin. Seder Eliahu contains also a number of concepts to which we have not accorded separate treatment, and which may be grouped under the topics of Israel, The Righteous and the Wicked, The Learned and the Ignorant, Motives, The Nations of the World, and The World to Come. Of these, the concept of Israel has figured in every concept and sub-concept we have discussed so that its integration with the other three fundamental concepts and, therefore, with all the other concepts, is not to be questioned.

Moreover, such is the organic coherence of the whole complex of concepts that, frequently, when any one concept was given "separate" treatment, we had perforce to touch upon those not given such treatment.[421]

Our concern with the organic coherence of rabbinic theology as a whole should not lead to the conclusion that we deny the necessity for analyzing the various concepts separately. The method employed here points to the opposite conclusion. Only by the detailed analysis of every concept separately can the flexibility of rabbinic theology be demonstrated, an analysis that reveals at the same time the mutual interdependence of all the concepts. Only through such detailed study, moreover, have we discovered the distinguishing features of the individual concepts — corporate justice, the efficacy of Torah, ethical *Derek Ereẓ*, *ẓedakah* as love, to take a few instances — that are essential to the understanding of rabbinic theology as a whole. In subsequent studies on other Midrashim, we hope to analyze fully the concepts not treated separately here, and also to enlarge on the outlines of the individual concepts already traced.

In this study, however, our chief interest centered on the organic coherence of the concepts. We have become more familiar with the manner in which the theory of organic thinking is exemplified by rabbinic theology. It is now possible, therefore, to analyze more deeply the theory itself and to address ourselves to the problems on which this theory sheds light.

CHAPTER IV

ON THE ORGANIC COMPLEX

I. The Organic Concept

For a thing to escape attention it needs only to be most commonplace. How else can we account for the fact that so little attention has been paid to the plain, every-day ideas of a man, the concepts which he must use in all his relationships, the grounds or motives for that spontaneous activity that constitutes so large a portion of his life? The "necessary" ideas or concepts which establish man in the world of nature have been the subject of much careful study. But are there not other concepts, notably those that affect his social relationships, which are also habitual, canalizing his moment-to-moment experience and in that sense "necessary" concepts? Being habitual or unpremeditated these concepts are the abiding elements of a man's character, the threads that make up the pattern of his personality — or, to use a word upon which we shall soon elaborate, his values. Because rabbinic theology presents precisely such concepts, our analysis may therefore have bearings beyond the limits of its subject-matter. It is not unlikely that in describing the kind of coherence characteristic of rabbinic theology and the consequences of that coherence we are delineating the features of the valuational life in general.

To attempt to define exactly the scope of the sphere of value and conduct is to attempt an impossible task. It includes all social relationships, to be sure, but also much more than that. Man's attitude toward the earth from which he draws his sustenance,[1] toward the animals,[2] toward the very skills with which he is endowed[3] are to be included in the scope of value and conduct, if rabbinic theology is a criterion. In fact one may say that under certain circumstances almost anything may fall within that scope. Yet that does not mean that the valuational life is chaotic, formless. Whatever the particular instance in question may be, it is always subsumed under a generalizing concept, and all such concepts are organically related to one another.

The valuational life, it must be noted, is not "raw experience". The religious experience of the Rabbis always involved some concept or other — God's love, prayer, repentance, Torah, *Derek Ereẓ* or some other crystallization of their experience. Indeed, either experience is made significant by a generalization, a concept of some kind, or else what happens does not register at all. Without concepts which organize and interpret, the concrete, daily life of man would be without valuation whatsoever and could hardly be characterized as human. There would certainly be no difference, for example, between the giving of short and of honest weight if there were no concept of honesty, and without the concept of kindness such action as giving bread to the hungry would bear no significance or value, even granting that it were possible. If the impression nevertheless persists that the valuational life especially is composed of "raw experience", that impression can be ascribed to the pervasive qualities of the concepts themselves. Concreteness, as we shall see later, is one of the prime characteristics of the organic complex of concepts and we shall also learn that with this concreteness is associated the *effortlessness* of organic thinking. This is another way of saying that we take the organic concepts for granted.

The organic concept partakes of the nature of concepts in general. Cohen's statement regarding universals is true with respect to the organic concept, as well: "The universal idea and particular fact generally develop into clearness together, the particular instance helping to give body and prehensibility to the idea, and the idea making the instance clearer and more definite."[4] But the organic character of the concept enriches it with additional qualities absent in other types of concepts. We shall learn, moreover, that the organic concept is not a specialized department of the mind, sharply divided from other types of mental activity, but that it may fulfill an important function in both inferential and imaginative thought.

Throughout this study we have taken pains to indicate that each concept is integrated with the four fundamental concepts. Now, however, that we have before us the analysis of a fairly large number of concepts, we can describe in greater detail the specific nature of the organic concept and thus finally arrive at a more adequate definition of it. We have called the four concepts of God's loving-kindness, His justice, Israel and Torah fundamental because they are the constitutive elements of every concept in the organic complex. They enter into the constitution of such concepts as *Ḳiddush Hashem* and *Ḥillul Hashem* and *Malkut Shamayim*, to name concepts already analyzed, giving these concepts their form and manner of application.[5] The Rabbis' view of nature and their use of angelology conform to the four fundamental concepts.[6] And besides being the constitutive elements of the rest, the fundamental concepts interweave with one another, are constitutive of each other. Thus, to give one out of many possible examples, God's love is integrated with His justice in Mercy in Judgment;[7] that mercy is exercised toward Israel;[8] and when Israel is the object of God's love, that love is frequently manifested in Torah.[9] But this knowledge of the interrelation of all concepts only introduces us to the remarkable pattern of integration exhibited by the organic complex.

The individual fundamental concept is not an undifferentiated single concept but a complex in its own right, being composed of what we have been calling sub-concepts.

The concept of Torah is an excellent case in point. It includes the sub-concepts of the study of Torah,[10] the efficacy of Torah,[11] *miẓwot*,[12] Good Deeds,[13] and ethical *Derek Ereẓ*.[14] Ethical *Derek Ereẓ* is again a complex, being made up of charity and Deeds of Loving-kindness[15] and of all those matters such as honesty, humility, reverence and the like, which we have grouped together under the caption of Ethical Dicta.[16] The other fundamental concepts are likewise complexes. God's loving-kindness subsumes providence,[17] prayer,[18] repentance and atonement,[19] the latter having its own sub-concept in vicarious atonement; and God's justice includes justice due the individual, corporate justice,[20] and chastisement.[21] Though we have not given separate treatment to the concept of Israel, our discussion has often had to do with the learned and the ignorant, the righteous and the wicked, and the Patriarchs, terms representing no doubt sub-concepts of Israel.[22] Hence, we now possess an additional criterion for the fundamental concepts: they are complexes in their own right, made up, as they are, of sub-concepts.

The sub-concept must not be regarded as an inference from the main concept; it is a primary aspect of the concept itself. God's loving-kindness, for example, is directly expressed in His providence, and in the capacities within man for repentance and prayer; God's justice, to take another example, is directly expressed in justice due the individual, corporate justice, and so on. The sub-concepts, then, share in the common ground provided by the respective fundamental concept under which they are subsumed, but they cannot be logically inferred from that concept. Perhaps one more illustration will clarify this matter further. Having begun to disengage ethical *Derek Ereẓ* from *Derek Ereẓ* in general, we were able to confirm our discovery that the former is a sub-concept of Torah—how? Not by demonstrating that it could be logically inferred from Torah, but by citing passages which indicated that the Rabbis looked upon ethical *Derek Ereẓ* as segmenting, so to speak, the sphere of *miẓwot*, a sub-concept of Torah, and as being included in Torah, all three concepts thus sharing in a common ground from which non-ethical *Derek Ereẓ* is excluded.[23] But whilst the sub-concepts of a fundamental concept are aspects of that concept, they are *different* aspects of it, each possessing its own individuality. There is no need to labor this point; even sub-concepts so much alike as charity and Deeds of Loving-kindness are each distinguished by features not found in the other.[24] Possessed of characters of their own, the sub-concepts of the *same* fundamental concept combine with one another, just as do the fundamental concepts themselves or any other organic concept, for that matter. Repentance is integrated with prayer,[25] the study of Torah with ethical *Derek Ereẓ*.[26]

When we realize, moreover, that the sub-concepts are, in every instance, integrated with the fundamental concepts and that they can also combine with any other concept or sub-concept, the term "sub-concept" seems hardly appropriate. In the present volume we have demonstrated how the study of Torah, *miẓwot*, Good Deeds, *Derek Ereẓ*, charity and Deeds of Loving-kindness and the ethical dicta, and in the preceding study how repentance[27] and prayer,[28] are integrated with the fundamental concepts. We need only recall that the efficacy of Torah is integrated with the sub-concepts of the learned and the wicked and with the concepts of *Ḳiddush Hashem* and *Ḥillul Hashem*[29] to observe how any sub-concept can combine both with other sub-concepts and with other concepts. The sub-concepts, then, function in exactly the same way as do the concepts themselves. In the actual living process of organic thinking, there is no hierarchy of ideas, no true sub-concept, and if we have temporarily suggested such a hierarchy it was only for the purpose of making the process amenable to logical analysis. Our so-called sub-concepts could very well have been made "main" concepts and analyzed accordingly and we should have obtained quite as fair a view of rabbinic theology. This has, indeed, been the procedure of the authorities in the field of rabbinic theology.[30]

Let us now briefly set down our conclusions. All the organic concepts, by means of the fundamental concepts and sub-concepts, are integrated with one another, inextricably intertwine with each other. Every organic concept possesses its own individuality and cannot be inferred from any other concept, for if this is true of sub-concepts it is certainly true of organic concepts in general. And, finally, the individuality of the organic concepts and the process of the integration of the organic complex as a whole are not separable, in other words, the *wholeness* of the organic complex and the *particularity* of the individual organic concept are mutually interdependent. Our definition, then, would be: Organic concepts are concepts in a whole complex of concepts none of which can be inferred from the others but all of which are so mutually interrelated that every individual concept, though possessing its own distinctive features, nevertheless depends for its character on the character of the complex as a whole which, in turn, depends on the character of the individual concepts. Each organic concept, therefore, implicates the whole complex without being completely descriptive of the complex, retaining, at the same time, its own distinctive features. The definition at which we have arrived is corroborated by definitions of the organic drawn from other fields. Thus Ritter and Bailey, who demonstrate that the organismal conception has been a fruitful hypothesis in various branches of scientific research, define that conception as "the conclusion that . . . wholes are so related to their parts that not only does the existence of the whole depend on the orderly coöperation and interdependence of its parts, but the whole exercises a measure of determinative control over its parts."[31] And in Coghill's suggestive discussion of behaviour as the function of the organism as a whole we find an analogous — or shall we say parallel? — description of the relation between "the processes of integration and individuation of parts."[32]

"Rabbinic theology" as a designation for the rabbinic organic complex, though to some extent justified, is not the happiest of terms. We shall see later why the word "rabbinic" is not altogether satisfactory in this regard. Here we wish to point out that the word "theology" is not entirely appropriate. By "theology" we ordinarily mean the theory behind creeds or dogmas, a logical system of ideas or concepts having a hierarchical relation to one another, whereas organic thinking involves no such hierarchy but is rather a net-work of concepts. Rabbinic theology is not theology in the accepted sense but organic thinking.

II. General Characteristics of the Organic Complex

Stemming from the organic character of rabbinic theology (we shall continue to use the term for the sake of convenience) are certain other general features. As we go on to limn these features there will emerge into clearer view the manner in which values impart meanings to things, the connotative quality in values, the extent to which values act as necessary ideas, and other attributes of values. And if we learn of the attributes of values through a study of the general features of the organic complex, are we not entitled to say that the general characteristics of the organic complex are the characteristics of the valuational life in general? Let us proceed to take up these general characteristics one by one.

1. *The Concretization of the Concept:*—"The universal idea and particular fact", says Cohen, "generally develop into clearness together, the particular instance helping to give body and prehensibility to the idea, and the idea making the instance clearer and more definite."[33] In rabbinic theology this relation between general idea or concept and particular instance amounts to a continuous process — in other words, there is a continuous process of the concretization of the concept. We must always remember that we are dealing here with facts of moment-to-moment experience; hence, as the concept is concretized the facts of experience take on the meaning thus given them by the concept, are colored by the concept, and to that extent are determined by the concept. The action of the priests of the Philistines assumes a meaning or character in the eyes of the Rabbis when they designate it as *Derek Ereẓ, Derek Ereẓ* thus determining that particular action;[34] the fact of Israel's dispersion among the nations takes on meaning for the Rabbis when they designate it as an opportunity for *Ḳiddush Hashem*, the concept again determining the particular fact;[35] and in the fact that fruit and grain rot the Rabbis see a manifestation of God's justice, once more the concept determining the situation.[36] These are only a few examples taken at random, and therefore it is important to notice the *kind* of facts they typify. They are of the stuff of daily, hourly experience, "the facts of moment-to-moment experience," as we correctly called them. Being concrete situations, they need not always be *explicitly* characterized by the concepts which illumine them with significance or meaning. Even when organic concepts are but implicit or imbedded in events, situations, attitudes, facts, the latter are nonetheless seen to be concretizations of the concepts. We recognize a prayer just as we recognize an expression of

mother-love without either being explicitly introduced as such. Similarly, though the concepts are often named, as in the examples above — indeed we should not have so clear an idea of them had they not been named occasionally — the Rabbis also very frequently find no need explicitly to designate as such the concrete manifestations of the organic concepts. The organic concepts, then, are continually applied to the constant stream of experience. They canalize that stream, or, to drop the figure, they continually interpret or determine the facts, give meaning to them. Since values lend meaning and significance to life, we have one reason why organic concepts are values.

But life is not one high splendid level of significance, and there are times when the continuity of the process of the concretization of the concept is broken. And here another quality of the organic concept asserts itself. Every concept is possessed of a *drive* toward concretization. By that, of course, we mean that individuals with whom such concepts are habitual are not passive but strive always to concretize the concept afresh. The wife of one of the learned, inconsolable after his early death, could not rest until she had been shown a detail in which he was remiss, her tragedy being thus explicable in terms of God's justice;[37] R. Simon, condemned to death together with R. Ishmael, wept in despair over the inscrutability of God's justice until R. Ishmael pointed out where they had both been at fault;[38] the man "who knew Bible but no Mishnah" and who begged to be enlightened concerning God's providence since he noticed that man provides for himself, was finally satisfied when told that God's providence was evident in the wisdom and understanding He gave to man.[39] In the first two instances, the continuity of the process of the concretization of the concept of justice had been broken, and in the last, that of the concept of providence. The drive toward concretization was, happily, satisfied in these instances. But notice that here the process of concretization consisted in applying concepts to events that were awaiting interpretation, determination. Much more frequently the process functions in just the opposite way. Not only do ethical *Derek Ereẓ*, *miẓwot*, repentance, charity, etc. continually interpret the events as they occur but they act as drives in creating new events, in concretizing each concept afresh. The concepts of *miẓwot* or *Derek Ereẓ*, for example, actuated the Rabbis to perform *miẓwot* and ethical actions. Hence they determine events in a double sense. We have, then, another attribute of values, if values are organic concepts. Values are *active* ideals, continuously striving for fulfillment.

Rabbinic haggadic literature represents an inter-action between the life of the people and the creators of literature to a degree unknown today. The concepts which gave meaning to and determined the moment-to-moment experience of the people were the subject of discourses by the Rabbis delivered before the masses. Exemplified by illustrations from history and from their own times, refined by distinctions carefully drawn, applied to the situations of daily life and prefiguring a vision of the future, these concepts as taught by the Rabbis were but a literary — or oral — extension of the values held by the masses, and of untold effect upon the direction taken by the latter. The haggadic Midrashim, among them Seder Eliahu, possess the concreteness of organic thinking; they are, in fact, examples in literature of that kind of thought. Such matters as the concrete rewards for Torah[40] are to be explained on the ground that they are examples of the process of the concretization of the concepts.[41]

The individual is *aware* of the organic concept. The process of the concretization of the concept is not altogether inevitable, may at times be broken. On such occasions, the individual is made highly aware of the concept that finally determines the situation in question. In this respect, the organic concepts are to be distinguished from the categories of Aristotle, the concretization of the latter being so completely inevitable, the category so infallibly bound up with the concrete fact, that the individual in his ordinary, day-to-day existence is entirely unaware of the categories he must perforce employ. It was, indeed, this distinction between the organic concepts and the Aristotelian categories that prevented us from designating the former as categories. At all times the Rabbis, and the people whom they taught, were aware of their organic concepts. Not only had they to be highly aware, for instance, of the concept of justice in discussing matters like the "problem of evil",[42] but the manner in which they use the concepts generally obviously indicates that they were always aware of them. They could not very well teach the importance of the study of Torah, or regard certain actions and attitudes as *Derek Ereẓ*, or enlarge upon the need for repentance without being aware of what they were doing or saying. And a man could not very well engage in prayer or in acts of charity and Loving-kindness without being highly aware of his actions and of their implications, as well. Hence, though organic concepts are habitual because they continually impart meaning to things, are continually being concretized, they are not *merely* habitual or mechanical.

Though the organic concepts do not possess the automatic character of the Aristotelian categories, they are not entirely subject to free choice, either. True enough, there is room for choice as to which organic concept shall determine a particular fact or phenomenon[43] — but the choice lies within the orbit of the organic complex and does not apply to a concept outside of it. The process of the concretization of the organic concept is a constant one and there is no one moment, ordinarily, when the individual can, by main might, stop the process, drive and all, and insert a new concept up to that moment foreign to his experience. Isolated as he may be at that moment, his reactions to things continue and those reactions are determined by the organic concepts he has always held.

Similarly, there is no such thing as suspended judgment with regard to the organic concepts. There can be no waiting for sufficient facts to accumulate in order to classify them properly, as is the procedure in science. The phenomena of experience within the scope of the valuational life have meaning immediately or else do not register at all. Organic concepts can therefore not be directly produced by experimentation. Our conclusion is, then, that although the individual is highly aware of the organic concepts or values the latter are not completely subject to free choice.

If we take into account the process of the concretization of the concept and the organic character of the complex of concepts, we shall understand why rabbinic theology does not offer formal definitions of its concepts. A formal definition of a concept is a general statement, abstracted from particular instances, which enables us to recognize new instances that can be subsumed under the concept, and which allows us to relate the concept to other concepts within some coördinated system. Now, in rabbinic theology these functions are performed without formal definitions. By means of the process of the concretization of the concept new facts or instances are continually being subsumed under or determined by the concept, and, when the process is broken, the drive toward concretization takes care that the concept be applied and new instances be subsumed or determined. And in the organic complex all concepts are integrally related to one another. Incidentally, this analysis throws light on the difference between Philo's allegoric method and the rabbinic midrashic method, observed by

Kaplan.[44] In both methods of interpretation of the Scriptures the literal meaning of the text is departed from, but Philo, intent on finding in the Scriptures formal statements of theology is bound to make abstractions of the concrete biblical stories and laws, whereas the rabbinic interpretations having no such purpose are always couched concretely.

While the Rabbis do not define formally their theologic concepts, they may draw distinctions between them, especially when the concepts are very much akin. Thus they distinguish between the concepts of charity and Deeds of Loving-kindness[45] and between those of *mizwah* and Torah.[46] But, again there is no recourse to formal definitions. The distinctions are usually drawn with the purpose of teaching that what is involved in one concept is superior in merit to what is involved in the other concept. In the case of *mizwah* and Torah, the Rabbis make the simple statement that the rewards of Torah are superior to those of *mizwot*. And in declaring Deeds of Loving-kindness to be superior to charity, they enumerate specific acts or rather kinds of acts proving that the range of the former includes that of the latter. Hence, in no case do we have a general, abstract definition free from allusion to particular instances.

It could not have been otherwise. Had the Rabbis been obliged to employ formal definitions, they would have had to test each event, as it occurred, in the light of the definitions in order to decide under which concept it belonged. That would have been impossible, of course, for, as we saw above, the phenomena of the valuational life are usually interpreted immediately as they occur else they give no meaning at all. We cannot have, as we have said, suspended judgment with regard to the organic concepts. The truth is that we are dealing here with an aspect of life that is both spontaneous and infinitely varied in shadings, an aspect of life therefore hardly to be confined within the fixed boundaries of formal definitions. Only organic concepts are adequate for such phenomena. We can go so far as to say, then, that values cannot be adequately summed up in general, formal definitions. The fact that the Rabbis were not obliged to employ formal definitions would obviate, by the way, any necessity on their part for such an analysis as we have been indulging in here.

2. *Combination of Concepts:*—It cannot have escaped anyone that, to elucidate the concepts, we were forced to return to the same midrashim over and over again. What makes this sort of treatment necessary is the fact that a number of concepts are usually involved at once in any single concrete situation. That is to say, any single concrete situation does not, as a rule, involve the concretization of merely a single organic concept but that of several concepts at once. "As reward of Moses, the righteous, standing in prayer on four, five occasions and (thus) saving Israel from death, Scripture speaks of him as though he created them. Therefore it says, 'And He remembered the days of old, Moses, his people' (Is. 63:11)."[47] In this brief passage which summarizes and interprets several similar situations, no less than five concepts are concretized—God's justice (reward), the righteous, prayer, Israel, and Torah (Scripture). The passage depicting the Quality of Justice as engaging in a dialogue with God in which she assumes the rôle of prosecutor of Israel utilizes the concepts of justice, Israel, ethical *Derek Ereẓ* ("the evil tongue" etc.), *Ḥillul Hashem*, *Malkut Shamayim*, the study of Torah, prayer, *miẓwot*, and repentance.[48] There is no need of adding more examples; practically every passage in our Midrash describing any situation whatsoever involves not one but several concepts. A single concrete situation is interpreted, made significant, usually not by one but by several organic concepts or values.

Does it not seem obvious that the more concepts concretized in any given situation, the more meaningful will that situation be? The significance that inheres in the situations that make up day-to-day experience depends, then, for its richness, on the range of the organic complex of concepts involved. An organic complex containing a large number of concepts will grasp or interpret a concrete situation in more ways than will a complex with a small number of concepts. The greater effectiveness of the larger complex does not stop there, however. Because of the drive toward concretization, every organic complex creates new situations, new events informed by combinations of concepts, but the larger complex carves out a world beyond grasp of the smaller. For the individual with a large organic complex, therefore, day-to-day experience contains situations, yields significances, of which the man with a small organic complex is absolutely unaware. Rabbinic theology was an organic complex with a wide range of concepts, as is evidenced by the large number of concepts which combine to interpret any one situation. If the passages descriptive of situations are rich in concepts, it is only because these passages are but literary reflections of day-to-day experience, of situations made richly significant by combinations of concepts.

The organic relation between the concepts, we can now see, is no mere vagary of the valuational life. Concrete situations are grasped not by one but by a number of concepts at once. For any given situation *as a whole* to be meaningful there must, of course, be some kind of coherence between the concepts, but were that coherence to be of the inferential order, the situation would become apparent to the individual in piece-meal fashion. The concrete situation is grasped as a whole because the coherence between the concepts interpreting it is organic and not logical or inferential. In analyzing the concepts, we were forced to take them up more or less singly, but in so doing we lost precisely the manner in which each concrete situation as a whole was grasped by a number of concepts. In other words, our analysis of the concepts, of necessity restricted to logical procedures, could hardly convey either the feel of any concrete situation as a whole or the organic quality of the concepts that grasped it.[49] Rabbinic theological literature, the haggadic literature, having no such purpose as ours, is a literary reflection of organic thinking intact. Hence, its literary form can now be accounted for. Not only does rabbinic theology offer no logical system of ideas, but its material, consisting as it does of interpretations of concrete situations with consequent innumerable repetition of concepts, cannot be put into systematic, classified form so far as the concepts are concerned.

3. *Potential Simultaneity of Concepts:*—What makes it possible for a number of organic concepts to grasp any given situation at once is the potential simultaneity of the organic concepts. It is as if the whole complex were constantly at trigger-point, ready to pour forth *all* its concepts on any occasion or situation. In saying this we are saying no more than that the complex is organic, of one piece. Each situation has focussed upon it the whole organic complex, and the concepts that are concretized in that situation represent the maximum possible concretization of the whole organic complex. The concepts not concretized or actualized in that situation are not totally irrelevant to the situation for they have the status of concepts that were potentially relevant. This conforms to the conclusion reached above that each organic concept implicates the whole complex.[50] Organic concepts or values, then, possess the characteristic of potential simultaneity.

The simultaneity of the organic concepts is potential and not actual. For the concretization of the whole complex is always limited by two factors — the temperament or mood of the individual and the circumstances in which the individual is placed. Abraham, Isaac and Jacob, Moses and Aaron, David and Solomon, say the Rabbis, practiced charity and Nabal did not.[51] In the case of all the former the concept of charity was concretized but not in the case of the latter. The circumstances of an individual also limit the concretization of the complex, the individual who has the burden of an extensive business, for example, not being prone, as the Rabbis noted, to study Torah.[52] The potential simultaneity of the organic concepts, then, in view of the limitations imposed, enables the *maximum* possible number of concepts to be concretized in any given situation.

The potential simultaneity of concepts means that the whole complex is brought into play upon every situation. The organic concept, therefore, represents a refutation of Bergson's doctrine of "the cinematographical mechanism of thought."[53] Bergson claims that concepts necessarily make fragmentary and static what is in reality the constantly flowing and changing stream of life. Whatever may be the case with other types of concepts, this is certainly not true of the organic concept. The latter does not make the valuational life fragmentary for in any concrete situation the whole complex of values is brought into play. And there is nothing static about the way in which the organic concepts function because every change in circumstance brings with it new concretizations of the concepts. More, the concepts are dynamic drives actually creating new situations. If by experiential concepts we mean concepts which correspond completely with actual experience, then organic concepts or values are *experiential concepts.*

The potential simultaneity of concepts also means that organic concepts or values are connotative of one another. Aside from the concepts involved explicitly in any given situation, all the rest which were potentially involved are implicit in varying degrees. Those concepts which share the same ground as the concept concretized are immediately connoted, forming, as it were, a circle about that concept, with the rest of the concepts of the complex as a penumbra. Thus, the giving of charity, alms, immediately connotes God's love, *imitatio Dei* and Deeds of Loving-kindness, and the study of Torah just as quickly connotes *mizwot*, *Derek Erez*, the efficacy of Torah. In addition to these inner circles, the penumbra of the remainder of the concepts lends further shades of meaning to the concept concretized. For it takes but a little change in the situation to render any of the implicit concepts explicit. Connotation does not involve that step-by-step effortful reasoning characteristic of logical or inferential thinking; hence, organic thinking is *effortless*.

4. *The Element of Paradox:*—Because a situation is determined by several concepts at once, paradoxes occur in organic thinking not infrequently. The simultaneity of the concepts is limited, to be sure, but the limitation is the result of other factors, not that of logical antithesis. The Rabbis studied the Torah with both love and fear or awe in their hearts, emotions having conceptual parallels, respectively, in God's love and in His justice; and these contradictory feelings are perfectly natural.[54] The same midrash which declares that God will not punish the many for the iniquity "bound up with an individual" concludes with a vehement avowal of corporate justice;[55] and the contradiction here between judging every individual purely on his own acts and the notion of corporate responsibility is one from which we cannot escape today. In another midrash, poverty is regarded both as an expression of God's punitive justice and as a manifestation of His loving-kindness, a stimulant to Israel's spiritual life.[56] No one can deny the blighting effects of poverty, but it is equally true

that, on occasion, poverty may make for spiritual growth. We are dealing, then, with things that are logically contradictory but psychologically correct, with interpretations of paradoxical character because a situation may be determined by several organic concepts at once.

5. *The Fluid Character of the Complex:*—One of the factors limiting the simultaneity of the concepts is the temperament or mood of the individual. The same situation, therefore, may be interpreted or determined by different concepts, according to the temperaments of different individuals and even according to the different moods of the same individual. Such differences are especially marked when the same or a similar situation is determined at one time by one fundamental concept and at another time by another fundamental concept. The plea is made at one time, for example, that Israel survive lest Torah disappear, Israel being determined by the concept of Torah;[57] at another time, the "words of the Torah" are regarded as important solely "because they weigh Israel over to the side of merit,"[58] Torah being determined now by the concept of Israel. Prophecy among the Gentiles is determined by the concept of justice in the passage that states that, whether Israelite or Gentile, prophecy rests upon anyone according to his deserts;[59] and it is determined by the concept of Israel in the passage expressing disapproval that the gift of prophecy was given to the Gentile, Balaam.[60] An Israelite who has been afflicted by any of the plagues mentioned in Leviticus is regarded in one midrash as "an altar of atonement for Israel,"[61] the situation being thus determined by the concept of vicarious atonement; in another midrash, a man so afflicted is said to have been punished in such fashion for lying and for insolence,[62] the same situation now being determined by the concept of justice due the individual. When the righteous are bereaved of children, the death of

the little ones is at one time laid to the sins of the fathers, determined, that is, by the concept of corporate justice;[63] at another time the same fact is included among "the chastisings of love".[64] Were rabbinic theology a logical system, these various passages would doubtless appear to contradict one another. Since rabbinic theology is an organic complex, however, these passages are but examples of the fluid character of the complex which allows for differences in temperament and mood, gives room for choice, without thereby impairing the coherence between concepts.[65]

The other factor limiting the simultaneity of the concepts consists of the circumstances or situations in which the individual is placed. Obviously, no sharp line can be drawn between this and the factor just discussed, for the individual's temperament both affects his circumstances and is itself affected by them. Nevertheless, there are many instances where we can see how circumstances directly influence the choice of the determining concepts. The seven sons of Miriam, faced with the alternatives of apostasy or death, by virtue of that circumstance, were able to sanctify the Name.[66] Similarly, the Rabbi who was offered inducements to leave Jabne, the place of scholars, by virtue of that circumstance, was able to concretize the concept of the study of Torah.[67] Fluid enough to interpret circumstances of the most varied sort, the organic complex leaves room for the interpretation of historical events; hence, the concretization of the concepts will differ, in a measure, in different periods of Jewish history. Darkness is in store, say the Rabbis, for the sons of Esau and the sons of Ishmael, the two great world-empires, Rome and Islam, which oppressed Israel.[68] This concretization of the concept of justice would not have been possible, of course, prior to the rise of Islam. Again, in the Rabbis' complaint that when in Palestine Israel observed one day of the festival and that properly whereas now because of their sins two days are observed but not one properly, the concretization of the concept of justice arises definitely out of Diaspora conditions.[69] In a word, the fluid character of the complex permits of great variety in the concretization of the concepts, depending on the circumstances and the historical epochs.

The two factors limiting the simultaneity of the concepts render it inevitable for every individual to have a configuration of the complex all his own. The circumstances of the lives of no two men are identical, and neither are their temperaments. With the circumstances of an individual limiting the concretization of the concepts in a peculiar and original way and his temperament responding to the circumstances in a like manner, the combination of concepts determining similar situations will likewise be original and tend to be consistent. The result will be a fairly consistent and original configuration of the complex as it is brought into play in the moment-to-moment life of the individual. The last ten chapters of Eliahu Zuṭa, for example, evidently a unit, make of practically all of the concepts in the complex a configuration in which the concepts of Redemption, Paradise and Gehenna form the chief features,[70] and this configuration, therefore, betrays the author's or the compiler's temperament and interests. Exactly the same phrase —"whether Gentile or Israelite, whether man or woman, whether male-slave or female-slave"— characterizes two midrashim, one declaring that God takes no account of these distinctions in the reward given for a *miẓwah*, and the other affirming that these distinctions are of no account but that deeds alone decide whether "the Holy Spirit rest upon him."[71] That these two midrashim embodying the concept of justice were uttered by the same man is evident from something besides the style: the same examples concretize in one combination the concepts of *miẓwah* and justice, and in the other, the concepts of justice and Holy Spirit, combinations of concepts concretized in facts that make for a unique configuration of the complex bespeaking a man of breadth of vision and experience. The fluid character of the complex renders such individual configurations of concepts or values possible.

6. *The Aspect of Inevitability:*—The fact that the Rabbis were aware of the organic concepts is evidence that the latter, though habitual, were not merely habitual. Though the process of concretization is continuous, the concretization of any one concept is not inevitable. This dual character can be observed both when the concepts interpret situations or events and when they act as drives in creating new events.

We have a particularly clear illustration of this characteristic in the concepts that are aspects of Torah, although, of course, it is not confined to these concepts.[72] Keenly aware of the impulses in the individual that tend to nullify all aspects of Torah, the Rabbis epitomize and personify such impulses in the term of the *Evil Yeẓer.* The Rabbis say that it is the *Evil Yeẓer* which incites a person to sin,[73] that is, to transgress the Torah.[74] They do not, incidentally, make that great dichotomy between matter and spirit which would allow them to identify the *Evil Yeẓer* with the former.[75] The concepts of *miẓwot*, ethical *Derek Ereẓ*, the study of Torah, and the other aspects of Torah, when acting as drives, encountered, therefore, such opposition within the individual that the Rabbis took cognizance of it and had a name for it. With the outcome of a conflict of this nature always in doubt in any particular instance, the concretization of the concept involved was not inevitable. On the other hand, it is inconceivable that a person could have formed part of the community of Israel unless the concepts of the organic complex, acting within him as drives, were on the whole in some degree effective. And the same dual character of the organic complex is to be noticed when the concepts interpret situations or events. The Rabbis believed that the study of Torah has pragmatic efficacy, in other words, that good conduct is implicit in the study of Torah. But they also met with scholars who were dishonest in business, with scholars who transgressed "the words of Torah." Hence, the concretization of the concept of the efficacy of Torah was not inevitable. That very fact, however, immediately became a situation for other concepts to grasp or interpret, the dishonest scholar becoming an example of one who profanes the Name and he "who knows the words of Torah and transgresses them" an example of "an absolutely wicked (man)."[76] Since the concepts both interpreted situations and acted as drives in creating new situations, the process of concretization was, then, continuous at the same time that the concretization of any one concept was not inevitable.

This dual character of the complex, affecting as it did a wide range of concepts, made it possible for the individual not only to have an inward life but one wherein intensity of emotion blended with richness of conceptual content. Since the process of concretization was continuous, the experience of the individual was never chaotic but subsumed under a wide variety of concepts. But the concretization of any one concept was never inevitable, never infallible. In a degree however slight, the concretization of any particular concept was always voluntary. There was always a moment of awareness in which the choice was made. And when action was involved or when the internal or external opposition was great, awareness became acute, and the concretization of the concept charged with profound emotion. It was for this reason that the ritualistic *mizwot*, since they called for action, could become so important a means for the cultivation of the inward life.[77] And because the inward life is nothing if not voluntary, the Rabbis insist that even obligatory matters be accomplished with joy and hence partake of the nature of voluntary actions.[78] Organic concepts or values are, therefore, charged with emotion.

Our conclusion is, then, that the organic complex as a whole is inevitable in the sense that some concept must be concretized, but that the concretization of any particular concept or value is not inevitable. The lack of complete inevitability should not be taken, however, as a flaw in the functioning of the organic complex. On the contrary, the fact that the concretization of any particular concept is not inevitable, and hence not predictable, introduces the factors of novelty and change which inhere in the very constitution of an organism. These factors mark off the organismic from the mechanistic.

III. The Rôle of Logical Thinking

By allowing for individual configurations, the organic complex enabled the individual to have a valuational life of his own and yet to live in spiritual coöperation and harmony with other individuals. Now, no individual can possibly manage the circumstances confronting him, interpreted though these be by means of the organic complex, without some modicum of logical or inferential thinking. At the very least he must employ the Aristotelian categories to the extent demanded by the common-sense grasp of things. Hence, when wide scope is given for individuality, wide scope is also given for logical or inferential thought. The organic complex of rabbinic thought provided the living, subtle, flexible framework for inferential reasoning of a very rigorous order.

Within the framework of rabbinic theology, the reasoning of the Rabbis, both with respect to Halakah and Haggadah, is as soundly logical as that of the modern scientist. The rabbinic method "calls for ingenuity and skill, the power of analysis and association, and the ability to set up hypotheses — and all these must be bolstered up by a wealth of accurate information and the use of good judgment . . . And there is a logic underlying this method of reasoning. It is the very same logic which underlies any sort of scientific research, and by which one is enabled to form hypotheses, to test them and to formulate general laws. The Talmudic student approaches the study of texts in the same manner as the scientist approaches the study of nature."[79] While this statement bears particularly on the rabbinic method as applied to Halakah, legal material, it also states the case for the relevant aspects of the method as applied to Haggadah. For in Haggadah and Halakah alike, the Rabbis use logical procedures in order to interpret biblical texts and also in their search for ways to extend and deepen the concretizations of the concepts. Inherent in the rabbinic method are the terms that designate divisions of Torah; and these terms are employed in haggadic passages with full regard to their exact meaning.[80]

The deductions which the Rabbis draw from biblical texts in order to confirm their own statements are perfectly reasonable, if we bear in mind that their statements have to do with the organic concepts. Granting the concept of the World to Come, what is more reasonable, for example, than to interpret "I will render *double* unto thee" (Zech. 9:12) as referring to reward in this world and the World to Come?[81] Or, granting the concept of repentance, is it unreasonable to conclude that the verse "Come now, and let us reason together, saith the Lord" (Is. 1:18) speaks of repentant sinners?[82] Indeed, the rabbinic interpretations often suffer, from the modern point of view, not from the lack of logical method but from an excess of prosaic logic. Capable of poetic fancies on their own accord — as witness, for instance, the dramatic scene of the angels crying out in anguish over their exclusion from the immediate proximity of *Shekinah*[83] or the idea of God's giving Adam a divorce as is done with a woman[84] — the Rabbis frequently reduce poetic passages in the Bible to prosaic literalness. Thus, according to the Rabbis, "He knoweth what is in the darkness" (Dan. 2:21) refers to the measure of punishment for the wicked in Gehenna[85] and "The heavens declare the glory of God" (Ps. 19:1–2) to the fact that the heaven together with the earth sustain God's creatures,[86] interpretations, incidentally, that embody respectively the concepts of God's justice and His providence.

The rabbinic method of interpretation subjects the biblical texts to minute analysis. In the Ten Commandments, for example, the Rabbis discover a finely articulated structure, wherein the First Commandment is connected with the three others of the same table, the Fifth with the five of the second table, and the Fifth again with the Fourth in such fashion as to bind the Commandments concerning man's relation to God with those that deal of man's relation to his fellow-man.[87] Deductions hinging on a single word of a verse are justified either by analogy with the word as it is used in another verse or else by recourse to a meaning of the root linguistically possible. Thus, the bold figure hinging on the word *nokaḥ* in Lam. 2:19, in which God is said to be engaged in heated discussion with any one of the learned who studies alone, is justified by analogy with the use of the word in I Kings 20:29 where it denotes a battle array;[88] and the roots of *ẓafonah* and *ṭeref* render it linguistically possible for the former to be interpreted as "hidden" or "treasured"[89] and for the latter as "wandering".[90] The rabbinic method permits the use of symbolism, though to a much more limited extent than does the allegoric method. Not only, however, have the rabbinic symbols a certain poetic warrant but their use is invariably consistent. In fact, so consistent are the Rabbis in the use of their symbols that the presence in the proof-text of the word "water", a symbol for Torah, helped us to reconstruct a passage textually corrupt.[91] The rabbinic method of interpretation involves, then, rigorously logical procedures within the framework of the organic complex.[92]

We must note, finally, that while the methods of interpretation were generally accepted, the particular interpretation of any verse was not a matter of consensus. The same verse could be interpreted in any number of different ways, providing the rabbinic methods of interpretation were employed and providing the interpretation embodied an organic concept. Ps. 133:1, for instance, is first interpreted to refer to Aaron's intimacy with God[93] and then to the way in which one's youthful and mature periods are made harmonious through the study of Torah.[94] Indeed, for the Rabbis this stringing together on the same proof-text of a number of otherwise dissimilar midrashim served frequently as a method of organizing their homilies.[95] The point we wish to emphasize is that the particular interpretation of any verse was an individual one both in the sense that it was necessarily the product of an individual and in the sense that it was not a matter of consensus. The biblical texts as vehicles for the organic concepts assumed the character of events or occasions interpreted by those concepts and therefore enjoyed a similar latitude of interpretation. Despite the logical methods of biblical interpretation, Rabbis may well regard each other's interpretations as far-fetched just as they may differ on the interpretation or determination of an event. Haggadic interpretation was non-dogmatic. It is no wonder, therefore, that sometimes haggadic interpretations were indulged in without any serious intention to convey the true meaning of the verse.[96]

Logical thinking within the framework of the organic complex was not confined to the interpretation of biblical texts. The Rabbis were acutely aware of the concepts, and thus there was a constant drive toward concretization. To satisfy the drive they had to seek for specific ways to concretize the concepts; and this effort involved observation and analysis. In order to describe, for example, how the concept of charity may be concretized, the Rabbis were obliged to analyze specific situations and this, in turn, enabled them to mark off that concept from the kindred one of Deeds of Loving-kindness.[97] The same careful analysis of concrete situations enabled them to set forth the methods[98] and to lay down the ethical, technical and ascetic requirements for the study of Torah,[99] to describe how repentance may be stimulated[100] and how to avoid mechanizing the prescribed prayers.[101] Keen observation of the way men act is apparent in their directions concerning ethical *Derek Ereẓ*, in the minute regulations regarding the manner whereby that action may be refined.[102] In sum, the treatment of every concept illustrates how the Rabbis relied on logical thinking to discover ways in which the concepts might be concretized.

Some, even many, of the directions or rules for concretizing the concepts are laws, matters of consensus. But this much is to be noticed. While the Rabbis employ logical reasoning in order to extend or deepen the concretization of the concepts, *in no case do they undertake to demonstrate logically the existence of the concepts themselves*. They take the concepts for granted. In an organic complex of concepts, not only are the concepts not inferred from one another but they are not logically inferred from concepts extraneous to the complex. The coherence between the concepts is organic, not logical, though within the framework of the organic complex there is room, nay, necessity, for sound logical methods.

On a small scale, the organic complex permitted three distinct types of logical approach that would have destroyed the complex had they been exercised on a large scale. The Rabbis were, of course, bound to interpret all human events and actions by means of the organic concepts, and their statements concerning these events or actions usually were simply interpretive, therefore, and nothing more. Sometimes, however, they support such simple interpretations (of facts) or concretizations (of concepts) with inferential reasoning. Thus, they add to their statement that the wicked who swear falsely are punished and end in dire poverty the following reason: By swearing falsely, the wicked cause themselves to be disqualified as witnesses with the consequence that people, losing faith in them, cease to do business with them.[103] Similarly, the Rabbis employ inferential reasoning in support of concretizations of the concept of *miẓwot*, giving social and ethical reasons for the observance of the ritualistic *miẓwot* of *ẓiẓit*, *tefillin* and *niddah* and Sabbath.[104] In these examples of logical method, the Rabbis demonstrate the reality of a concretization of the concept of justice and the need of several concretizations of the concept of *miẓwot* but they do not undertake to prove the existence of the concepts themselves. Moreover, from the nature of the examples and from the fact that an individual, R. Meir, is mentioned as the author of one of them,[105] it is apparent that this type of logical approach is not a matter of consensus. Nor could it have been the consistent practice even of individuals. Had anyone attempted to make a practice of rationalizing leisurely over every concretization of a concept, the process of concretization itself would have been so impeded as to have been inoperative.

Another logical approach, occasionally found, consisted in actually employing logical inferences in order to interpret or determine a fact or situation. An excellent example is the cogent argument presented by one of our authors to the man who regarded the Bible only as having divine authority but not the Mishnah.[106] Now in proving to his opponent that the Mishnah also has divine authority the Rabbi was not attempting to prove the divine authorship of the Torah, both men taking this concept for granted since even the opponent believed in the divine authorship of the

Bible. What the Rabbi tried to do was so to interpret the Mishnah or give such meaning to it that his opponent would be forced to extend the concept of Torah to the Mishnah also, in other words, to determine the Mishnah by means of that concept. We have already observed instances of situations or facts that awaited determination in the stories of the inconsolable widow, R. Simon's impending death, and the man who desired proof of God's providence.[107] Logical inferences, though of a more simple nature than here, determined those situations also.[108] Since the concretization of any particular concept is not inevitable, the organic complex permitted this type of determination. Had it been a general practice, however, to attempt to determine every event or fact by logical inference, the process of concretization would again have been so impeded as to have been inoperative.

A third type of logical approach permitted on a small scale consisted in determining a situation or event by means of a logical relationship between concepts. While organic concepts cannot be *inferred* from one another, logical *relations* between them are not impossible. We found a logical relation to exist between the concepts of repentance and the efficacy of Torah; and we said that this explains the assumption that the learned surely repent of misdeeds they may have committed.[109] But notice that this particular combination of concepts represents only one of a number of combinations by which that situation may be determined.[110] Hence, even if the logical element is not, as we are tempted to say, coincidental, the combination still exhibits an organic aspect. The only other example in the Seder of a logical combination of concepts interpreting or determining events is to be found in the passage wherein the whole existence of the world is schematized. With the concept of Torah made central in this schema, the period before Torah can only be chaos and the period succeeding Torah the messianic epoch.[111] Like all interpretations of historical events by means of the organic concepts, this view is not a matter of consensus, as we pointed out before.[112] In corroboration, we need only recall how the Rabbis interpreted the original sin of Adam which Christianity firmly regarded as the cause of both sin and death in the human race. At one time, the Rabbis declare that Adam's sin is responsible for the presence of death (not of sin) "until the end of all generations", a view determined by the concept of corporate justice; at another, they say that each man dies because of his own sin, a view determined by the concept of individual distributive justice; and at still another time, instead of regarding death as a calamity, they state that it is a moral purgative for the world, a view determined by the concept of chastisement.[113] Whether the events be those of history or of every-day life, the fluid character of the complex permitted them to be interpreted or determined in different ways, even by means of logical combinations of concepts occasionally. Nevertheless, had it been a general practice to attempt to determine events by means of logical combinations of concepts, the process of concretization would once more have been so impeded as to have been inoperative.[114]

We have now accounted for the fact that certain kinds of rabbinic interpretations are met with far less frequently than others. Still more rare are statements that cannot be included in the organic complex at all. Such statements approach the philosophical arguments which attempt to prove the existence of God. The statement, for example, that the greatness of God can be appreciated when we observe that each individual in any species is unlike his fellow approaches very closely the teleological argument.[115] Despite a very adequate proof-text, this rabbinic dictum is, strictly speaking, outside the range of rabbinic theology for it does not involve any organic concept.

The organic complex gives ample scope for the exercise of individuality; hence it gives ample scope for the exercise of logical thinking. In order to possess an original configuration of the organic complex, the individual must employ the Aristotelian categories at least to the extent necessary to manage the circumstances of his experience. Though the logical method of biblical interpretation was general, the particular interpretation of any verse was the product of the individual and not a matter of consensus. Again, though the search for ways in which to extend or deepen the concretizations of the concepts may often have resulted in laws, the search itself was always undertaken by an individual teacher. Finally, the individual, according to his powers, could employ inferential reasoning to support his determination of situations, and logical inferences and logical combinations of concepts in the very process of determination. Since the organic complex made room for the individual — even for the unlettered individual who also must possess his original configuration of the complex — it cannot have made either for sterile uniformity or for what is known today as "the mob-mind". Charged with emotion as the organic concepts are, they nevertheless give ample opportunity for sober reasoning.

On the other hand, the organic complex renders possible the most intense degree of spiritual harmony and coöperation among individuals. With the unlettered and the Rabbis alike, the individual teacher has in common the organic complex and the laws; and with the Rabbis he has further in common the logical method of Bible interpretation and the search for ways to extend the concretizations of the concepts. What is noteworthy is that the basic spiritual unity provided by the organic complex of concepts does not result from the formulation of dogmas. Dogmas are conclusions logically coherent with one another, each of which has also been arrived at through a logical process. Such a combination of dogmas constitutes a world-view which is fixed since any deviation would argue a flaw in the logical process. The organic concepts, however, are not the result of a logical process, the coherence between them being organic and not logical. Individuals may, no, must, differ in their world-views for each world-view is an original configuration of the complex. The organic complex, then, enabled the individual to have a valuational life of his own and yet to live in spiritual coöperation and harmony with other individuals.

IV. The Relation to Folklore

The organic complex enabled the Jews to live in spiritual coöperation with each other, unifying the group through a common mode of thought and action. If this be tantamount to claiming that the organic complex was the "group-mind" of the Jewish people, the "group-mind" was certainly no disembodied ghost. Unity of thought and action was possible because the inevitably unique configuration of values possessed by every individual was but an original configuration of the organic complex of concepts common to all.

For the refinement and deepening of the organic complex the Rabbis, as a class, were largely responsible. They represent a remarkable instance of how the best spirits of a group may interact with the people as a whole and thus influence, even determine, the spiritual outlook and character of that people. To judge from this instance, two basic conditions are necessary for an interaction of this kind. In the first place, there must be some process whereby the best minds are selected and trained. The great academies of Palestine and Babylon attracted, trained and gave occasion for the mutual development of the most gifted minds of the people. In this fashion was the rabbinic class formed, the members of which had in common, besides the organic complex, the logical method of Bible interpretation and the search for ways to deepen or extend the concretization of the concepts. But such a class, as a second condition, must not be a professional one, removed by economic and social interests from the people at large. Unpaid teachers of the adults of the community,[116] the Rabbis remained rooted in the folk, engaging in all manner of work for their livelihood.[117] However intricate or fine-spun their legal discussions might be, their concern with the concepts which lent significance to their daily affairs was neither beyond the ken nor removed from the experience of the people whose lives they shared. Hence, they were the spiritual leaders of the people, refining and applying the concepts of common experience. When the Rabbis used popular teaching devices — fable, parable, story, exaggeration and the like[118] — it was probably less a conscious effort to be popular than the natural result of being at one with the folk. There was no gap between the Rabbis and the folk.

The organic complex is a framework — "a living, subtle, flexible framework" for logical thought, a living framework just as flexible and subtle for certain aspects of popular, imaginative thought. The Rabbis' pre-occupation with logical, inferential thought no doubt reflects their intellectual interests as a class; their pre-occupation with popular, imaginative thought just as truly reflects their interests as members of the folk. Legends, folk-tales, are no less vehicles for the organic concepts than are biblical verses. For example, the story of Abraham's being cast into the fiery furnace and that of Miriam, daughter of Tanḥum, and her seven sons both involve, among other concepts, *Ḳiddush Hashem*.[119] Whether these inspiring tales of heroism did or did not originate with the Rabbis really does not matter; as the Rabbis told them, their popular appeal consisted in the dramatic concretization of the concepts. The same is true even of those legends the sources of which are lost in antiquity. There is a rabbinic version, for example, of the ancient Babylonian story of Marduk's sport with Tiamat; as told by the Rabbis, however, the legend is a concretization of the justice God metes out to the wicked.[120]

In the framework of the organic complex, logical and imaginative thought are not departmentalized. The Rabbis are fond of embellishing biblical accounts with additional details, these imaginative details being, of course, further concretizations of the concepts. Thus, to cite a few instances, the Rabbis tell us that Barak was Deborah's husband and that the gift of prophecy was her reward for advising him to perform a good deed, a conclusion drawn from the name "Lappidoth" (Judges 4:4);[121] that Lamech received reward for mourning over his father's father, his lament consisting of Gen. 4:23–24;[122] and that the Sodomites merited their punishment not only because of homosexuality but also because of robbery and incest, borne out by the words "wicked" and "sinners" in Gen. 13:13.[123] Again, ancient legends doubtless contributed to these and to many more rabbinic versions of biblical narratives but the rabbinic versions, with the organic concepts they involved, soon gained currency among the people. The organic complex, then, was the framework for legends on biblical themes current among the people. And what is especially noteworthy is the fact that such rabbinic legends were supported by biblical texts. Framework at one and the same time for both logical and imaginative thought, the organic complex integrated them both in the very process whereby its own constituent concepts were integrated.

The organic complex acts as the framework for angelology. In our earlier study we concluded that "every homily in Seder Eliahu that speaks of angels is an exposition of a concept, no matter how detailed the angelology may be."[124] The throne of glory, the *Ḥayyot*, the ministering angels, the Angel of Death serve as vivid, dramatic background for the concepts of God's loving-kindness, His justice, Torah, Israel and *Ḳiddush Hashem.* We noticed, moreover, that there is room for differences of opinion with respect to angelology in accordance with the predilections of individuals.[125] Similarly, we learned that, except for a few statements revealing an objective interest in natural phenomena, in the bulk of the passages having to do with natural objects the latter also serve as background to the fundamental concepts.[126] Qualities of human personality are, as a result, attributed to natural objects with the sea, Mt. Sinai and Mt. Zion, for example, given speech in a passage concerning God's justice whilst the attribute of culpability is given heaven and earth, the sun, moon and constellations in passages concerning Israel. It is plain, therefore, that in angelology and nature-anthropomorphisms we have more legends that are concretizations of the organic concepts and therefore integrated with the complex.

The organic complex was, then, the framework for much of the imaginative, popular folklore. In such folklore, the organic concepts possessed a great and fertile field for concretizations, a field yielding illustrative stories as well as richly colorful background. The folklore integrated with rabbinic theology enabled it to be the complex of values not alone of the Rabbis but of the people at large. Hence, just as above we found the term "theology" to be inappropriate so here we find the term "rabbinic" inadequate. In any case, we can now more readily understand how it was that the organic complex gave character not only to the Rabbis but to the folk and ensured continuity of spirit and outlook for centuries, permitting men of the second and men of the eighth centuries to talk in the same terms. We can also appreciate more keenly the old observation that a group's values are imbedded in its folklore.

Did the Rabbis, an intellectual class, themselves believe in the legends? Did they regard as recitals of sober fact the stories in which angels or nature-anthropomorphisms figure? Had such matters been taken by the Rabbis for sober fact they could not, keen analysts that they were, have allowed so many contradictory statements as to facts. In one passage, for instance, the sun appears as an involuntary and protesting object of worship; in another, as acquiescing at being placed in the rôle of a god.[127] One teacher affirmed that the angels ate the food Abraham prepared; other teachers said they did not.[128] On the other hand, these stories certainly were not sheer imaginative fancies to the Rabbis. To them neither fact nor fiction, the legends belonged to quite another category provided for by the organic complex — the category of significance. Things, events acquire significance or meaningfulness, we have learned, as they are integrated or determined by the organic concepts. The organic concepts themselves can be characterised in no other way than by saying that they endow things with significance. They are, therefore, grasped only by the category of significance. The concretizations of the concepts belong, of course, to the same category, whatever such concretizations be — daily events, history or legend. When any event or thing is grasped by the category of significance other categories to which it might belong are naturally irrelevant. In sum, rabbinic legends, angelology and nature-anthropomorphisms represent neither idle stories nor matters of dogmatic belief but are concretizations of the organic concepts.

The category of significance may appear foreign to us of the present time because, paradoxically, we resort to it, on occasion, in a much more deliberate fashion than did the Rabbis. When in the mood to read poetry, we consciously strive to capture the significance wrested by the poet from his experience. But that experience itself, a genuine awareness of concrete significance, cannot be summoned at will by the poet. Though he may struggle with its expression, the awareness of the significant experience must be poignant, spontaneous, not artificial. In the poets, therefore, we find the closest *analogy* to rabbinic legend and anthropomorphism. Nature-anthropomorphisms, though of a different sort, are as common to the poets as to the Rabbis. When Keats speaks of Autumn, "season of mists and mellow fruitfulness", he says:

"Who hath not seen thee oft amid thy store?
    Sometimes whoever seeks abroad may find
Thee sitting careless on a granary floor,
    Thy hair soft-lifted by the winnowing wind;
Or on a half-reaped furrow sound asleep,
    Drowsed with the fume of poppies, while thy hook
Spares the next swath and all its twined flowers;
    And sometimes like a gleaner thou dost keep
        Steady thy laden head across a brook;
    Or by a cider-press with patient look,
        Thou watchest the last oozings, hours by hours."[129]

Can we assume that to Keats this figure, being no fact, was just fancy, mere ornament to the idea? But the figure can in no wise be separated from the idea, is, indeed, a concretization of the idea. It is the expression of an experience belonging to the category neither of fact nor of fiction but to that of significance. A poetic experience as well as rabbinic legends and anthropomorphisms is in that category, though distinct in type. The former is the concretization of an idea perhaps never again to be experienced, the latter are concretizations of concepts, concepts driving toward ever new concretizations. The poetic experience is so unique and individual an affair, the idea so ungeneralized and thus so dependent on the figure clothing it, that the poet cannot expect a repetition of that experience nor can even confidently count on anything similar to it. The organic concept, on the other hand, repeatedly re-crystallizes itself in new concretizations, each in a sense unique yet united to the rest by the common concept.

Anthropomorphisms attributing man-like qualities to God have been the subject of discussion for centuries. Medieval philosophers like Maimonides explained them on the ground that the masses could not have understood God's activity in other terms whereas modern thinkers are inclined to regard them as poetic metaphors. But if they are not expressions used solely for the benefit of the masses, they are also not figures rising out of the fleeting experiences of a poet, though akin to such figures. Since, in our text, anthropomorphisms invariably involve the fundamental concepts,[130] they are concretizations of the concepts and like nature-anthropomorphisms belong in the category of significance. Between poetry and anthropomorphism there is naturally close kinship. Good taste and appropriateness are the final arbiters in both. In poetry what may be the expression of the experience of one man may offend the sensibilities of another. The precautionary terms employed by the Rabbis—"if it could be said," or "as it were" and the like[131] — to mitigate anthropomorphisms certainly do not imply an abstract, philosophic approach to God. Were that so these terms would preface every anthropomorphism and not only "strong expressions" which, incidentally, are also by no means always so mitigated. Granted that the precautionary term mitigated the anthropomorphic concretization of a fundamental concept, its use nevertheless depended on the individual teacher's good taste, his sensitiveness as to what is compatible with God's dignity.

The organic complex does not act as framework for all aspects of folklore, not even for all the folklore to be found in rabbinic texts. Demonology, superstitions having to do with the evil eye, witches, dreams, and good luck practices consist largely of techniques and the dangers against which these techniques are efficacious. Devoid of material which can be grasped or interpreted by the organic concepts, passages telling of these techniques appear to be bits of folklore untouched by rabbinic theology, and are, in fact, entirely absent in our text.[132] The single passage there on astrology, though indicating some belief in that "science" expressly negates its connection with Israel, one of the organic concepts;[133] and the same negative attitude is taken in the two passages on magic.[134] That the Rabbis in general decidedly object to the exploitation of religious practices as "techniques" is apparent from the way they decry the belief in the propitiatory value of the sacrifices, offering, instead, a reinterpretation involving the organic concepts.[135] If we remember that the organic complex, framework for logical and imaginative thought at once, utilized to the full all the folklore possible in consonance with it, we must conclude that all the forms of rejected folklore having "technique" for their common characteristic are something altogether other than rabbinic theology. Not contributing to the continuity of outlook and character of the people nor, by the same token, to its unity of thought and action, that folklore which is technique is native, we suspect, to no particular folk but is as general in its nature as modern science. The problem as to how it could have crept into rabbinic texts is indeed a puzzling one. Krochmal, however, after declaring that the language of these comparatively few passages proves their non-rabbinic origin, does go on to give a plausible explanation.[136]

Our test, then, by which we may distinguish rabbinic material in folklore is: That folklore belongs to rabbinic theology which is a concretization of an organic concept and thus integrated into the organic complex. By this test not only are the "techniques" or superstitions excluded but also all anthropomorphisms, nature-anthropomorphisms, angelology and legends that do not embody an organic concept.[137]

V. Relation to Bible — Organic Levels

Rabbinic haggadic statements are usually homilies on biblical texts. In an earlier section we learned that such interpretations of the Bible involved rigorously logical procedures — minute analysis and comparison of texts, attention to the linguistic possibilities of words, controlled use of symbolism, hermeneutic rules. The whole elaborate methodology of interpretation was to the Rabbis a means of finding biblical authority for their own statements and views, or, to put it otherwise, the way for arriving at the meaning and the full implications of Scripture. But the very necessity for so elaborate an apparatus itself merits investigation. We have been aware, on numerous occasions, that the rabbinic interpretation differs from the plain meaning of the texts. Does the rabbinic method, then, impute to Scripture meanings essentially foreign to it? Are the Rabbis engaged in a deliberate, conscious effort to read into the Bible their own views, an effort that at best must be characterized as artificial?

Far from being foreign to each other, an intimate relationship exists between rabbinic theology and Scripture. The concepts of God's love and justice, Torah and Israel are as basic and as frequently met with in the latter as they are in the former. Not only are the fundamental concepts common to both but other concepts, such as the righteous and the wicked, as well. And where complete conceptual parallels are lacking, the Bible contains at the very least some foreshadowings of the rabbinic concepts. Even more subtle, pervasive characteristics are also common to both. In rabbinic theology, what we called the "independent attributes of God"— eternity, truth, holiness, omniscience, creativeness, omnipotence and the like — are always linked to a fundamental concept, that is to say, are to be found only in concretizations of the fundamental concepts and are, therefore, to the Rabbis always manifest in some practical, concrete situation.[138] Similarly, in the Bible such divine attributes as "unity, power, foresight have a practical end in view", as Davidson points out.[139] He goes on to say that the same is true of biblical descriptions of God's activities in nature,[140] a conclusion paralleled by our observation that in the rabbinic view all things in nature have been created and carry on with reference to the fundamental concepts.[141] To touch upon the vast field of the relation of rabbinic to biblical law would take us far beyond the scope of this work. Nevertheless, we have already noticed that in Bible and rabbinic theology alike the concept of *miẓwot* denotes both ritualistic and ethical matters.[142] In short, without further inquiry, we can safely affirm that rabbinic theology and the Bible have many features in common.

Yet the resemblances do not obscure the differences. Rabbinic theology possesses many conceptual terms not to be found in the Bible. The terms *Malkut Shamayim*, *Teshubah* (repentance), *Talmid-ḥaḥam* (the learned), and *'Olam Habba*, to mention several, do not occur in the Bible at all. Other terms, such as *Derek Ereẓ*, *'am haareẓ* (the ignorant), and *ẓedaḳah*, again to take only several examples, although found in the Bible, have different denotations or connotations in rabbinic theology. Now it is true that, despite the fact that we have here new conceptual terms, we are not dealing with totally new and original concepts. The value which the Rabbis called *Teshubah*, for instance, is distinctly biblical though the Bible does not contain this noun-form, the term as such. But it is equally true that the new terms bring marked advantages to rabbinic theology, even when the values they stand for are rather well established in the Bible. With the terms in current use, the values become more intimately a part of the individual's personality and hence play a far greater rôle in daily life. This is especially apparent as regards those terms that stand for values not so well established in the Bible, the manifold manifestations of *Ḳiddush Hashem*, for example, hardly being envisaged in the germinal form that this value assumes in Scripture.[143] By means of the new conceptual terms, therefore, rabbinic theology affects situations more varied and of greater range than does the Bible.

The changes wrought by the new conceptual terms, instead of being confined merely to the values which these terms represent, extend to the whole rabbinic complex. Rabbinic theology is an organic complex; hence, the emergence of new factors means that changes are produced not only in the individual concepts obviously involved but in the entire complex as well. Indeed, it is probably more correct to regard the new conceptual terms as effect rather than cause, as being a result of the new organic complex of rabbinic theology as a whole rather than as discrete elements that ultimately effected such changes in the biblical concepts as to produce the new rabbinic theology. In any case, with respect to the Bible, rabbinic theology is a *new* complex of concepts. But of this the Rabbis could not have been aware. Events recorded in the Bible are couched there in terms of the fundamental concepts and of other concepts that determined the incidents of the Rabbis' own existence. The Rabbis would have needed, therefore, more than all our gains in the conceptions of history and time, let alone our present vantage-point, not to have viewed the biblical events in the same light as they viewed the events of their own day. In other words, the Rabbis read into the Bible their own organic complex. The rabbinic interpretation of Scripture thus allows us to discover precisely those matters which distinguish rabbinic theology from its biblical antecedents.

The rabbinic concepts are, we have pointed out, much wider in application than the biblical, a characteristic of which the fundamental concepts afford striking examples.

The rabbinic concept penetrates into events or data that had not been interpreted by its biblical parallel at all or else into hitherto uninterpreted details of an event already interpreted. Yet the biblical data alone, concretizations in one way or another of biblical concepts, cannot satisfy the much wider demands for concretization on the part of the rabbinic concepts. In order to have enough scope for its concepts, rabbinic theology frequently adds details to the biblical accounts, embellishing the latter with legends which, as we saw above, are themselves concretizations of rabbinic concepts. The rabbinic concept of the justice of God gives ethical significance to the visitation of the plagues mentioned in Leviticus,[144] accounts for the character of each of the ten plagues sent upon Egypt,[145] assigns a cause for the successful reign of Jereboam, the son of Joash.[146] The rabbinic concept of God's loving-kindness adds to the biblical narratives the details that God mourned over the destruction of the generation of the Deluge;[147] that, when Israel repented after having sinned by worshipping the golden calf, "His compassion was moved and He gave them the Day of Atonement (as a day) of pardon;"[148] that, after "the grave matter that happened to Israel on account of the spies," God Himself recalled to Moses the kind of plea he should make.[149] The rabbinic concept of Torah recasts the biblical characters in accordance with its own requisites of study and practice: Joseph not only conformed to the Ten Commandments but also to certain ritualistic regulations regarding the slaughtering of animals;[150] David taught Torah in an academy;[151] Jabez prayed that God enlarge his border "with the learned."[152] The rabbinic concept of Israel widens the biblical ideal of Israel as a priest-people until the demarcation between the priest-class and the rest of Israel is all but eliminated: The Rabbis extend the ritual practice of the washing of the hands,— a biblical obligation upon the priests when entering the tent of meeting or when approaching the altar —, to all Israel in order to demonstrate that "not to the priests alone was holiness given but to all — to the priests and to the Levites and to the Israelites."[153] This enlargement in the status of Israel was profoundly affected by the concept of Torah: The knowledge and practice of Torah renders one not of the priestly caste "worthy to offer up a burnt-offering upon the altar."[154] In the interaction here of the concepts of Torah and Israel we have an illustration of the phenomenon that a change in any concept involved not that concept alone but the other concepts, the whole complex, as well. In fact, the wider application of concepts is itself but an index of the new character of the complex as a whole. The rabbinic concepts are not mere extensions of the biblical; they are really new concepts, as the new interpretations of biblical data and the added legendary material on biblical themes testify.[155]

The new character of rabbinic theology — new, that is, with respect to the Bible — can be glimpsed in two other distinctive characteristics. For one thing, rabbinic theology gives much more attention to the individual and as a consequence, or rather concomitant, allows for the greater development of the inward life. To the Rabbis every individual mentioned in the Bible is important and they elaborate on the personalities and activities of even incidental characters like Lamech[156] and Ahitophel,[157] to say nothing of great figures like Aaron and Moses.[158] This profound interest in the individual is, of course, like the other features of rabbinic theology, not limited to the interpretation of the Bible but a quality inherent in the complex generally. It is manifest in the application of every concept, particularly the fundamental concepts. God's love provides for,[159] His mercy encompasses,[160] every individual; God's justice reaches "each and every one", whether in reward or punishment.[161] No one is exempt from the study[162] and practice[163] of Torah. The concept of Israel is sharpened by the sub-concept of the learned to a type which gives more definite outlines to the individual.[164] The rabbinic interpretations of the Bible cited in the preceding paragraph reveal how the regard for the individual common to all rabbinic concepts is embodied in their concretizations. Now this preoccupation with the individual means that the individual himself senses more keenly the whole organic complex as it is focussed in him, that the rabbinic concepts assume for him a heightened personal and subjective coloring. In a word, the organic complex becomes material for a rich inward life. Whilst all of the concepts contribute to the inward life — notice how Torah[165] and *mizwot*[166] foster it — the depth of that life is sounded most strongly perhaps by the emphasis on such concepts as prayer and repentance. So needful did prayer and repentance appear to the Rabbis that they attribute them to biblical characters on every occasion, and especially on critical occasions: The whole community of Israel prayed at the Red Sea when Pharaoh was about to attack them,[167] and after Moses placed before them the laws they uttered a prayer, the words of which are given;[168] and the virtue of the men of Deborah's army was that they prayed in the synagogue morning and evening.[169] Israel repented in secret after worshipping the golden calf,[170] and is bidden by Joshua to repent before entering the Holy Land.[171] Even these few examples of the many occasions the Rabbis find appropriate for prayer and repentance which the Bible passes over are enough to indicate that these values were given far greater emphasis in rabbinic theology. The conception of *imitatio Dei*, in rabbinic theology a most poignant awareness of God on the part of the individual, is another illustration of our thesis, the Rabbis imposing this conception on the texts of Ps. 15:2 ff.[172] In fine, the greater concern with the individual and the concomitant intensification of the inward life are apparent in every phase of rabbinic theology.

Finally, rabbinic theology reveals a definite emphasis upon love, an emphasis which brings the Rabbis to interpret in terms of love matters which the Bible describes in terms of justice. In the Bible, stern justice is meted out to Adam after his disobedience; but the Rabbis transform the decree into an expression of God's love and into a promise of everlasting life.[173] Similarly, the statement "visiting the iniquity of the fathers upon the children . . . unto the third and unto the fourth generation" (Exod. 34:7) is interpreted in such a way as to render it evidence of God's love.[174] The use of the term *ẓedaḳah* is an excellent case in point. Although as used in the Bible the term connotes justice, to the Rabbis *ẓedaḳah* is a concept connoting tender love and denoting compassionate help to those in need, a meaning the Rabbis also attribute to the word in its biblical settings.[175] The emphasis on love is a current running through the whole complex of rabbinic theology, and naturally affects the other characteristics we have been discussing. Thus, the imitation of God, a conception which intensifies the inward life of the individual, consists of the imitation of aspects of God's loving-kindness, according to the interpretation of one biblical passage whilst the interpretation of another has it that God pleads that Israel imitate His qualities on the ground of His love for them.[176] We may also recall that prayer and repentance, which again intensify the inward life, are sub-concepts of God's loving-kindness. All of the trends we have observed in rabbinic theology are but different phases of one organic complex and affect and color each other continuously. For that reason they demonstrate, since they are all characteristics whereby rabbinic theology is to be differentiated from its biblical antecedents, that they are characteristics of a *new* complex, related to the Bible yet distinct from it.

Our study of the relation of the Bible to rabbinic theology has brought to light a new feature of the organic complex.

The organic complex is characterized by the individual concepts of which the complex is composed; it is further characterized by certain general characteristics; and now we have learned that it is also characterized by certain special trends which mark the complex off from what is even decidedly related to it. When the Rabbis interpret the Bible they must perforce recast the biblical events, characters, everything, in terms of their own theology differentiated from the Bible by certain special characteristics.[177]

Of what nature is this relationship between the Bible and rabbinic theology? No element, taken singly, is absolutely new and original with rabbinic theology. All of its elements, the special trends included, if disparately regarded are certainly at least adumbrated in the Bible. What *is* new is the complex as a whole. It is the new organismal character that makes for the differences between the Bible and rabbinic theology, some of which we have outlined. Each concept, its own range of concretization enlarged, is vitally affected, charged rather, by similar changes in the other concepts and by the special emphatic trends of the complex in general. Thus, the wider range of concretization of any rabbinic concept implies besides greater width of range new qualities which render that concept not just an extension of its biblical antecedent. But the Bible does contain the antecedents of all the elements of rabbinic theology. The Bible, therefore, represents the organic complex out of which the rabbinic organic complex has emerged. It gives "the set" to the rabbinic complex, supplying not only the elements of the latter but the possibility, the factor, of integration itself. The dependence of rabbinic theology upon the Bible is thus explained. Nevertheless, this dependence can be seen only after the rabbinic complex has emerged. True to the organismal nature of the complex, the rabbinic concepts, with their specific qualities, could not have been deduced or inferred from their biblical antecedents. Like the organismal integration of the complex, the process we have just described also has its biologic analogy or parallel: "Evolution is a series of stages. At each stage a new form of relatedness supervenes, and from this new relatedness something new emerges, and this new relatedness is effective in determining the 'go of events' in the next higher level. It is what we have called the formation of unitary complexes, each with its characteristic reaction."[178]

The Bible and rabbinic theology are, then, successive organic levels, with the second emerging from the first. We cannot say, of course, that the rabbinic complex is higher than, or superior to, the biblical. Because the rabbinic complex has a wider range of concretization and hence enriches with significance a wider sphere of situations it is, however, richer than the biblical. If a higher development spells, in accordance with the philosophic criterion, a more abstract conception of God, the rabbinic complex is certainly no higher than the biblical. On the contrary, the wider range of concretization makes necessary, if anything, a more profuse use of anthropomorphisms, especially in connection with the rabbinic emphasis on God's love and on His regard for the individual.[179] And yet, the habitual use of anthropomorphisms does not lessen the Rabbis' awe for the majesty of God, a fact to which the prevalence of the precautionary terms testifies.[180] Richer significance goes with deeper reverence, not with greater philosophic abstraction.

The objection may be raised that the biblical period is not a unit, primitive conceptions giving way to more developed ones, and that evidence for this is to be found in the Bible. Such evidence still does not disprove, however, that the Bible represents a single organic complex. The biblical period may not be a unit but the Bible itself, books selected, edited and put into one collection, certainly is. Early traditions, echoing primitive notes, were reinterpreted to conform with the dominant outlook of a later period, just as still later the rabbinic complex reinterpreted the primitive Marduk legend.[181] Jastrow, who has compared most carefully the Hebrew with the earlier Babylonian traditions, is convinced that the predominant view from Genesis onward is unified and that even the ritualistic sections are given in the prophetic spirit.[182] He says, "The spirit is everywhere the same. The entire Old Testament is soaked with this spirit. The nation's past is viewed and reviewed from the standpoint of the ethical monotheism of the Prophets."[183] Differences that may appear at first glance to be due to different ethico-cultural levels will prove, upon analysis, to be the result of different configurations of the same organic biblical concepts. For, again to draw a parallel from the rabbinic complex, different configurations of the same complex, allowing for great differences in ethical judgments, are rendered inevitable by the differences in the circumstances and the temperaments of individuals.[184] Thus, Davidson, after a thorough sifting of the biblical ideas declares, "Scripture has a meaning and a view of its own on most moral and religious questions; and not more than one view really, although, of course, different writers may present the view with all the variety natural to different minds and diverse circumstances . . . This view is not to be inferred from any single text, but from the general tenor of thought of the Scripture writers."[185] But let us even suppose that as we scan the Bible today we shall discover more than one ethico-cultural level, that the work of reinterpreting earlier traditions was done imperfectly. The fact remains that the very gathering together and editing of the biblical books, with the necessity for selection which this process implies, bespeaks a period when the Bible, taken as one whole, reflected the Hebraic mind. That this period immediately preceded the rabbinic is evident from two considerations: On the one hand, every rabbinic concept is seen to be rooted in the Bible and, on the other hand, the full rabbinic connotation of any concept is not found in the Bible. The Bible, therefore, taken as one whole, represents the organic complex out of which the rabbinic organic complex has emerged.[186]

We have learned above that the Rabbis could not have been aware that they were reading their own viewpoint into the texts of the Bible. This was all the more natural, we now realize, because the rabbinic organic complex emerged directly from the biblical. The "elaborate methodology of interpretation was to the Rabbis a means of finding biblical authority for their own statements and views," but it was also more than that. The elaborateness of the methodology did not arise out of a mere fancy for complicated things. A simple methodology would have meant a very nearly uniform interpretation for all, since everybody would then have been restricted to a few definite methods. The elaborate methodology, however, is of a piece with the whole organic complex, being flexible enough to ensure the individual an interpretation of the Bible in consonance with his own configuration of the rabbinic organic complex. Moreover, by the same token, it made possible more or less fresh impacts of the biblical upon the rabbinic complex in successive generations, impacts productive of fresh interpretations.

VI. The Experience of God

The rubric, so often employed, of "God, Israel and Torah" is utterly misleading. It gives the impression that just as the Rabbis possessed the concepts of Israel and Torah so, too, their experience of God was grasped by a God-concept. It gives the impression, also, that their experiences grasped by the concepts of Torah and Israel can be distinguished from their experience of God. These are wrong impressions, if our analysis has been sound.

While the Rabbis had profound experience of God, they had, strange though it may appear at first, no all-inclusive God-concept. Their experience of God was brought to them, for one thing, by the four fundamental concepts. But notice that if God's love and justice are manifestations of God so also are His Torah and His chosen people, Israel, the people wherein His immanence, *Shekinah*, is manifest.[187] The all-inclusive God-concept cannot, therefore, be confined to the manifestations of His love and justice. The "independent attributes"—eternity, omniscience and the like—do not constitute an all-inclusive God-concept both because they are many and because, as we saw, they are always incidental to the fundamental concepts.[188] Such concepts as *Malkut Shamayim* (the sovereignty of God)[189] and *Ḳiddush Hashem*[190] fuse the fundamental concepts, to be sure, but each does so independently and for its own purposes, as it were. Moreover, the fundamental concepts are still left free to combine with other concepts of the complex. In fine, there is no all-inclusive God-concept which might definitively grasp, and therefore limit, the interpretive functions of the four fundamental concepts.

Free of the confines of an all-inclusive God-concept, the Rabbis' experience of God was nonetheless unified. The four fundamental concepts intertwined, were integrated, with each other and with all the rest of the concepts. The integrated organic complex, hence, always involved the awareness, the experience of God. Accompanying every concretization of an organic concept was the adumbration of the integrated complex fraught with experience of God. In other words, the experience of God was a characteristic of the organic complex as a whole. Now we have noticed that characteristics of the complex as a whole, such as the rabbinic emphasis on the individual and on love,[191] may not only be more marked in certain particular concepts but may even decide the full character of some concepts. Exactly the same feature may be observed here. The fundamental concepts are not responsible for the experience of God. The experience of God is an emphatic characteristic of the complex as a whole informing, particularly, certain concepts among which are, besides the fundamental concepts, those of *Malkut Shamayim*, *Ḳiddush Hashem*, prayer, repentance. We can now understand why the Rabbis had no need of an all-inclusive God-concept to give unity to their experience of God. Inseparable from the integrated organic complex, the experience of God could not be otherwise than unified. In fact, the organic complex not only made an all-inclusive concept unnecessary but impossible, as well. Since the complex of concepts organized into one unified whole the entire valuational life, an additional concept extraneous to the complex, a super-concept — if we may even use the term — was obviously impossible.

Thus, the Rabbis' experience of God was unconfined by the restrictions of an all-inclusive concept yet at the same time coherent. It was not inchoate or "raw experience." Dependent on an organic complex of *concepts*, it rose into expression in particular concepts though an undercurrent in all. The values that attached to things and events in ordinary, every-day life, the concepts that gave these phenomena their coloring, were organic concepts or values. Accompanying each experience of value, a decisive shade in the coloring, as it were, was the experience of God. Because the complex as a whole was inevitable, the experience of God was inevitable; because the concretization of any given concept was effortless though not automatic, the experience of God was effortless though not automatic. The experience of God was an inevitable, effortless, though non-automatic factor in the normal valuational life of the Rabbis.

Each individual, however, had his own valuational life, a unique configuration of the complex. Unity of thought and action among individuals was possible, we have said, because the unique configuration of values possessed by every individual was but an original configuration of the complex of concepts common to all. But the organic complex did not only make possible unity among the individuals of the group. Each individual's unique configuration of the complex was integrated, unified. What was certainly a major aspect of the individual's personality was thus at once unique and integrated. This aspect of the individual's personality was fraught with the experience of God. What relation was there between the experience of God and the experience of integrated personality, the awareness of the self?

The awareness of the self was heightened, tremendously enriched by the experience of God. In demonstrating this we shall gain a larger view of the way in which the emphatic characteristics coalesced,[192] a trait to be expected from an organic complex. We cannot go back of the awareness of the self, of course. The rabbinic emphasis on the individual meant, among other things, that there were occasions when there was *poignant* awareness of the self. For certain concepts, we have learned, such as the fundamental concepts, were particularly apt to emphasize the individual,[193] and hence, on occasion, the self. The concretizations of the fundamental concepts, however, were precisely those wherein the experience of God rose into expression or greater awareness. Indeed, any concept expressive of a *poignant* experience of God — like *Malkut Shamayim* or *Ḳiddush Hashem* — allowed for concretizations wherein frequently there was also a poignant awareness of the self. Thus, whenever the concretization of an organic concept involved a poignant experience of the self there was, necessarily, also a poignant experience of God.

Nor was this all. The coalescence consisted not of two emphatic characteristics but of three. The third was the rabbinic emphasis upon love.[194] Since the individual's personality, so far as it was informed by the organic complex, was integrated, his poignant awareness of the self and his poignant experience of God at the same time could not be otherwise than related. This bond was expressed in terms of love in consonance with the emphasis on love throughout the complex as a whole. In the experience of God, the individual deeply felt that God loved him and he reacted with love toward God, a love at times not unmixed with fear. Mark, how, in the concepts about to be mentioned, all three emphatic characteristics blend. The individual felt God's love for him when he repented[195] and when he prayed,[196] just as he was keenly aware of the self on those occasions. The afflictions of the individual, regarded as visitations of God's justice in the form of chastisement, were felt to be "chastisings of love."[197] The Torah which the individual studied and the *miẓwot* he practiced were, he felt, manifestations of God's love,[198] and hence to engage in either was a labor of love and joy.[199] The individual must acknowledge *Malkut Shamayim* in a declaration, and that is tantamount to the affirmation "I love and fear Heaven."[200] And in *Ḳiddush Hashem*, awareness of the self and love of God were again fused, crucially and ultimately fused especially in that aspect of *Ḳiddush Hashem* which was martyrdom.[201] Now in thus describing the coalescence or blending of the three emphatic characteristics we have been depicting, as well, the important elements of the inward life. Because the inward life was the "concomitant," as we said above, of the emphasis on the individual, the awareness of the self was so rich and deep. The organic complex rendered the awareness of the self a full, many-toned, composite and, on occasion, even ecstatic, experience. On the other hand, logical thinking added but little to the awareness of the self. To be sure, in giving ample scope for the exercise of individuality, the organic complex gave ample scope for the exercise of logical thinking.[202] Nevertheless, the logical processes by themselves did not give room for the inward life as we have described it.

The awareness of the self was, then, frequently an element in the poignant experience of God. On those occasions the poignant experience of God had a character that was peculiarly personal, as privately personal as was the very awareness of the self. These high, climactic moments rose out of the steady experience of God in the ordinary, normal valuational life of the individual and would, of course, have been impossible without that background.

Has rabbinic theology, because it is composed of concepts, any affiliation with philosophy? One of the primary functions of philosophy is to discover generalizations or concepts which will apply to all the various spheres of knowledge however discrete these spheres may seem to be. To be a subject of knowledge at all, that is, to be amenable to understanding or reason, the data of every sphere must exhibit some kind of order, some form of interconnectedness. Our own study of rabbinic theology, for example, consists in elucidating the organic order which it exhibits. But the very use of logical reasoning as we approach any new field involves a certain assumption. It involves the assumption that the universe as a whole, including the new field we are about to approach, is amenable to reason and possesses, therefore, an underlying order. Philosophy endeavors to justify this assumption by attempting to prove that, in fact, cosmic order does exist. It seeks to formulate a generalizing principle, a concept, that will epitomize all the known kinds of order, which are themselves formulated concepts, and this generalizing, all-inclusive concept it calls God. Hence, philosophical proofs of God are cosmological and teleological, those of order and design with the latter but another term for order. Rabbinic theology, we have surely noticed, presented no such proof. It possessed no all-inclusive God-concept. Indeed, the attempt to formulate an all-inclusive concept arises from the need to justify and epitomize — in a word, to integrate — all forms of logical thinking. Rabbinic theology, however, stood in no need of such a concept because it was already organically integrated.

How far medieval Jewish philosophers diverged from rabbinic theology can be gaged from the fact that they strove to formulate an all-inclusive God-concept. Believing that this philosophical God-concept was to be found in Jewish tradition, they attempted to bring the Jewish traditional concepts into harmony with philosophical concepts. That they did not succeed is evidenced by the artificiality and arbitrariness of their allegorical method. For they tried to harmonize two kinds of concepts that are essentially different in type. Philosophic concepts are, in every case, formulated. Each is a summary or epitome of some kind of order. Each is complete in itself, though it may be joined with others in a system. But rabbinic concepts, as we have learned, are not given formal definition.[203] Since only the rabbinic complex as an integrated whole exhibits an order, the single concepts are not complete in themselves. To inject an organic concept into a nicely formulated philosophical system without changing the character of the former is an impossible feat.[204] In attempting this very thing, medieval Jewish philosophers were bound either to do violence to the rabbinic concepts or else to be inconsistent. In order to harmonize the concepts of God's love and justice with philosophy, the former, to all intents and purposes, are practically explained away.[205] Yehudah Halevy attaches preëminence to the ritual laws though holding that the ethical laws must be the prerequisite in conduct, whereas these distinctions are foreign to rabbinic theology.[206] Maimonides is inconsistent in his statements concerning the study of Torah. At one time he says that the primary function of the Torah is to inculcate right ideas, ideas having to do neither "with deeds nor with qualities of character," which is a statement embodying a philosophic doctrine; and at another time he declares that the study of Torah is important primarily because it leads to pious action, a statement embodying the rabbinic concept of the efficacy of Torah.[207] These are but some of the illustrations, incidental to our previous discussions, of the ways in which medieval Jewish philosophy differs from rabbinic theology. Medieval Jewish philosophy, in short, cannot be regarded as a development of rabbinic theology.

On one point rabbinic theology and medieval philosophy seem to concur — on the unity of God. But this congruity is only external. The Rabbis' experience of God was unified, we have said, because it was an emphatic characteristic of the organic complex as a whole, of the valuational life entire. But among the phenomena of the valuational life was the patent fact that there existed other religions. With the experience of God an undercurrent in the *whole* valuational life, unavoidable contact with other religions served not to weaken but to strengthen that experience. Then the experience of God rose into expression in the concepts of *Malkut Shamayim* and *Ḳiddush Hashem*. On the other hand, the organic complex also possessed a concept with which to interpret or grasp the other religions, the concept of "strange worship." It denoted that these were false, abhorrent religions and that the gods thus worshipped were false gods.[208] Inferential reasoning which, as we have learned, may sometimes support the application of an organic concept,[209] is perhaps more frequently employed in the service of this than in that of any other concept. Thus, the worship of idols and of man is proved to be absurd and that of fire utterly wrong.[210] This inferential reasoning, however, is limited, for it is in behalf of a concept belonging to an integrated organic complex, a concept, therefore, really taken for granted. It is a far cry from this limited reasoning to the intricate, discursive attempt to prove the unity of the philosophical conception of God, an attempt involving the formulation of concepts.

Granted that the rabbinic experience of God cannot be grasped by any philosophic concept, how may we characterize that experience? It was none other than a form of mysticism, provided we recognize that mystical experience need not be altogether ineffable. It is a common error to assume, as Wieman does, that "the distinguishing character of the mystical experience is this intense stimulation producing vivid consciousness, yet without any integrated system of response."[211] Such a description certainly does not hold for all the forms of Western mysticism. In his work on the great Christian mystics, probably the profoundest study made of that type of Western mysticism, von Hügel builds up the thesis that Religion is constituted of three elements — the Intellectual or Conceptual, the Institutional or Historical, and the Experimental or Emotional. None of these elements, he insists, can be suppressed without hurt to the whole. Completely ineffable mystical experience, "Exclusive Mysticism," he depicts as utterly ruinous in its effects.[212] "Is there, then," he asks, "strictly speaking, such a thing as a specifically distinct, self-sufficing, purely Mystical mode of apprehending Reality? I take it, *distinctly not*; and that all the errors of the Exclusive Mystic proceed precisely from the contention that Mysticism does constitute such an entirely separate, completely self-supported kind of human experience . . . Even the most exclusively mystical-seeming soul ever depends, for the fulness and healthiness of even the most purely mystical of its acts and states, as really upon its past and present contacts with the Contingent, Temporal and Spatial, and with social facts and elements, as upon its movement of concentration, and the sense and experience, evoked on occasion of those contacts or of their memories, of the Infinite within and around those finitudes and itself."[213] Besides the ineffable element, then, there is also a communicable element, and the two reënforce each other so that the deepest experience of God is not only most poignantly ineffable but also, paradoxically, to some degree communicable. Now, though there is a marked difference between the kind of mysticism described by von Hügel — witness its philosophic approach! — and the rabbinic experience of God, this characteristic paradox of mysticism was true of the rabbinic experience of God, as well. When did the rabbinic experience of God become communicable, rise into expression? Often, as we have learned, precisely when it was most poignantly, privately personal, unshared with others — in fine, when it was ineffable. Apart from this paradox, the very fact that the rabbinic experience of God was not subsumed under an all-inclusive concept is sufficient evidence that it was a mystical experience.

But if it was different from the kind of mysticism heretofore analyzed, what kind of mysticism was it? The rabbinic experience of God was *normal* mysticism because it was a factor in the normal valuational life. Indeed, "rabbinic" experience, as we pointed out above, is a misnomer.[214] Though it varied in depth as personalities varied, it was the experience of every member of the nation, not alone of such as had special training or temperamental aptitudes. There were some individuals, however, whose valuational life was affected by abnormal psychologic states, such as visions and locutions, and rabbinic theology by no means excluded religious experience of that type. There was thus room for that experience of God which was a factor in an abnormal state of the valuational life, in other words, for abnormal mysticism. The Talmud states that the prophet Elijah appeared to R. 'Anan and taught him "what is called

Seder Eliahu Rabba (and) Seder Eliahu Zuṭa,"[215] a statement which leads Friedmann to conclude, erroneously we think, that the entire text of Seder Eliahu was the result of abnormal mysticism. Friedmann goes on to give other instances in which Elijah is said to have appeared to individual Rabbis and instructed them in specific haggadic and even halakic matters.[216] Such a source of haggadic or halakic interpretation did not lend to the latter added prestige in the eyes of the Rabbis, however. On the contrary, the Rabbis gave the preference to the coöperative method of the study of Torah pursued "every day continually"[217]—to the normal interpretations of texts and laws by means of inferential reasoning.[218] They declared that new interpretations or laws derived in the course of this normal study were inspired by the Holy Spirit.[219] No special virtue, hence, attached to abnormal mysticism. In fact, although not excluded from rabbinic theology, abnormal mysticism was quite superfluous. The experience of God was a characteristic of, and rose to poignancy within, normal valuational life. And the teachings resulting from abnormal mystical experience certainly had no greater prestige, to say the least, than those resulting from the normal method of study.

In contrast, one of the noteworthy characteristics of philosophic mysticism, as presented in von Hügel's analysis, is an emphasis on the special virtue of abnormal mysticism. To be sure, von Hügel takes pains to demonstrate that visions, locutions and the like are but the final stage, the climax of much meditation, contemplation, prayer and other normal matters; and to warn that the "ecstasy" must answer to an ethico-spiritual test. Nevertheless, after mentioning some great Christian mystics, he concludes, "All these, and countless others would, quite evidently, have achieved less, not more, of interior light and of far-reaching helpfulness . . . without . . . the experience furnished to them by their ecstasies and allied states and apprehensions."[220] The rôle of such individuals, which accrues to them in great part because of their mystical experiences, is, according to von Hügel, that of rendering possible emotional or spiritual inter-communication among men,[221] a rôle which the organic complex filled in rabbinic theology. Jewish philosophic mystics, we must add, while not placing so strong an emphasis on abnormal mysticism yet also regarded it as having special virtue. Thus Baḥya ibn Paḳudah, who lived in the eleventh century, holds forth the promise that he who cultivates "the duties of the heart" assiduously will, after contemplating deeply on God's watchful supervision, reach the high station of the saints and "see without (bodily) eye, and hear without (bodily) ear, and speak without (bodily) tongue" and feel without bodily senses and apprehend without proofs or demonstration;[222] and the veil separating him from the divine wisdom will be removed;[223] and his soul will be happy in the apprehension of truths concerning the nether and the upper worlds.[224] This exaltation of the abnormal mystical state was foreign to rabbinic theology. For in rabbinic theology the experience of God was normal mysticism, a factor in the normal valuational life.[225]

VII. The Relation to the Ethical

We have dealt with this topic in the third chapter of the present volume. But we can now indicate how the sphere of the ethical, as apprehended by the Rabbis, exhibits perhaps most clearly some of the features of the organic complex. We may thus bring those features into bolder relief.

The concept of *Derek Ereẓ* strikingly illustrates how the organic complex as a whole made for the special function of each of its constituent concepts. By means of the concept of *Derek Ereẓ* all acts characteristic of humanity were *potentially* included within the scope of the ethical; when such acts were grasped or interpreted by a fundamental concept they were *actually* within the scope of the ethical. Again, certain persistent human traits such as love, humility, arrogance, truthfulness, and so on were regarded as always *actually* within the scope of the ethical; and, being aspects of *Derek Ereẓ*, served as sub-concepts of the latter in the organic complex and were likewise integrated with the fundamental concepts. The sphere of the ethical was, therefore, in a sense co-extensive with the sphere of characteristic, universal human conduct, a sphere so large as to have made the ethical meaningless had *Derek Ereẓ* not been a concept within an organic complex. The organic complex in a continuous, living manner grasped now this and then that characteristic human act to draw it within the sphere of ethical *Derek Ereẓ*. The ethical, then, was not merely intertwined with the organic complex; without the organic complex there could have been no category of the ethical at all. This would seem to render futile the attempt to build up ethical systems in formulated, philosophical fashion, ethical systems that are not part and parcel of an integrated organic complex.

Because the ethical concepts were part of the organic complex, the experience of God accompanied every concretization of an ethical concept. Now the Rabbis held that the practice of *Derek Ereẓ* was incumbent not only upon Israel but upon the Nations of the World as well. Their own experience, however, necessarily led them to regard the experience of God as involved in the practice of *Derek Ereẓ*. Accordingly, they characterized trust in God as *Derek Ereẓ*,[226] and the flouting of God as a heinous sin that could, from the viewpoint of the Rabbis, be imputed to the Nations of the World when these worshipped idols.[227] *Ḥillul Hashem* was, therefore, numbered among the eight things that bring destruction upon *all* nations and individuals.[228] The experience of God which accompanied the practice of *Derek Ereẓ* was thus powerful enough to rise to expression in these and in other instances.[229]

Just as the sphere of the ethical illustrates so well the organic aspect of the complex, it illustrates equally well the rôle of logical thinking within that complex. Since the ethical concepts were organic, they were not produced by deliberate experimentation nor were they summed up in general, formal definitions.[230] But the ethical sphere was nevertheless the subject of painstaking, logical, reflective thought. The Rabbis, as we said above, constantly sought for specific ways to concretize the concepts. Not only was the scope of ethical action enlarged through these ways but it was also made more pointed and refined. For example, the giving of charity, whilst an opportunity for giving vent to a generous impulse, was also made the occasion for a careful weighing of various claims for aid.[231] Even such a matter as the delicate balance between friendly rebuke and fault-finding was resolved by the mature wisdom of the Rabbis.[232] Indeed, the ethical concepts themselves were subject to analysis insofar as they had to be distinguished from one another for the purpose of finding specific ways for their concretization.[233] And the problem of several conflicting ethical demands called for rational decisions whereby one demand was granted the right of way over the others. The Rabbis solved this problem by making gradations in ethics not by means of an ethical casuistry but in their own characteristic fashion. Since many *miẓwot* were included in the category of *Derek Ereẓ*, the gradations in *miẓwot* whereby some were designated as "grave" and others as "light" made for corresponding gradations in *Derek Ereẓ*;[234] and thus, in case of conflict, precedence was given to that which was of larger social significance.[235] The organic character of the ethical concepts, then, did not prevent acute logical thinking. On the contrary, were it not for the organic concepts, purposeful, logical thinking on these problems would have been impossible, for the problems themselves would have been non-existent. Logical thinking was possible because there was organic thinking.

The dual aspect of the sphere of the ethical that has just been described was grounded in the very character of the organic concepts which were effortless yet non-automatic. Because the organic complex was inevitable, the organic concepts were always "on tap," as it were, and usually interpreted events immediately as they occurred. The concretization of the organic concept in this respect was effortless. That it was not automatic, however, can be seen from the few instances where the interpretation of events was not immediate.[236] When it was a matter not of interpreting an act already performed but of serving as motive for action, the effortless aspect of the organic concept was at its weakest. The opposing forces within the individual, epitomized by the Rabbis as the *Evil Yeẓer*, were strong enough, on occasion, to thwart concretizations of organic concepts.[237] On the other hand, this non-automatic aspect of the organic concept made possible all the gains achieved by reflective, logical thought. The organic concepts, including the ethical concepts, were, as we said above, habitual but not *merely* habitual. The ethical concepts were drives because they were organic concepts; but they were drives the fulfillment of which was not inevitable because the concretization of any given concept was non-automatic.[238]

The sphere of the ethical in rabbinic theology demonstrates once more how the Rabbis as a class interacted with the people at large. The ethical drives were concepts; hence, they could be taught or at least cultivated and strengthened through instruction, contrary to the modern view which describes behaviour largely in terms of environment. The training of the folk along ethical lines was one of the primary functions of the Rabbis. The Rabbis, however, taught not abstract ethics but were concerned with *Derek Ereẓ*, concrete human traits. They did not build up imposing ethical systems beyond the ken of the folk but emphasized concepts in the common organic complex, concepts that thus possessed the quality of common drives. They instructed not by means of an ethical casuistry but often through folk-tales, stories, parables and legends, the very warp and woof of the culture of the folk. The detailed laws and rules, fruits of inferential thinking, but refined and gave greater scope to the common drives. So indubitably part and parcel of the common culture, so closely linked with the common drives, rabbinic ethics could not have been just moral theory to the people at large. Yet even Moore, deeply discerning as he is, has this to say: "The Jews unquestionably felt that in morality they were superior to the nations among whom they lived, and in some things they doubtless were so; but as flatteringly fallacious modern examples again show, the comparison may be between moral ideals on the one side and immoral reality on the other."[239] Moore apparently fails to realize how closely the Rabbis interacted with the people at large. True, since the ethical concepts were drives the fulfillment of which was not inevitable, they were no doubt less often fulfilled by the common people than by the Rabbis. But the Rabbis, "those who," as Moore puts it, "most faithfully translated principles and rules from doctrine into practice,"[240] were only better examplars of that ethical life in which the whole people participated. Our Midrash itself refers on various occasions to the upright conduct of the masses, quite incidentally, and with no attempt at glorification. It speaks of the ignorant men who are upright; of those who have not studied but are "men of Good Deeds;" of the ignorant who guard themselves from sin; of the ignorant "in whom there are *Derek Ereẓ* and the rest of the *miẓwot*, who keep themselves far from transgression;"[241] of the business men who lead an ethical life but who do not occupy themselves with the Torah;[242] of the many lads and maidens in Israel who remain virgin until their marriage.[243] All comparisons aside, "rabbinic" ethics could not have been confined to the rabbinic class because the masses as well as the Rabbis possessed the organic complex. The ethical concepts were part of the organic complex and like the other concepts were concretized at some time or other.

For the Rabbis and the masses alike, the experience of the ethical was not limited to the sphere encompassed by *Derek Ereẓ*, the relations, largely, of a man with his fellows. The whole organic complex was colored by the experience of ethical significance. Are not the fundamental concepts ethical in quality, characterized, that is, by the same qualities that are *actually* within the scope of ethical *Derek Ereẓ*? Love and justice and ethical teaching and the ideal of the people are to be found, respectively, in the concepts of God's love, His justice, Torah and Israel. And, since the four fundamental concepts were integrated with all the other concepts, the concretization of every concept of the complex possessed an undercurrent of ethical significance. The experience of ethical significance was, then, the fourth emphatic trend of the complex. Like the other emphatic trends, it rose to expression in certain concepts — in the fundamental concepts and in the concept and sub-concepts of ethical *Derek Ereẓ*.

The experience of ethical significance coalesced with the other emphatic trends. Whenever there was an emphasis upon love in the concretization of any concept, there was at the same time, obviously, an emphatic experience of ethical significance. The experience of ethical significance rose into expression, we have said, in the fundamental concepts; but in the latter, as we have learned, the emphasis upon the individual and the experience of God rose into expression, as well. And we have also noticed, in this section, that the experience of God was involved in the practice of ethical *Derek Ereẓ*. All the emphatic trends, then, including the experience of ethical significance, coalesced. In other words, whenever a concretization reflected the emphasis on love, the emphasis on the individual or the poignant experience of God, that concretization possessed an emphatic ethical significance.

Not all concretizations, therefore, were on an equal plane of ethical significance. We are not referring now to matters of practice or conduct wherein a "grave" *miẓwah* took precedence over a "light" one in case of conflict, but to concretizations having no such practical issue. Those concretizations were of higher, or rather highest, ethical significance which evinced an emphasis on the individual or on love or in which the experience of God was given expression. Thus, interpretations embodying the concept of justice due the individual were probably of deeper significance than interpretations embodying the concept of corporate justice, though the latter was bound up with the important idea of corporate or collective responsibility.[244] In one instance, the angels argue for the exercise of corporate justice whereas God Himself declares that He acts according to the justice due the individual—"I deal with man according to his deserts at the moment;"[245] and the angels, as we know, frequently serve as the foil to God's loving-kindness or to God's higher justice, bringing these into stronger relief. And in another instance, when Israel sinned with the golden calf, God accedes to Moses' plea against the imposition of corporate justice.[246] As to the dominant ethical significance of the emphasis on love and of the poignant experience of God we have the testimony of two profound rabbinic conceptions. The conception of Mercy in Judgment summarizes the rabbinic view that God's justice is itself softened by His love.[247] The conception of the imitation of God reflects the transcending ethical significance of the poignant, personal experience of God, for here the experience of God is the impetus for the practice of all good qualities, particularly of the various aspects of love.[248] We have termed these "conceptions" in order to distinguish them from concepts since, unlike the latter, each is a fixed idea, a permanent coalescence of emphatic trends.

The experience of ethical significance, in rabbinic theology, went hand-in-hand with religious experience. Indeed, ethical significance was but an ineluctible phase of that religious experience which gave events and situations general significance.[249]

VIII. Excursus on Philosophies of Organism

The new organismic approach to scientific problems in widely different fields has had an immense effect on modern philosophy. Philosophies have arisen which attempt to provide concepts descriptive of organism in general so as to epitomize all organismic forms of order. There are also more restricted philosophies of organism, those which limit their generalizing concepts to several demonstrably related fields. Now we have shown rabbinic theology to be organic or organismic in character. We can, therefore, test some of the better-known philosophies of organism in the light of the characteristics of the mental organism displayed by rabbinic theology, a test especially in place when those philosophies apply to spiritual or cultural matters. If, in such cases, the characteristics of the mental organism displayed by rabbinic theology do not conform to the new philosophic generalizations or concepts, the latter, insofar as they fail to epitomize this particular organismic form, must be faulty generalizations.

The most comprehensive philosophy of organism, and hence perhaps the most difficult to grasp, is that developed by Whitehead. Many of his metaphysical concepts can be taken as generalizations of the characteristics of rabbinic theology. Thus, in his notion of "prehension"[250] we see the generalization of *the potential simultaneity of concepts*; in his idea of "appetition"[251] (the urge to actualization) that of *the concretization of concepts*; in his idea of "a cosmic epoch"[252] that of *organic levels*; in his idea of a "society"[253] that of the relation between the *organic complex* and the *individual configurations* of it; in his idea of "rhythms"[254] (the idea that every great rhythm contains lesser rhythms without which it could not be) that of the relation of the *concept* to its *sub-concepts*. There are, indeed, a number of other parallels worth considering would not such considerations take us too far afield. Nevertheless, his metaphysical generalizations are not entirely at one with our characteristics of the mental organism. His idea of the "mutual relatedness" of "eternal objects" cannot be taken as a generalization of the *integration of organic concepts* because "eternal objects" are not organic concepts. Organic concepts are altogether inseparable from the organic process whereas "eternal objects" must, in some sense, be fixed, and are, to that extent, independent of the process. Critics sympathetic to Whitehead's main thesis admit that the idea of "eternal objects," an idea of Platonic origin, is out of harmony with his general philosophy of organism.[255]

Exactly the same inconsistency is to be found in Whitehead's view of religion. Whitehead declares that "the topic of religion is individuality in community"[256] and that "the individual is formative of the society, the society is formative of the individual."[257] These and similar statements depict religion as organismic. The unique configuration of values possessed by every individual, as we have learned, was but an original configuration of the organic complex of concepts common to all. Even Whitehead's famous dictum, "Religion is what the individual does with his own solitariness,"[258] may not be untrue to religion viewed as an organic process.

When the awareness of the self—"the individual with his own solitariness"—was an element in the poignant experience of God, the experience of God had a character that was peculiarly, privately personal. We doubt, however, that this is indeed the implication of Whitehead's dictum. For he is interested not in Process alone but in "eternal objects" or "eternal ideas", as well. These eternal objects are metaphysical generalizations, and for Whitehead religion must yield metaphysical generalizations. "A metaphysical description takes its origin from one select field of interest. It receives its confirmation by establishing itself as adequate and as exemplified in other fields of interest."[259] Hence, "the doctrines of rational religion aim at being that metaphysics which can be derived from the supernormal experience of mankind in its moments of finest insight."[260] "Theoretically," he continues, "rational religion could have arisen in complete independence of the antecedent social religions of ritual and mythical belief," adding that, of course, this was not the case historically.[261] The organismic Process which means that "the topic of religion is individuality in community" is, then, according to Whitehead, theoretically superfluous since rational ideas, those which are eternal, whether rising from religious or other fields can, theoretically, be arrived at by the individual *sans* community. We might add that, since rational ideas are independent of empiric history, any one select field, religion included, is theoretically superfluous. But the organismic Process does not remain with Whitehead only theoretically superfluous. "Institutions . . . bibles . . . codes of behaviour," he remarks, "are the trappings of religion, its passing forms."[262] If religion consists primarily of eternal ideas, this is correct; but if religion is an organismic Process, its materials, its social institutions, cannot be separated from the Process itself. All in all, in Whitehead's religious view the "eternal objects" seem to have crowded out the organismic Process. And to this his famous dictum—"Religion is what the individual does with his own solitariness"—probably bears testimony. How can we account for such a deflection from the organismic approach on the part of one who starts out with a philosophy of organism?

The basic fallacy of many philosophies of organism consists in the failure to take account of the fact that each organismic form has its own individuality, the organismic character of which must be demonstrated with respect to the constituents peculiar to itself. Generalizations or concepts epitomizing aspects of the organismic process *in general* are only *descriptive* or *analytic*, not organic, concepts. Whitehead apparently takes his generalizations epitomizing aspects of the organismic process in general, generalizations which parallel our *descriptive* general characteristics, to be organic or organismic concepts in themselves. According to Whitehead, must not these generalizations, since they apply to the universe as a whole in his philosophy, be included among the "eternal objects" or "eternal ideas" between which there is a "mutual relatedness?" With this premise he can maintain that a rational religion composed of such metaphysical concepts would be organic. But to possess organic quality, concepts must be constituents of an organismic complex or form having its own individuality, the organismic character of which must be demonstrated with respect to the constituent concepts peculiar to itself. Can Whitehead actually identify all the "eternal objects" and demonstrate their organismic character, their "mutual relatedness"? Can metaphysical concepts be organic? To say, as does Whitehead, that "eternal objects" are envisaged in "the primordial mind of God" or are "components of the primordial nature of God"[263] is to confess that demonstration here is impossible. Metaphysical concepts are, therefore, for us at best but descriptive and analytical, not organic. And this is borne out by the evidence in our own study. If our study of true organic concepts teaches anything, it teaches that if a religion is organic or organismic its concepts will not be metaphysical. Organic concepts are effortless whereas metaphysical concepts involve great strain not only in their acquisition but in their retention as well. Organic concepts give room for differences in the views of individuals whereas metaphysical concepts, "eternal ideas," dogmas, demand rigid uniformity. In short, organic concepts, as we tried to explain above, are distinct in type from philosophic or metaphysical concepts. No wonder, then, that Whitehead is inconsistent in his views on religion: his description of religion as an organismic process must necessarily conflict with his description of it as a rational system of metaphysical concepts. Thus, in the former "the topic of religion is individuality in community"; in the latter, the community and its social institutions are theoretically superfluous.

Social philosophies of organism are especially apt to suffer from what we have termed "the basic fallacy." The organismic approach in the social sciences demands, first of all, minute and painstaking analysis in order to discover the particular organismic forms, each with its own individual characteristics, in which social life abounds. Until these organismic social forms are identified in detail, all generalizations, even if couched in terms of the organismic approach, are bound to prove sterile. We have seen, for example, that generalizations epitomizing aspects of the organismic process in general are only *analytic tools*, not organismic concepts. In other words, the logical method here remains the same as in all other types of scientific research. It must, of course, remain the same if it is to be valid. The organismic approach differs from other types of scientific study only in its hypothesis: We are utilizing the organismic approach when we attempt to prove by logical means that the subject under analysis is organismic. Yet Wheeler, in an interesting article on the history of the organismic approach, assumes that the measure to which individuals of any period utilize that approach in their analytic studies is a sure indication of the organic quality of that period. On that basis, he even plots "culture cycles" which allow him to predict wars and revolutions with almost mechanistic accuracy.[264] The most patent abuse of the organismic terminology is, of course, to be found in the fascist philosophies where the word "organic" is simply an honorific term to cast glamour over pseudo-scientific ideas and over rank prejudices. True organic concepts act as inner drives, we have learned; and were the fascist concepts such drives what need would there be for concentration camps, absolute censorship, terror-tactics and other methods of constant intimidation and regimentation?

We shall touch briefly on two other philosophies of organism. Vague though the positive side of Bergson's philosophy may seem to us, he is emphatic enough in his criticism of conceptual thought. Indeed, as we saw above, he is over-emphatic, for he dismisses all concepts as only analytic tools.[265] Since, in his view, concepts but hamper our true integration with the movement of life, he advocates his own particular kind of intuition. The exercise of this kind of intuition, he affirms, necessitates tremendous concentration and great exertion of will in order to overcome our ordinary conceptual or intellectual way of thinking, and even at the end, true integration with the movement of life, or experience of God, cannot be complete. There is no gainsaying any individual's personal experience, of course, and such Bergson's "intuition" seems to be. But we can assert, at least, that his thesis does not represent a valid organismic approach to religious experience. For we have learned that organic concepts, concepts that correspond completely with actual experience, are possible; that the integration of personality is not achieved only by choice intuitively-gifted individuals; and that the experience of God was, certainly among the Jews, an effortless factor in the ordinary, normal valuational life of the individual.

Dewey has done much toward elucidating the implications of the organismic approach. He has attempted, as he says, "to contribute to what has come to be called an 'emergent' theory of mind."[266] He recognizes that "the distinction between physical, psycho-physical and mental is . . . one of levels of increasing complexity and intimacy of interaction among natural events."[267] But, for all that, when he comes to treat of "ends" or values he succumbs to the old, stultifying "basic fallacy." Aware that these values are "ends so inclusive that they unify the self,"[268] he apparently fails to grasp the import of his own statement. If the ends are so inclusive as to unify the self it must be because they are constituents of an organismic form on the mental level. The thing to do, therefore, is to try to discover the special character peculiar to this organismic form, an analysis such as that undertaken in our study of rabbinic "ends" or values. Here, however, organism for Dewey ceases to be "emergent" and becomes a matter for synthesis, for manipulation. "It remains," he declares, "only to weld these things (i. e. values) together;"[269] and this welding is to be achieved, apparently, through imagination—"as far as these ends, through imagination, take on unity."[270] Dewey's failure to utilize the organismic approach towards ends or values results also in the failure to perceive that, in an organic complex, there is no definitive concept of God but rather the experience of God. "The word 'God'," he says, "means the ideal ends that at a given time and place one acknowledges as having authority over his volition and emotion, the values to which one is supremely devoted, as far as these ends, through imagination, take on unity."[271] This conception of God is very much akin to the philosophical conception except that, instead of being a generalizing principle epitomizing all the known kinds of order,[272] it is a generalizing principle epitomizing all "ideal ends". Rabbinic values, as we learned, do not "*take on* unity." They are not synthetically unified by the concept of God, whether through imagination or other means, but are integrated because they are constituents of an organic complex. We should say, therefore, that Dewey's approach to the matters pertaining to our study leans to the rationalistic rather than to the organismic.

When full cognizance is taken of the fact that each organismic form has its own individuality which must be made the subject of careful analysis, the organismic approach is sound and fruitful. We are familiar with the results of this approach in psychology — in Gestalt and psycho-analysis. But it has produced results equally as rich, if less well-known, in other fields — in biology, chemistry, physics, astronomy and mathematics.[273]

IX. Conclusion

Is organic thinking a phenomenon of modern times? Did peoples in the past other than Israel possess an organic complex of concepts? The overwhelming importance of society, again and again indicated in the researches of all the social sciences, makes it likely that organic thinking is an abiding feature of man's mental life, a supposition likely enough, at any rate, to merit further investigation. Substantiation of this supposition will amount to a demonstration that all religion and ethics which are social products are not an arbitrary, chaotic hodge-podge of historical accidents but possess an order inherent in the very nature of society. Techniques and conclusions developed in the course of such investigation may even aid us to grapple with the complicated processes of present-day society.

Our theory is already rather well substantiated by a

study made some years ago in the field of anthropology. Lévy-Bruhl's analysis of primitive mentality, though not his reflections on the rôle of that mentality in civilized society, is strikingly consistent with our own thesis. "Logical thought," he says, "implies, more or less consciously, a systematic unity which is best realizable in science and philosophy,"[274] a systematic unity expressed "through a hierarchy of concepts."[275] Primitive thought, as he points out, is on the contrary non-hierarchical. It is governed by an ensemble of collective representations by means of which all objects, situations, relations, events, are determined.[276] Even the logical thought of the primitives, examples of which are the classification of objects and the method of numeration, is of a piece with the collective representations.[277] Now these collective representations do not really abstract and generalize as do our own concepts;[278] and have, in fact, not yet crystallized out as genuine concepts, since they contain, as integral parts, affective and motor elements.[279] They operate instead through what Lévy-Bruhl calls "the law of participation," whereby occult and mystic relations render the primitive mind frequently oblivious of all the laws of rational thought, such as those of identity and contradiction.[280] Primitive mentality as described by Lévy-Bruhl and rabbinic theology as we have described it are, therefore, similar in two respects and vastly different in a third. Like rabbinic theology, primitive thought is non-hierarchical and, again like rabbinic theology, this non-hierarchical thought acts as framework for logical thinking. Unlike rabbinic theology, however, primitive thought does not possess a pattern of clearly discernible concepts, a complex of concepts each member of which, though related to all the rest, has a marked individuality of its own expressed through its own power to abstract and generalize. It seems justifiable, then, to regard primitive thought as a form of organic thinking wherein individual concepts have not yet altogether differentiated out. Since organic thinking is thus not confined to rabbinic theology, we have the more reason to assume that it is an abiding feature of man's mental life.

The study of primitive mentality is, however, limited in its bearings on organic thinking. Primitive mentality, to be sure, is a form of organic thinking, but it is an undeveloped form, lacking aspects observable in mature forms. Anthropologists sometimes fail to appreciate the distance between primitive and civilized man. Noticing that certain features of social thought and practice are common to both, they sometimes allow their knowledge of the primitive form, the only form they have studied scientifically, entirely to color their view of the civilized form, concerning which their remarks are at best conjectures. Durkheim, for instance, specifically affirms that in penetrating to the fundamental, essential traits of primitive religion we penetrate at the same time to the basic, elementary forms common to all religions.[281] But scientific method demands an explanation of new phenomena as *new* phenomena, and is not satisfied with an explanation which, however valid for a certain stage, leaves the new phenomena out of account. The failure to measure up to this scientific standard mars the concluding pages of Lévy-Bruhl's work. Brilliant and subtle in his analysis of primitive mentality, his view of the influence of that mentality on civilized thought is mere conjecture, and conjecture that is negated by his very analysis. In his analysis, Lévy-Bruhl takes great pains to demonstrate that primitive thought is characterized by its lack of the kind of concepts employed by civilized man, and that *instead*, the primitive mentality is governed by "the law of participation." The use of concepts by civilized man should obviously have been regarded by Lévy-Bruhl as a *new* phenomenon. Indeed, he does recognize that when thought begins to be ideological there is no longer "mystic symbiosis," living communion with things and totems.[282] Nevertheless, he goes on to say that "there is nothing to prevent abstract and general concepts, once formed, retaining elements still recognizable as vestiges of an earlier age."[283] Such vestiges of mystic, primitive mentality he discerns in modern concepts that possess affective and motor elements.[284] An area rich in possibilities for research is all too easily dismissed here by being called "vestiges." Far from being vestiges of mystic symbiosis, concepts of this type employed by a civilized group display, as we have found, a distinct dynamic order, a coherent relationship between the concepts, and not that identification of subject with object characteristic of mystic symbiosis. The organic concepts possess affective and motor elements, true enough, indicative of a kinship with primitive mentality. This kinship, however, is accounted for by our theory of organic levels, primitive mentality being a very early level of organic thinking. Of all this, Lévy-Bruhl had, of course, no inkling. Finding immensely potent human concepts which he viewed only as "vestiges," he declares with some despair "that the rational unity of the thinking being . . . is a *desideratum*, not a fact."[285] Not only is he unaware of the coherent order possessed by these concepts but he fails completely to perceive their function. Without the concepts enriched by affective and motor elements, there could be neither group unity nor the individual thinking being whose individuality consists of an original configuration of these social concepts which his logical thinking, in turn, refines and deepens. As long as we have society, then, so long will we have concepts with rich affective and motor elements. But these concepts, as illustrated in different ways by Lévy-Bruhl's analysis and by his closing remarks, cannot be studied to the best advantage at the level of primitive mentality.

Further study of organic thinking may well proceed with rabbinic theology as a point of departure. We need for our investigation a form of organic thinking possessing all the characteristic traits, a mature form. Such an organic complex must, of course, be expressed through concepts, and the more full its expression the more adequate for our purpose. In fine, organic thinking can best be studied in a form sufficiently developed to have produced a literature. The vast literature produced by rabbinic theology is not a mere accident, a freak development of a particular form of organic thinking. It derives from the basic relationship between the group and the individual, the basic relationship, on the plane of organic thinking, between the organic complex and the individual configurations of it. Perhaps in no other developed civilization of the western world was the individual so completely integrated with the folk — both cause and effect of the remarkable spiritual leadership of the folk on the part of the gifted, literary individuals who acted as its teachers. Hence we possess a literature which exhibits probably the most fully developed characteristics of organic thinking, and which for that reason, we think, yielded so readily to the methods of this initial study. Equipped with the organismic approach, we have discovered characteristics of an organic form on the mental level. These characteristics can be employed as tools in the study of other forms of organic thinking. We must always bear in mind, however, that the organic characteristics are characteristics of *divergent* organisms, as a consideration of some of the conclusions of our study will show.

In our study of rabbinic theology, incomplete as it is, a number of characteristics of organic thinking were brought to light. Organic thinking is conceptual: the complex, the constituents of which are demonstrably organically interrelated with each other, is always, certainly in civilized groups, a complex of *concepts*. It is this conceptual character of every complex of organic thinking that renders it an organismic form on the *mental* level. Now each organic complex has an individuality of its own. The concepts of each complex differ from those of other complexes. The number of concepts differs with each complex, the larger complex carving out a world beyond grasp of the smaller.[286] Each complex probably has its own special emphatic trends in addition to its "separate" concepts, but these trends are peculiar to itself. It is hardly likely, for example, that the coalescence of the experience of God, the emphasis on love and the emphasis on the individual is to be found anywhere but in rabbinic theology and perhaps in the systems based upon it. No doubt all organic complexes act as framework for logical thinking and for folklore, but both differ in extent and content with every complex. Again, the ethical sphere is doubtless part and parcel of every organic complex, but, once more, the content of that sphere differs with each individual complex. There are doubtless traces of earlier organic levels in every complex, but probably rabbinic theology alone reinterpreted *continuously* the previous organic level in its entirety. What we have designated as General Characteristics — The Concretization of the Concept, Potential Simultaneity of Concepts, The Fluid Character of the Complex and the like — while characteristics of all organic complexes and in that sense of social values in general, are not all equally as pronounced in some complexes as in others. There are differences in flexibility, in the room given for individual personality, differences, in brief, that correspond to the divergencies already mentioned. We do not mean to imply, of course, that there are no similarities in the contents of the various organic complexes. If, however, even successive organic levels possess their own distinct individualities, this must be all the more true of unrelated organic complexes. The characteristics of organic thinking, then, are tools for the investigation of divergent organic complexes, since each organismic form has its own peculiar individuality.

There can be no such thing, therefore, as "organismic logic." Since each organic complex has its own individuality, there are no general concepts which are constituents of a general complex. How, then, can there be an "organismic logic" or a kind of organic thinking that represents all organic complexes? Moreover, an organic complex cannot be achieved by manipulation of concepts on the part of an individual. The basic relationship between the group and the individual which an organic complex expresses precludes this sort of manipulation. We thus return to the conclusion that, though organic thinking may be the framework for logical thinking, it is thinking of an order different from the latter.

This study of rabbinic theology, as has been said, is far from complete. We have attempted to discover the principle of coherence, the organizing principle of rabbinic theology, and we have proceeded with the analysis to the point where this principle and some of its general implications can be recognized. But further analysis of the many matters left unfinished or else not touched upon at all will certainly throw more light both on rabbinic theology and on organic thinking in general. Our knowledge both of rabbinic theology and of organic thinking will be greatly enhanced if the method employed in this work on Seder Eliahu is applied in studies of other Midrashim and of the haggadic material of the Talmuds. Such studies will delineate the distinguishing features of a number of rabbinic concepts at best only alluded to in our present work. The rabbinic theology expressed in the prayers and implied in the ritual and imbedded in the Halakah ought also to be investigated from our point of view. A comparison of the theology of the Rabbis with that of the earlier books of the Apocrypha would also prove useful. Historical studies, already written, of the lives and views of individual Rabbis can yield much information on the relation of the organic complex to the individual configurations of it and on the way in which economic, social and political situations in different periods were interpreted by the organic concepts. Greatly needed, though involving many difficulties, is a comprehensive study of the relation of medieval Jewish philosophy and Kabbalah to rabbinic theology, and particularly of the way in which Kabbalah has utilized the rabbinic concepts. Equally valuable would be an inquiry as to the manner in which the rabbinic concepts are employed in the popular medieval Jewish ethical works. These are some of the things to be dealt with if the theory presented here is to be amplified.

Finally, there remains the problem as to the reinterpretation of rabbinic theology in accordance with our modern needs. If the rabbinic reinterpretation of the Bible is a criterion, reinterpretation is apparently essential to the process whereby the old organic complex is transposed in its entirety to a new level. Reinterpretation today begins with an attempt to find "equivalents"—as Kaplan calls them[287]—equivalents in modern life of the old organic concepts. Supposing conditions to be favorable to the emergence of a new organic level, its emergence will mean, however, that reinterpretation will lose its piece-meal character and become a method for transposing the old organic complex as a whole. Reinterpretation must thus undergo a development, and that development can be accelerated with a deepened knowledge of organic thinking. Are new organic complexes necessarily new organic levels? Is it possible for a new organic complex to incorporate only fragments of the old? Can we discern the formation of new organic patterns or complexes in the present? The answer to these and similar questions are germane to the problem of reinterpretation today.

APPENDIX

In the chapter entitled "Introductory — On the Text" in *The Theology of Seder Eliahu*, we dealt with a number of theories regarding the date, authorship and land of origin of the Seder Eliahu; and we also touched on the matter of the state of the text as presented by Friedmann. It would serve no real purpose to append now an exhaustive study of all the opinions this much-discussed book has elicited from scholars, in view of the fact that many of these opinions differ only in slight details from those we have considered. Moreover, recently discovered data which we shall shortly adduce allow us to give definite answers to some of the questions hitherto moot, and so render discussion on these points futile.

Nevertheless, we ought to mention a view differing radically from any we have already considered. Entirely at variance with the conclusions of Rapoport, Zunz, Bacher and Oppenheim, and Yawetz[1] is the theory advanced by both Graetz and Güdemann. Graetz holds that the author of our text lived in Rome in the tenth century, and, taking the "Babylon" of our text to refer to Rome, regards the wars and persecutions mentioned in the book as reflecting the attacks of the Hungarians upon Italy.[2] Güdemann likewise states that our author lived in Italy in the tenth century, though not necessarily in Rome, and, adding that he was an itinerant preacher, accounts for the mentioning of Babylon on the ground that travellers like to relate of the far places they have visited rather than of their experiences at home.[3]

This theory, among others, has now been disproved by data furnished in a work recently published by Asaf. The source of the statement in the 'Aruk[4] — even to the last phrase saying that the passages in the Talmud introduced by תני דבי אליהו are all to be found in Seder Eliahu — has proven to be a responsum by R. Natronai, Gaon of Sura, who lived in the middle of the ninth century.[5] The date of Seder Eliahu, then, must be fixed at no later than the eighth century; and it cannot have been composed in any European country.

Ginzberg's theory according to which our text once had a "Baraita" and commentary[6] is disputed by Mann. Mann declares that תלמוד רבא and תלמוד גדול refer to the "great Talmud, i. e., *Talmud Babli*", and that [ ]ל הקטן refers indubitably to a statement by Samuel the Small, and that, hence, Ginzberg's theory "is entirely unwarranted".[7] But Mann certainly fails to prove his contention. He states that, having consulted the manuscript at Cambridge, he found that "there is enough space after this line (i. e., the line closing with אליה רבה) to indicate that subsequently there begins a new section having the superscription תלמוד גדול, viz., that the text on folio 5a, lines 2 ff., contains Aggadic statements from the 'great Talmud', i. e., *Talmud Babli* (Sanh. 43b, Ber. 12b, etc.)".[8] Mann's language here, especially the use of the word "etc.", is somewhat unfortunate for it leads to the inference that the entire text of folio 5a, lines 2 ff., contains statements from Talmud Babli, which, if correct, would establish Mann's contention. The facts are, however, that Sanh. 43b and Ber. 12b — cited by Ginzberg himself — are the *only* parallels to the text on folio 5a, lines 2 ff., that can be found in Talmud Babli, that these parallels form about *half* of the folio in question, and that the latter half of this very folio which Mann describes as containing statements from the Babli consists of a passage closely similar in style to a confessional at the end of Yerushalmi Yoma,[9] and of another passage for which no parallel has been found. Moreover, the designation "the great Talmud" for Talmud Babli is altogether unusual and Mann offers no parallels for it. From this, and from the inadequacy of the evidence in folio 5a, lines 2 ff., we must conclude that Mann has not proved his contention that תלמוד רבא and תלמוד גדול refer to the Talmud Babli. As to his contention that [ ]ל הקטן refers to a statement by Samuel the Small, and that this statement actually occurs as an anonymous Baraita in Yoma 35b — again a parallel given by Ginzberg himself — we need only recall, first, that the Baraita is *anonymous*, second, that many statements given anonymously in the Talmud have parallels in our text.[10] [ ]ל הקטן may very well originally have been אליה קטן, as Ginzberg says in his introduction, and as Friedmann, indeed, took it to read.[11] These considerations ought to remove the objections advanced by Mann against Ginzberg's theory. On the other hand, Ginzberg's theory is supported positively by the instances of "Baraita" and commentary in which our text abounds, as exemplified by a number of passages to which we have called attention in the course of discussion;[12] and by those passages some of which reflect a Palestinian and others a Babylonian or Diaspora locale.[13]

We have found the state of the text of Seder Eliahu, even as edited by Friedmann, far from satisfactory; hence, studies in the textual problems of this book should be mentioned. Of particular value in this respect are two reviews of Friedmann's edition, those of Theodor and of Marx. Theodor discusses the orthography of our text, and also suggests that the readings of the Yalḳuṭ be given careful consideration, a suggestion that has been followed in our renderings of relevant passages in Seder Eliahu.[14] Marx compares our text with the סדר אליהו זוטא edited by Ch. M. Horovitz (1882), and offers some illustrations of differences in their readings.[15]

NOTES

NOTES

In these notes, "above" and "below" designate references to the present volume. Where no book is mentioned and these designations are absent, page-numbers refer to Friedmann's edition of Seder Eliahu. "Additions" followed or preceded by page-numbers refers to the "Additions" in Friedmann's edition of Seder Eliahu.

NOTES TO CHAPTER I

[1] William James, essay on The Importance of Individuals, in The Will to Believe, (New York, 1919), pp. 257–258.

[2] As we shall demonstrate in our last chapter, the term "rabbinic theology" is not an appropriate designation for rabbinic thought. We shall continue to use the term, however, because it has achieved general currency.

[3] See Kadushin, The Theology of Seder Eliahu (New York, 1932), p. 17. This book is hereafter designated as TE.

[4] See ibid., p. 19.

[5] See ibid., p. 20. Note 11 there should be corrected to read: "Schechter, opus cit., Preface, pp. xi–xii."

[6] W. Bacher, Die Agada der palästinensischen Amoräer I, (Strassburg, 1892), Introd., p. IX.

[7] Ibid., Introd., p. XI–XII.

[8] M. Friedmann, Seder Eliahu Rabba und Seder Eliahu Zuṭa (Wien, 1902) and Pseudo-Seder Eliahu Zuṭa (Wien, 1904), published by Achiassaf, Warsaw, and bound in one volume.

[9] It has recently been proved that the 'Aruk copied from an earlier source, and that the date of Seder Eliahu must be fixed at no later than the eighth century—see Appendix, below, p. 262.

[10] See the preceding note.

[11] These instances are all referred to below, p. 324, note 12. The succeeding note there refers to instances some of which indicate a Palestinian and others a Babylonian or Diaspora locale.

The entire problem of our text is taken up in detail in TE, Chapter I, and supplementary information is given in the Appendix below.

[12] Finkelstein, in his review of TE would add a fifth fundamental concept, Man. We cannot agree, though we are grateful for his calling attention to this concept. The importance of the concept of Man, he argues, warrants our regarding it as fundamental. But all rabbinic concepts are equally essential to the rabbinic world-outlook, and the "fundamental" character of the four fundamental concepts has

nothing to do with their importance. Man is indeed, as Finkelstein says, a rabbinic concept; and we need go no farther than the material gathered in this work to indicate that, like all the other rabbinic concepts, it is woven out of the four fundamental ones: God *loves* man — He made the earth a dwelling place for man (TE, p. 83), and feeds man daily out of His charity or *love* (ibid., p. 112); He acts with *justice* toward man — "he judges the sons of men ... and pays to everyone according to his deeds" (ibid., p. 166); an aspect of Torah, ethical *Derek Ereẓ*, is incumbent upon all mankind (below, pp. 122–4); *Israel* has a special rôle to play among mankind (TE, pp. 68–69). For Finkelstein's view, see his article in The Jewish Quarterly Review, New Series, Vol. XXV, No. 1 (July, 1934), pp. 13–16.

[13] See above, note 3.

[14] Cf. TE, pp. 64–71.

[15] See ibid., p. 58 and pp. 63–64.

[16] Cf. ibid., pp. 58–63.

[17] Cf. ibid., p. 66.

[18] Cf. ibid., pp. 71–74.

[19] Cf. ibid., pp. 61–64.

[20] Cf. ibid., p. 66.

[21] Cf. ibid., pp. 75–88.

[22] Cf. ibid., pp. 88–101.

[23] Cf. ibid., pp. 34–38.

[24] Cf. ibid., pp. 38–48.

[25] Cf. ibid., pp. 49–57.

[26] Cf. ibid., pp. 109–113.

[27] Cf. ibid., pp. 114–118.

[28] Cf. ibid., pp. 118–137.

[29] Cf. ibid., pp. 134–135.

[30] Cf. ibid., pp. 137–161.

[31] Besides the passage in our text concerning Eliphaz and his son Amalek, Haman and his ancestor Agag, etc. quoted in TE, pp. 206–207, there is another famous midrash concerning Ishmael and his children found in a number of sources. Bereshit R. 53, 18, commenting on Gen. 21:17, tells of how the angels appeared against Ishmael, saying: " 'Master of the universe, wilt Thou bring up a well for a man who in the future will cause Thy children to die of thirst?' Said He to them, 'What is Ishmael now?' They answered, '(Now he is) righteous.' Whereupon He said, 'I deal with man according to his deserts at the moment.' " This passage, as Theodor points out, has in mind Is. 21:13–14, which verses are taken by the Rabbis to refer to the treatment of the exiled Judeans on the part of the Arabs, Ishmael's descendants, and these verses are indeed supplied by several other sources. Comp. J. Theodor, Bereshit R. (Berlin, 1913), p. 573. Here, then, the angels identify Ishmael with his descendants —"A man who in the future"— as one corporate personality, and argue that help should be withheld from him, an argument in the interests of corporate justice. Incidentally, here is also another instance of angels acting as background to bring God's higher justice into greater relief.

[32] Modern moralists have not advanced beyond the Rabbis in the solution of this ethical problem. "In the presence of obvious conflict between the principle of

individual responsibility and that of collective responsibility, the philosopher is tempted to decide for one or the other of these principles. But humanity continues to profess both and to disregard both whenever necessary . . . These reflections suggest that in the face of the complicated situation before us we cannot unqualifiedly accept either the principle of individual or collective responsibility, nor absolutely deny either"— Cohen, Reason and Nature (New York, 1931), pp. 393–394. Cohen's example of the assumption by the Allies that all Germans are to be held responsible for the Great War, even those who opposed it and even generations to come, proves to us, despite what Cohen says previously, that collective responsibility is grounded in the idea of collective or corporate personality. Indeed, nationalism as such argues that the notion of corporate personality cannot be dispensed with.

[33] For the aspects of the concept of God's justice cf. TE, pp. 163–211.

[34] Cf. ibid., pp. 8–9.

[35] Cf. below, p. 53.

[36] Cf. ibid., p. 87.

[37] Below, p. 197 f.

NOTES TO CHAPTER II

[1] Below, pp. 23–7. Some of these terms are defined in the next section.

[2] TE, p. 33.

[3] Ibid., pp. 108–109.

[4] "Additions," p. 34.

[5] Pp. 21–22.

[6] P. 160.

[7] Pp. 70–1.

[8] P. 12 and p. 37.

[9] "Additions," p. 15. The proof-text from Prov. 1:9 speaks of Torah as לוית חן and it is thus another לויה, company.

[10] "Additions," pp. 35 and 33. On the personification of Torah see Bacher, Terminologie (Hebrew trans.) I and II, s.v. תורה, particularly II, p. 312. Comp. also Schechter, Some Aspects of Rabbinic Theology (New York, 1910), Chapter IX.

[11] Pp. 33 and 32. "Friedmann's text is impossible. Read ולא אמר — There is one most secret chamber of the Torah which God did not reveal to Israel. The idea is made quite clear on p. 32 — that there is for every student of the Torah some secret in it which only he might be able to find!"— (L.G.)

[12] "Additions," p. 20; and on p. 187. The other four are heaven and earth, Abraham, Israel, and the Temple.

[13] Pp. 189–90.

[14] P. 164. "Read פותחת בבי"ת instead of אומרת בי"ת"— (L.G.).

The claim has been made that the Kabbalah can be traced to talmudic times and even earlier. See Horodetsky, החסידות והחסידים Vol. I, Introd., p. viii.

[15] P. 160. It was one of the things created before the Cherubim. The others were Gehenna, Paradise, the throne of glory, the name of the Messiah, and the Temple. The Torah, the fountain of life, was with God before creation — p. 33 of "Additions."

[16] P. 160.

[17] P. 105.

[18] P. 185.

[19] P. 105.

[20] "Additions", p. 33.

[21] P. 3.

[22] "Additions", p. 45.

[23] P. 195.

[24] P. 30.

[25] P. 179.

[26] Ibid.

[27] "Additions", p. 17.

[28] Ibid., p. 18.

[29] Ibid., p. 45. "And your crown is greater than their (i. e., the kings') crown" —ibid., p. 18.

[30] P. 89 — כתר דברי תורה. This statement is attributed to David. A very similar statement, also attributed to him, has the version וקשרת לנו קשר בדברי תורה — on p. 157. Again, on p. 32, the statement with a slight variation is repeated, and there וקשרת לנו קשר גדול בדברי תורה occurs. The most acceptable version, it seems to me, is on p. 89, and quoted above; the others seem to have been affected by the proximity of the word וקשרת.

"ק' כתר means 'to crown', and מסוף וכו' modifies the entire sentence."— (L.G.).

[31] P. 171.

[32] P. 170.

[33] Ibid.

[34] "Additions," p. 37 — שקולה.

[35] P. 6. For the way in which the two thousand years of Torah are derived, see Friedmann, note #1, on p. 7. See also TE, pp. 103–4; and cf. Ginzberg, Genizah Studies, Vol. II (1929), pp. 397 and 400.

[36] P. 71. "In the text, קדושים is misspelled for קדומים, caused by the verse quoted: . . . קודש"— (L.G.).

[37] Pp. 70–1.

[38] "Additions", p. 40.

[39] P. 85.

[40] P. 113.

[41] P. 112.

[42] P. 149. "This statement is a rhetorical exclamation by God: If I would forget Israel I would have to forget the Torah since Israel is the people of the Torah. It corresponds to the phrase frequently used by the Rabbis: תורה מה תהא עליה — for the realization of the Torah, the existence of Israel is a *sine qua non*."— (L.G.).

"Torah as a purely spiritual entity, the outflow of Divine Wisdom is, of course, superior to anything material, including Israel. On the other hand, the purpose of the Torah is its realization in life which is impossible without Israel. There is from this point of view no difference in the estimate of the two — Torah and Israel"— (L.G.).

It seems to me that what we have described as the organic unity of rabbinic theology enables us to understand why there is "no difference in the estimate of the two", despite emphasis at one time upon Israel and at another upon Torah. The fundamental concepts are organically one, being only different vantage points or different points of view from which the world may be looked at. Hence, as we shall see immediately, Israel and Torah are also placed on a par on some occasions.

43 P. 105.

44 P. 191. "קלקל בה means: he misused it — as the same expression used on p. 190 with regard to כהונה and מלוכה indicates. Balaam, according to the Haggadah was immoral and of an evil character (comp. Legends, Vol. III, p. 354 ff.), and hence proved himself unworthy of the Torah."— (L.G.).

45 P. 12.

46 P. 23.

47 These divisions will be taken up in the next section, where the terms are defined also.

48 P. 8. This translation is explained by a correction in the text — below, Chap. II, note 130.

49 P. 13.

50 P. 106. There are, of course, numerous places where all the divisions are given without being specifically called Torah but where this is altogether understood — on pp. 82, 29, 88 and frequently elsewhere.

51 P. 137.

52 "Torah" as equivalent to Bible and Mishnah, pp. 140, 194, "Additions", p. 6, and elsewhere. "Words of the Torah" as equivalent to Bible and Mishnah, pp. 70, 193, 196, 195, 97, 37, and elsewhere.

53 P. 15. See Friedmann note #19; his second interpretation is the correct one, for "three" is clearly in apposition to "My Torah".

54 P. 19.

55 P. 15.

56 P. 4.

57 P. 71. That is, the prophets have assured Israel that when they return to God, He will return to them, as seen from the proof-text, Joel 2:12. "פתח אחר gives no sense. I think the correct reading is פתח אחד: There are many doors opened to Israel through which one is led to God, and by the study of the Prophets one can well find *one* of them."— (L.G.).

58 P. 124. Comp. Moore, Judaism, Vol. III (1930), p. 81, where he quotes Tanḥuma, ed. Buber, Re'eh I.

59 P. 4.

60 P. 76.

61 P. 121.

62 P. 138. Similar injunctions or other places where single verses and *halakot* are regarded as Torah are on pp. 30 and 12.

63 P. 175.

[64] P. 23.

[65] Above, p. 16.

[66] See Bacher, op. cit., I, p. 133 and II, p. 311, s. v. תורה.

Three unusual expressions for Torah occur in our text: תורה תמימה, on p. 127 and on p. 178; תורה ברורה on p. 139; and on p. 126, Jacob (Israel) is said never to have put away ספר תורה from his hand, and this, too, probably does not refer to the scroll of the Pentateuch only.

[67] Pp. 8, 11, 22, 23, 31, 37, 68, 82, 99, 100, 124, 129, 155, 198; "Additions", pp. 14, 37; and elsewhere.

[68] Pp. 120–1.

Ginzberg offers here a definition admirable for its terseness and lucidity, and some pertinent remarks. " 'Torah' as well as 'words of the Torah' have in Seder Eliahu as in other rabbinic sources a generic as well as a particular meaning. In the generic, they mean any teaching — Pentateuch, Prophets, Hagiographa, Mishnah, Talmud, etc. At the same time 'Torah' as well as 'words of the Torah' stand for תורת משה (the Pentateuch), and then, of course, opposed to any other part of the Bible. On p. 121, 'Torah' has this meaning and is *certainly* opposed to the words of the Prophets, 'the words I told you at first'. By the 'Torah', of course, is meant the Torah as correctly interpreted, and a verse of the Pentateuch interpreted by קל וחומר was for the Rabbis, of course, a Pentateuchal teaching"— (L.G.).

[69] See below, Chap. II, note 109.

[70] P. 146. On p. 28, Abraham is made king over the inhabitants of the world after they listened to words of Torah, which consisted in the recitation of the things that had happened to him. On "Additions", p. 7, the verses from the Pentateuch contained in the *tefillin* are referred to as "words of the Torah".

[71] "Additions", p. 20: "הפך in Hebrew as well as in Aramaic means 'search'; cf., for instance, II Sam. 10:3 where ולהפכה can have no other meaning"— (L.G.).

[72] See below, p. 39.

[73] P. 32. See above, Chap. II, note 11.

[74] P. 15; similarly, "Additions", p. 33. God, Himself, will ultimately tell them the final decisions on these matters — p. 69. "במקומו modifies the previous clause — the unclean as 'becoming it', etc."— (L.G.).

[75] Introduction, p. 109.

[76] "Additions", p. 19.

"I am not quite convinced of it. Why could not שומר be synonymous with עושה? Cf. Friedmann, Introd. p. 110: וזו השמירה היא משנה. If any differentiation is meant, עושה = מעשה and שמירה = תלמוד. Cf. Sifre Deut., par. 58: ושמרתם זו משנה ועשיתם זו מעשה"— (L.G.). But see below, pp. 29–30, and the references cited. In any case, however we take these terms, Torah conveys the ideas of both study and practice.

[77] P. 180.

[78] "Additions", p. 39.

[79] P. 144. Gehenna seethes for those who recognize it (Torah) but transgress it — p. 108.

[80] P. 96 — פשעה של תורה. See Friedmann, note #43. But there is a strong presumption that this passage does not refer to the Deluge but to the First Destruction, and that, in this case Torah does mean study. See below, Chap. II, note 420.

[81] P. 74. See Friedmann, note #14.

[82] Bacher, op. cit., I, p. 133, puts it thus: "In its wide meaning, (Torah) includes all the studies of Judaism, both whatever refers to belief and practices and whatever refers to the study itself."

[83] A partial list of passages where "Torah" refers to study: Pp. 13, 30, 37, 48, 50, 55, 63, 64, 84, 93, 95, 100, 110, 112, 113, 117, 133, 141, 144, 148, 156, 168, 182; "Additions", pp. 16, 17, 18, 21, 32, 33. A partial list of passages where "words of the Torah" refers to study: Pp. 8, 14, 16, 22, 33, 38, 47, 50, 52, 62, 63, 64, 92, 97, 101, 102, 105, 107, 109, 111, 117, 118, 130, 133, 137, 167, 187, 189, 195, 196; "Additions", p. 3.

[84] Pp. 13, 115, 4, 197, 57, and elsewhere.

[85] P. 172. Friedmann, Introduction, l. c.

[86] P. 19; above, p. 28.

[87] Pp. 16–17.

[88] Pp. 29, 178; "Additions", p. 21, and elsewhere.

[89] Pp. 62, 197, 198, 31; "Additions", pp. 1, 2. Torah is one category and charity and Deeds of Loving-kindness another, on p. 90.

[90] Pp. 13, 36, 38, 67, 91 (twice), 92, 93, 104, 127, 128 (also the parallel in "Additions", p. 4), 139. In one place "the study of Torah" occurs alone — p. 31.

[91] " 'Torah' is a generic term for instruction in religion (including morals) rather than commandment (מצוה) or statute (חק); both of which are indeed included in it, but as particular species or forms may be distinguished within it (not *from* it)" — Moore, Judaism, Vol. III, p. 81. See also below, pp. 72–4, where the ambiguity of the term is accounted for, and its scope enlarged.

[92] Above, p. 18.

[93] Pp. 189–90, 33, 130, 61; cf. also p. 68.

[94] Pp. 189–90.

[95] P. 9. See Friedmann, note #19. Ginzberg, whose rendering I have taken in the translation above differs with Friedmann. "Accurately העביר is used here like I Sam. 20:36 — להעבירו. He made his words pass beyond nine hundred seventy-four generations. As to Friedmann's view, according to which God 'skipped' nine hundred seventy-four generations — that is putting something into the text which is flatly refuted by the other passages where God is said to have for nine hundred seventy-four generations 'sat' over the Torah. There can be no doubt that according to Seder Eliahu the Torah was created one thousand generations before Moses, i. e., nine hundred seventy-four generations before the creation of the world. Accordingly, העביר is to be taken literally: He established all His words for the sake of Israel. Cf. II Chron. 30:5 — 'ויעמידו דבר וכו"— (L.G.).

[96] P. 190.

[97] P. 68.

[98] Pp. 4, 15, 16, 26, 32, 33, 37, 56, 108, 112, 139. The Torah is one of the five possessions which God made especially His own in His world — p. 187; "Additions", p. 20.

[99] Pp. 85, 193, 179. Then they accepted upon themselves the Kingship of Heaven. See TE, pp. 59–60, *Malkut Shamayim*.

[100] P. 11.

[101] "Additions", p. 38.

[102] P. 130. See Friedmann, note #8. In his Introduction, p. 85, he states that it is an interpolation from the piska on the Ten Commandments in the Pesikta Rabbati. "I am not quite as sure as Friedmann that the text is interpolated, but there can be no doubt that it is corrupt. אל תיקרי does not introduce a notarikon and ד"א follows upon a general remark without a particular interpretation, which of course is impossible. Read אין אנכי אלא לשון נוטריקון, אנא נפשי כתבית יהבית"—(L.G.).

[103] Pp. 149, 192.

[104] P. 192. See TE, pp. 93–95: The authority of the Torah is further enhanced by angelology.

[105] "Additions", p. 44.

[106] P. 33. This statement introduces Deut. 33:29.

In a rather inept metaphor, God is said to be the bridegroom, Moses the attendant or best man and the Torah the bride, when the Torah was given to Israel —"Additions", p. 29. In other texts, it is Israel that is the bride or else the bridegroom whose Father is God, analogies far more fitting. See Friedmann, "Additions", p. 29, note #27, where these texts are cited.

[107] Pp. 119–20.

[108] Pp. 120, 122. Bacher, Terminologie, II, p. 220 (Hebrew trans.), quoting Frankel, says that מדת הדין is a characteristic expression in the Palestinian Talmud for דיני ממונות. Incidentally, we have here another example of the Palestinian background of the text.

[109] P. 19. The phrase "words of the Torah" refers to the Pentateuch, and we thus have another instance where this phrase stands for the Pentateuch in contradistinction to the Prophets, as can be seen from the following remarks by Ginzberg: "The connection between Ezek. 36:26 and the statement ד' תורה כפולין is inexplicable (without emendation). Read ונתתי לכם לב בשר זה יצר טוב. And the remark is made by the Rabbis that Ezekiel follows the usage of the Pentateuch (see above, p. 25) where numerous verses are repeated, and that, following this usage, there occurs a repetition in the very same verse — לב חדש and יצר טוב=לב בשר"— (L.G.).

[110] Ibid. I had thought at first to translate קויתי אתכם as "I hoped for you," but Ginzberg's remarks, which explain the present rendering, are conclusive: "It is true that in Is. 28:10, which verse our author explains, the Septuagint takes קו to mean 'hope'=תקוה; but קוה את is impossible. I believe that Seder Eliahu connects קו with נקוה, 'gather together'. The meaning is: I kept you gathered together before the building of the Temple and for four hundred ten years during which the Temple stood; but you made My commandments to naught — the exile took place. By the way, our author takes לצו and לקו=לא צו, לא קו; cf. Tanḥuma, Ẓaw, 14, ed. Horeb 386: וזאת התורה לעולה למנחה וכו' לא לעולה ולא למנחה וכו'" — (L.G.).

[111] P. 82. Comp. the references mentioned by Friedmann, note #12.

[112] P. 84 — פעמים יש תורה.

[113] See Bacher, op. cit., p. 84.

[114] P. 171 — מפי הגבורה נאמרו.

[115] Pp. 171–2. See TE, pp. 151–2.

[116] P. 15.

[117] P. 127.

[118] See Bacher, op. cit., p. 30 and p. 84.

[119] P. 10. See Friedmann, note #40.

[120] P. 68.

[121] P. 72. Friedmann hints, in note #1, that the man who knew Bible but no Mishnah may in this case have been a Christian. "It is extremely unlikely that it refers to Christians, i. e., Judeo-Christians, who differed not only in questions of law from the rest of Israel. Anti-Pharisaic Sectaries never disappeared completely from among the Jews till they finally crystallized in Karaism"— (L.G.). See below, Chap. II, note 383.

[122] P. 82. See Friedmann, note #15.

[123] The first is an aspect of God's love and the second, of His justice.

[124] P. 124. Saadia also dates the Mishnah from the time of the building of the Second Temple — see below, Chap. II, note 383.

[125] Comp. the Kuzari of Yehudah Halevy, chap. III, where this belief and the supporting examples are well stated. The contention of Halevy כי הענין רחב מן המלות is sound.

[126] P. 15. "Additions", p. 33: Here there is added, "in what is permitted and what is prohibited and in (other) Halakot".

[127] P. 68. Friedmann offers one explanation of על הטמא במקומו ועל הטהור במקומו on p. 15, note #12, and another in his Introd. p. 121. But see above, Chap. II, note 74.

[128] P. 63. See TE, pp. 50–2, on the Holy Spirit.

[129] P. 19. דבר תורה here in the singular. כבוד is translated as "glory" and as "honor". "מתאנח על כבודו is a euphemism for the lack of glory or dishonor which the wicked world heaps on God and Israel"— (L.G.).

[130] P. 8. The text at the close has been corrected. The text says מיד רוח הקודש שורה בתוך מעיו שנאמר רוח ה' דבר בי ומלתו על לשוני and I have corrected it to read as it does in the introduction to this passage: מיד רוח הקודש שורה עליו ותורתו בתוך מעיו. The Holy Spirit is, I think, never said to lodge anywhere within a man — it "rests", שורה. The phrase at the end was confused with the proof-text and corrupted. תורתו בתוך מעיו is translated "an inalienable part of him." Another, and slightly different version is found on p. 167, which Friedmann (Introd. pp. 45 and 48) regards as added later, with good reason.

[131] P. 55.

[132] Pp. 94 and 55. "חדש — to establish a new law or draw a new interpretation is found already in the Mishnah, cf. Yadayim 4:3, and is not rare in Talmud and Midrash"— (L.G.).

[133] P. 93.

[134] P. 148. Similarly: " 'As tents (אהלים) planted of the Lord' (Num. 24:6) — that refers to the houses of study"— p. 117.

[135] Pp. 14, 61, 62, 66, 68, 84, 91, 130, 137, 162, 193, 194, 195, 196: "Additions", pp. 1, 2, 6, 7, 8, 24, 25. In these examples, of course, the grammatical forms differ with different tenses, persons, and numbers. Comp. Bacher, op. cit., I, p. 119, s.v. קרא and p. 132, s.v. שנה.

[136] Pp. 91, 21, 4, 63, 68. We must again allow for grammatical differences in tenses, persons, numbers and moods.

[137] Pp. 13, 69, 70, 77, 88, 92, 106, 133, 163, 175, 194; "Additions", pp. 5, 18. Note the argument on the Mishnah between our author and an opponent on pp. 171–2, where the question of the whole oral Torah is involved. Comp. Bacher, op. cit., p. 80, s.v. מקרא and p. 84, s.v. משנה.

[138] P. 16; "Additions", p. 23.

[139] "Additions", pp. 14, 8. Note that in the last passage, the Mishnah is described as having chapter-headings and tractates. This refers, then, to the Mishnah of R. Judah. Since, as Prof. Ginzberg has said (TE, p. 15) the "Additions" are part of the later "Talmud" of the Seder, this passage should occasion no surprise. "פרק is a very old term used in the Mishnah, and does not necessarily refer to the chapters of *our* Mishnah. Of later origin is מסכת (tractate) which occurs in this passage" — (L.G.).

[140] Pp. 8, 11, 22, 23, 31, 37, 68, 100, 124, 129, 91, 155, 198. The five books of the Pentateuch are symbolically referred to in the parable on p. 182; the Book of Exodus is referred to by the locution "said before Mt. Sinai", and the Book of Deuteronomy as "the book of reproofs", on p. 19, where the Book of Ezekiel is also mentioned; on "Additions", p. 21, the Book of Genesis is mentioned. The word פסוק (a single verse) occurs on pp. 30, 12, 94, 138, "Additions", p. 18, always in connection here with "one *halakah*".

[141] Pp. 22, 29, 37, 69, 88, 91, 100, 138, 155.

[142] P. 13.

[143] P. 23.

[144] P. 15.

[145] P. 82.

[146] Comp. Bacher, op. cit., I, p. 84 s.v. משנה, and I, p. 25 where several examples identical with our own are cited.

[147] Comp. Bacher, op. cit., I, s.v. מדרש. מדרש חומשים occurs on p. 198 of our Seder.

[148] Bacher, op. cit., I, s.v. הלכה. The terms "Halakah" or "Halakot" occur alone here on pp. 99, 121, 23, 173, 68, and elsewhere.

[149] Bacher, op. cit., I, s.v. הגדה.

[150] In two passages where we should expect the whole Torah to be denoted, there occur such omissions — on pp. 10–11, the Bible, Halakot and Agadot, and on p. 129, the Bible, Midrash, Halakot and Agadot, comprise in each instance the entire Torah.

[151] P. 8.

[152] Bacher, op. cit., I, s.v. תלמוד, points out that it is frequently equivalent to מדרש. "That תלמוד=מדרש is not correct. What is true is that in a number of places *some* read תלמוד and some read מדרש, which only proves that the scribes misunderstood the meaning of מדרש and put the later תלמוד instead of it. תלמוד in tannaitic sources is *never* anything but 'study', *not* a particular branch thereof."— (L.G.).

[153] P. 106.

[154] P. 68. According to Friedmann, Introduction, p. 60, תלמוד here is a later interpolation. Similarly, (Introd. pp. 45 and 48), he so regards the passage on

p. 167, where "Talmud" and *pilpul* are also mentioned, and there his opinion seems well-grounded. But see below, Chap. II, note 237.

155 "Additions", p. 5.

156 TE, p. 15.

In the two passages in which Bible and Halakot alone are mentioned there appears to be no intention of listing all the parts of the Torah. On p. 198, man is told to study the Torah, then the Prophets, then the Writings, then the Halakot; having studied the latter, he is assured of *'Olam Habba*; and thus the intention here is to take the man up to the point at which he is assured of *'Olam Habba*, and not to enumerate the parts of the Torah. On p. 31, the man who studies Bible is urged to be grateful for his knowledge, and all the more so, the man who studies Halakot; and here, too, there is no intention of listing the divisions of the Torah but merely to enjoin the duty of gratitude for what one learns whatever that consists of.

157 TE, p. 113.

158 תלמוד תורה — pp. 13, 36, 38, 67 and elsewhere.

159 P. 84. The other references are given in TE, p. 38.

160 P. 52. See Friedmann note #31.

161 P. 139. "An unsightly thing" is a euphemism for sin.

162 P. 67.

163 P. 128, "Additions", p. 4.

164 Pp. 195, 139. See TE, p. 158.

165 It is found on pp. 4, 68; also see here below, pp. 61–2, regarding the order of studies so strongly enjoined by the Rabbis.

He that has studied the Torah, the Prophets and the Writings, Mishnah, Midrash, Halakot and Agadot and that "served the learned" is described as "doing the will of His Father who is in Heaven" and as though he were bringing a gift before the King — p. 91.

166 P. 15. "ישיבה means attendance at the lectures in the academy"— (L.G.).

167 P. 94.

168 P. 92.

169 Pp. 21–22. "Cf. the text which also speaks of the joy of God over those who study. The last sentence — מכן ולהלן — is somewhat corrupt"— (L.G.).

170 P. 33.

171 P. 127. Again, in a parable, the study of Torah, wisdom, understanding, etc. and Good Deeds are likened to food and drink, "sweet" to the learned — p. 91.

172 P. 129.

173 P. 92.

174 P. 68.

175 P. 133. Both in this midrash and in the one above the study is that of Bible and Mishnah.

176 P. 146.

177 P. 31. For Halakah is more advanced study than Bible.

178 P. 139 — פתחון פה בתורה ברורה.

179 P. 52.

180 Pp. 92, 93, 91 (twice).

181 Pp. 8, 167, 63. See above, pp. 37–8.

[182] Pp. 195–196. Part of the dialogue not translated here is in TE, p. 84.

[183] P. 69.

[184] He who possesses neither Bible nor Mishnah but just reads one verse (Gen. 36:22) all day "the reward of Torah is in his possession"— above, p. 26. Cf. also below, Chap. III, note 164. In the last two statements justice is apparently emphasized, and in the first, Torah.

[185] P. 64. "Read ש מ ה ימחלו לך. Roḳeaḥ, end זכירת השם, reads שימחלו which is also possible; but Friedmann's text is corrupt"— (L.G.). Thus this passage also insists that prayer for knowledge of Torah must come after a certain moral effort has been made. See below, Chap. II, note 196.

Everybody, old and young, men and women, ought to pray for knowledge from God — p. 70.

[186] P. 31. The same note is struck in the previous reference also. On p. 31, notice Jabez's prayer for the knowledge of Torah.

[187] P. 133 — שייכנסו לחוך מעיו; and so in the similar prayer above.

[188] Comp. TE, p. 147 and note 118 on that page.

[189] After Prov. 28:13.

[190] P. 63 "מתאנח על כבודו וכו' is a euphemism meaning 'the lack of glory' which the wicked world refrains from giving to God, Israel, Temple, etc."— (L.G.).

[191] See TE, p. 14. Friedmann also hints that here we are dealing with commentary material — see p. 64, note #34 and note #37.

[192] P. 63.

[193] Ibid.

[194] Pp. 63–4.

[195] See the following note.

[196] P. 64. "The passage אומרים . . . עליהם belongs after ושבעת and with מתוך continues the sentence ending with לפה. 'Ask for the biblical verse' refers to the student of Bible who asked for the explanation of a biblical verse; '*and the halakah*', to the advanced student who asked for the explanation of a *halakah*. If one is not too bashful to ask, the meaning is, one will succeed in understanding and retaining what one is taught, the verse or the *halakah*. And then the text adds [ו]מתוך ארבע — if one acquires, too, four other qualities (נאה etc.) he will likewise become a good scholar. The text, according to my reconstruction reads: אלא מתוך שהוא אוכל ושותה יבוא לידי תנומה שנ' פן תאכל ושבעת. אומרים לו לאדם עד שאתה מבקש . . . על עבירות (אכילה ושתיה) שעברת שמה ימחלו לו עליהם. ישאל אדם את הפסוק . . . אם זמות יד לפה מתוך כך אדם שומע ווכרה ומתוך ארבע.

"The text has only שלא כהונן (the rest is filled in by Friedmann) and in the Yalḳuṭ this phrase is missing. I take it to be a marginal note by a reader who remarked 'שלא כהונן'—'the text is not in order'— i. e., the passage אומרים לו לאדם is misplaced, as remarked above.

"The עבירות are eating and drinking to excess. 'Before thou prayest . . . pray thou first' etc. Cf. p. 133 (where there is a passage of exactly similar import)"— (L.G.).

[197] TE, p. 46; cf. also, ibid., p. 97, note 100.

[198] "Additions", p. 18.

[199] A corrupt version of the rule immediately following? See Friedmann, "Additions", p. 18, note #23.

[200] See Friedmann, ibid., note #24.

[201] If we accept the reading of our text; but see Friedmann, note #29.

[202] The apparent contradiction here is discussed below, on p. 129.

[203] This rule was confused textually with the preceding one resulting in the phrase ובקבלת חכמים which I have not translated. See also Friedmann, note #31. "Of course בקבלת חכמים is an error, but its origin is to be explained: The scribe repeated חכמים after בקבלת which he had just written, and then noticing his error he wrote correctly בקבלת יסורין without, however, erasing the two wrong words"— (L.G.).

[204] "I take it literally: who does not change his seat in the house of study and in this way helps to keep order"— (L.G.).

[205] "Undoubtedly a doublet: (1) Read ומתרחק (2) אינו רודף. In Abot VI, there is only one"— (L.G.).

[206] "נושא בעול is sharing responsibility in giving decisions and similar activities" — (L.G.).

[207] "שמועה is an old term for 'tradition'— found in the Hebrew Ben Sira — and מכוון שמועה is one who is accurate in transmitting a tradition"— (L.G.).

[208] "Additions", pp. 18–19. This selection is part of a whole section in our Seder which is found as a baraita in Kallah, where it probably belongs originally, and which was also added to Abot. See Friedmann, "Additions", p. 15, note #1, for a discussion of this matter, and see his notes on this passage for the different readings and variants.

[209] P. 31. God here is מקום.

[210] P. 85. After Ps. 119:1.

[211] P. 101.

[212] "Additions", p. 18.

[213] "Additions", p. 8.

[214] P. 47.

[215] P. 197.

[216] P. 137.

[217] P. 84. "Cf. also p. 46: the injunction against praying in the streets — exactly what in the New Testament the Pharisees are supposed to do!"— (L.G.).

[218] P. 128. On p. 4 of "Additions" the passage is repeated with a few slight variations, "engaging little in business" being omitted and "cleaving to associates" added. These passages will be discussed again on p. 129 below.

[219] Above, p. 50. It is more pungently stated on p. 189 —"a man who converses with his neighbor in rivalry".

[220] P. 37. Similarly, on p. 31: "When a man studies Torah, etc. and knows (sufficient) to answer questions about them, he should keep them in his hand (i. e., memorize them)".

[221] P. 4. See Friedmann, note #10.

[222] "Additions", p. 8. See Friedmann, note #33, in regard to the possibility that the statement is that of Elisha the son of Abuyah.

[223] Ibid. "If this statement is really by R. Ishmael ben Elisha, משנה does not mean the Mishnah but oral law. Of course, מסכתות is a later addition. Cf. above, Chap. II, note 139"— (L.G.).

[224] P. 31.

[225] P. 102. The Rabbis desire that a man should spend much time at study and but little in business — pp. 8, 198.

[226] P. 113.

[227] Pp. 13–14.

[228] P. 14.

[229] Pp. 136; 26, 91, 197; and pp. 24–25 of "Additions."

[230] P. 133.

[231] "Additions", p. 18.

[232] Maḥzor Vitry, ed. S. Horwitz (1923), p. 557 (in the commentary to Abot). The commentary adds that a rich man is all the more duty-bound to engage in Torah. Ginzberg explains the passage, however, by saying that the scholar's "independence and freedom" were safeguarded by his frugal needs, (Students, Scholars and Saints, 1928, p. 55), an explanation in line with the one shortly to be given.

[233] P. 196.

[234] Ibid. On the same page, the learned are warned "not to neglect the Torah, and not to eat or drink overmuch."

[235] P. 64.

[236] P. 8. "וישב והגה instead of וישב ויהגה after ששם"— (L.G.).

Repeated with slight variations on pp. 167, 198 (twice), where the phrase "and like unto a cow plowing in the valley" is added.

[237] P. 8. The homilies on this page seem to be the source for the homilies quoted later on in the text. From the fact, however, that in every case this statement introduces different subject-matter, it is apparent that on p. 8 we have the "mishnah", and elsewhere commentaries on it. It is also quite possible that the first statement on p. 8, and given here first also, is the "mishnah" and the homily following, commentary. See also Friedmann, Introd., pp. 45 and 48.

[238] P. 121. Note here the term לדבר תורה, in the singular.

[239] P. 156 — שמצטער עליה. Another term with a similar connotation is המזלזלין עצמן בדברי תורה, "who neglect themselves over the words of the Torah"— p. 117 and elsewhere.

[240] P. 22.

[241] P. 173.

[242] P. 37. עלמות in the proof-text (Song of Songs 1:3) is interpreted as reading עַל מָוֶת.

[243] P. 22.

[244] It may be in place to refer once more to Halevy's Kuzari. In Chapter II, he discusses the matter of asceticism, and his conclusions are rather similar in spirit to ours here. But he does not relate asceticism to Torah particularly. See also Ginzberg (Students, Scholars and Saints, pp. 188–9), who explains why it is that "the highest culmination of a non-ascetic religion (Judaism) should culminate in ascetic saintliness".

245 Above, p. 49.

246 P. 107, and pp. 97, 137.

247 P. 118.

248 Ibid. The homily means, of course, that there will be a famine of Torah in the land, that is, that knowledge of Torah will be lacking; but it contains also the implication we are utilizing here.

249 Above, p. 43.

250 TE, Chapters V and VI.

251 Pp. 54–5. "For talmudic times this is hardly correct!"— (L.G.). Ginzberg's explanation of this passage is found in the following note.

Bet ha-midrash, "the house of study", is mentioned by itself again on p. 92.

252 Pp. 14, 54, 97, 107, 113, 137; "Additions", p. 37. Since Ginzberg holds that the *bet ha-keneset* does not have the same function as the *bet ha-midrash* in talmudic times, he must explain those passages where these two institutions are mentioned together: "On p. 14, בה"כ belongs to קורין, the *bet ha-keneset* being the institution — the synagogue — where the Bible is read as part of the services; and בהמ' to שונין where the study takes place. On p. 54, בה"כ is the place where the children's school — ושכרו להן מלמדי תינוקות — was held. The reference on p. 97 is to be explained in the same way as the reference on p. 14. On p. 107, ושונין לשם שמים is undoubtedly to be added. The reference on p. 137 is again to be explained in the same way as the one on p. 14. On p. 37 of 'Additions', בה"כ is the place of prayer — מקדשין את שמי פעמים. There remains only p. 113 where בה"כ seems to be a place of study, but, of course, this one passage is not sufficient to prove it as בה"כ and בה"מ are often mentioned together. Cf. the following note"— (L.G.).

253 Pp. 93–4. "The בה"כ is the place where one learns פסוק and the בה"מ where one learns הלכה"— (L.G.).

254 P. 94.

255 P. 117. "The identification of gardens with schools has its reason in the fact that in Palestine as well as Babylonia the academies were in gardens. Cf. כרם של יבנה=Academy of Yabneh, which is to be taken literally; and ננתא דבי רב in Mata Meḥsayah — cf. Baba Batra 54a. Cf. also my remarks in Compte Rendu des Melanges Israel Lewy (Paris, 1914)"— (L.G.). "By the river-side" is also a symbol for Torah, for "water" as we have seen, is such.

"Behold how good and how pleasant it is for brethren to dwell together" (Ps. 113:1) is applied to one who has studied Mishnah, etc. and who studies with his comrades — p. 68.

256 See above, p. 38.

257 P. 148. "אהל in the Haggadah is the Temple (Shemot R. 31:9), and then applied to the מקדש מעט of the בהמ"ד (cf. Megillah 29a); cf. Berakot 63b, the haggadic interpretation of אדם כי ימות באהל where באהל=אהלה של תורה, i. e., the בה"מ"— (L.G.).

258 Above, p. 39.

259 P. 15, "Additions", p. 33. See above, p. 37. "His (God's) *bet ha-midrash*" is also mentioned on pp. 4, 55 and elsewhere.

260 P. 68. Youth and maturity are the "brothers", in this interpretation, mentioned in Ps. 133:1. "Talmud" is an interpolation — Friedmann, Introd. p. 60.

[261] P. 198.

[262] Ibid. The repetition is less likely to be two versions than Baraita and commentary.

[263] Pp. 37, 91, 22, etc. — ושמש תלמידי חכמים. One who has studied Bible and Mishnah but has not "served the learned" is likened to him "from whom the words of the Torah disappeared"— p. 37. Cf. Ginzberg's essay מקומה של ההלכה (ירושלים תרפ"ט), pp. 16, 38–9.

[264] P. 91 — זו היא מדה שלמה.

[265] Pp. 100, 155. See below, Chap. II, note 387.

[266] P. 37. "For עומד בחוץ, comp. Tosefta Hag. 2; Yer. Hag. II, 77a"— (L.G.).

[267] P. 139.

[268] See above, pp. 51–2, where the technical requirements for the acquisition of Torah are discussed.

[269] P. 63.

[270] Pp. 10–11. For the interpretation of the proof-text (Ps. 19:4), see Friedmann, notes #42 and #43.

[271] "Additions", p. 33. Here the Midrash describes an event in the great *bet ha-midrash* in the World to Come; but it manifestly reflects a custom current at the time. Cf. TE, p. 150, on the *Ḳaddish.*

[272] P. 11.

[273] P. 195.

[274] P. 10. See Friedmann note #38, and the references cited there. In note #39, he offers one explanation for the interpretation of "And night unto night revealeth knowledge" (Ps. 19:3), and in his Introd. p. 83, another. Neither seems to me to be satisfying. "Friedmann's explanations are impossible. With the exception of Daniel, Ezra (which for the Rabbis included Nehemiah) and Chronicles, *all* the rest are pre-exilic, i. e., from the point of view of the Rabbis. That a special reference is made to Targum, the Aramaic in Daniel is, of course, out of the question. I read שלכתובים [מדרשן] זה in which תנ"ך=כתובים, as is frequently the case in the old literature (cf. Bacher, Terminologie I, 92), and which is here used for the sake of brevity, as the author did not care to repeat תורה נביאים וכתובים. The day is the time for the study of Bible, the night for מדרש, i. e., the oral explanations of the text. The text to the verse בכל הארץ must be made to read: שמטין אזנם ליחיד ומאזנין לשמוע ד"ת — in the house of study, the congregation 'bends its ear' (cf. Derek Erez ed. Higger, p. 75: הט אזנך ושמע דבריהם) to listen to the words of the יחיד, the head of the school"— (L.G.).

[275] P. 155.

[276] P. 154–5. See Friedmann's note #36.

[277] According to Shemot R. 47:13, Moses was enabled to differentiate between day and night during the forty days on Sinai in this wise: When God spoke with him, Moses recognized that it was day, and when He told him to study, Moses recognized that it was night. Thus, again, the day was dedicated to the written Torah and the night to the oral Torah, for what Moses studied by himself at night were the implications, the מדרש, of the matters he learned by day.

[278] P. 16. Torah is accounted of greater worth in repentance than even the giving of charity.

279 P. 133. The Sabbath should be entirely devoted to Torah — p. 4. In this passage (p. 4), does the phrase ישכים אדם וישנה בשבת refer to the study of Mishnah?

280 P. 15.

281 Above, p. 19.

282 "Additions", p. 19.

283 P. 137.

284 P. 138. An interpretation of Is. 58:7. Here the teaching of Torah covers the *Ḳeri'at Shem'a*, the *Tefillah*, a biblical verse and an *halakah.*

285 P. 63.

286 P. 105.

287 P. 109. Except for the idea of *imitatio Dei*, the language and thought of this midrash are almost identical with those of the one on p. 105.

288 Pp. 62–3. This description is of him "who wishes to labor in the words of the Torah."

289 P. 139. See Friedmann, note #32.

290 P. 67.

291 "Additions", p. 6. On p. 54, our text says that the community "hired the scholar", presumably in order to teach. But Ginzberg points out that the editio princeps and the Yalḳuṭ have another word instead of "scholar", which makes the midrash more in consonance with the facts: "Not the teacher was paid but the comrade. On p. 54, the editio princeps and the Yalḳuṭ read חזנים and חזן, respectively (instead of 'scholar'). חזנים were paid officials of the community. Salaried Rabbis were entirely unknown to antiquity, and Friedmann was entirely wrong in retaining the false reading החכם instead of החזן. By the way, the article ה betrays the correct reading: A community had the Ḥazan (החזן) but only a חכם! Of course, teachers of the primary schools were paid — cf. Mishnah Nedarim 4:3 and here ושכרו להן מלמדי תינוקות. Cf. also p. 197 concerning the תלמיד חכם . . . ואין נהנה משל צבור כלום" — (L.G.).

292 "Additions", pp. 17–18.

293 "Additions", p. 6.

294 P. 54 — מלמדי תינוקות.

295 P. 110. See TE, p. 142.

296 P. 13, "Additions", p. 37. "I am not quite sure of it (that the school was in the teacher's home) in view of the fact that בי רב, 'the house of the master', is in the Talmud the common designation for the higher academy which certainly was not in the private dwelling of the head of the academy"— (L.G.).

297 P. 110.

298 "Additions", p. 23. These facts we learn from the instructions given by the "dead man" to R. Joḥanan.

299 P. 164. The word "blessed" begins the blessings in Deuteronomy which *precede* the comminations; the latter begin with א. The Torah also begins with ב, and for the same reason.

300 P. 195.

301 "Additions", p. 20. See Friedmann, note #45.

302 See TE, p. 142.

303 "Additions", p. 7.

[304] P. 95. A variant is found on pp. 167–8, and the ending which gives the reason for the Rabbi's refusal differs from the one on p. 95. See Friedmann, note #38, p. 95. As to Ḳasdir: "קשדיר, קסדיר, קודיר — corrupted into קודיר, the ו and ז are frequently misread — were different spellings for the Latin *quaestor*, government official"— (L.G.).

[305] P. 12.

[306] P. 23. According to Friedmann, this midrash had a beginning which is missing here — Introd. p. 84. "The reading of the Yalḳuṭ (cf. Friedmann ad loc.) is quite correct. There is nothing missing, but the scribe repeated מיכן אמרו from the preceding sentence. With ואל — as it is in Yalḳuṭ, not אל as in the editions — begins a new remark that illustrates Elisha's devotion to study. By the way, the remark that the last conversation between master and pupil (Elijah and Elisha) had 'words of Torah' for its subject is also found in the Talmud, Taanit 10b, which passage escaped Friedmann"— (L.G.).

[307] "Additions", p. 15.

[308] P. 99. A rich man's name survives because of his wealth — TE, p. 173.

[309] TE, p. 170, note 33.

[310] Maimonides, Moreh Nebukim, Part III, Chapter 27. To be sure, the secondary function of promoting right conduct must precede the primary one in time, but only because the secondary is a necessary basis, really only a means to the primary. Because the right ideas are primary, he places them at the head of his Code (Mishneh Torah, Hilkot De'ot, Chapters 1–4). Yehudah Halevy, as we shall note later, has a view that is more related to rabbinic thought.

"I do not believe that this sweeping statement does justice to Maimonides. He speaks not only of ideas but also of 'beliefs' (cf. Chapter 28 and end of 27) or in modern parlance 'of religious values', and he even mentions specifically the love of God. Attention should be called to the fact that in his Code III, תלמוד תורה, he, in agreement with the authors of the Talmud, insists that the importance of תלמוד תורה consists in its leading to pious actions"— (L.G.).

There can be no doubt that Maimonides is inconsistent in his statements, "happily inconsistent" I should say. For another evidence of this inconsistency see below, Chap. II, note 401.

[311] P. 139.

[312] P. 138.

[313] P. 87; p. 70 (in a slightly different context).

[314] P. 196. One of the proof-texts is appropriately enough Koh. 12:13; from this and from the fact that the passage enjoins a man not to show disrespect for elders and parents when he has studied Bible and Mishnah, it can readily be inferred that "the end of all things" refers to the study of Torah. Cf. also below, p. 115.

[315] P. 37.

[316] P. 111.

[317] P. 79.

[318] P. 56. שיקראו וישנו בה. "The world" is frequently a term here for Israel, e. g., "brings redemption to the world"—"Additions," p. 19.

A comrade who teaches a man Mishnah and Bible reveals to him the secrets of Torah and the secrets of *Derek Ereẓ* —"Additions", p. 6.

[319] P. 167.

[320] "Additions", p. 1. For "repents", see TE, p. 124, and note 58 there.

[321] Above, p. 64.

[322] "Additions", pp. 1–2.

[323] "Additions", p. 2. Note that "thoughts of the sword", "thoughts of the yoke of flesh and blood", etc. are mentioned, not just the "yoke of flesh and blood", and this indicates that what is spoken of here is the mental life of man and not the dangers themselves.

[324] P. 116.

[325] TE, pp. 127–8.

[326] Above, pp. 28–9.

[327] Ibid.

[328] P. 106.

[329] See above, p. 29.

[330] P. 115.

[331] P. 16. "Lacking two hundred"— instead of one thousand, David slew only eight hundred at one time. This midrash is very similar to the one on p. 56.

[332] P. 37.

[333] Above, p. 30.

[334] Pp. 16–17. This refers, as Friedmann points out in note #34, to the degree of light of the halos in the World to Come.

[335] Above, pp. 37–9.

[336] Above, p. 73.

[337] The same reasoning would account for the statement on p. 168 that the neglect of the study of Torah is tantamount to all the transgressions in the world.

This contrast between Torah and *mizwot* was suggested to me by Rabbi Aaron Abromowitz of the College of Jewish Studies, Chicago.

[338] TE, pp. 127–8. Also, ibid., pp. 130–31. The statement there on p. 131, that "Good Deeds are intimately related to Torah" has by now, I think, been amply justified.

[339] P. 16. See above, p. 63.

[340] TE, p. 198.

[341] Ibid., p. 194. In the text, pp. 67, 96, 146.

[342] "Additions", p. 8.

[343] "Additions", p. 39. "I read עקומות for עמוקות of editio princeps"— (L.G.).

[344] "Additions", p. 5.

[345] P. 69.

[346] See TE, p. 64 and pp. 69–70.

[347] P. 144.

[348] P. 82.

[349] P. 69.

[350] P. 13.

[351] "Additions," p. 6. See Friedmann, note #23. A man may, apparently, not know even Bible and yet "do two, three Good Deeds"— p. 155.

[352] See the illuminating article by John Baillie, The Idea of Orthodoxy, in The Hibbert Journal, Vol. XXIV (1925–26), pp. 232–249. Socrates' dictum that virtue

or goodness is knowledge develops by intermediate steps into Plato's view in the tenth book of the *Laws* (908–909). Plato declares that those who are "the natural possessors of righteous disposition . . . and ally themselves with the good" but who do not hold the correct religious beliefs ought to be confined for no less than five years, during which they are to be taught right doctrine. If they still prove recalcitrant, they are to be killed. And this is but the fate of the honest doubter! The Greek influence upon the Christian Church included this form of dogmatism. Augustine urges that people be coerced into the right beliefs (Augustine, Epistolae, xciii — translated in Library of Nicene and Postene Fathers); and Baillie offers other evidence from Paul and from the Pastoral and Post-Pauline Epistles. "Sound doctrine"— creeds — thus became the basic teaching of the Church.

Baillie rightly recognizes that the term "faith" as used by Jesus (Matt. ix, 23) means not credence but *reliance*, and, of course, claims that this conception is original with Jesus. We know it, however, to be the rabbinic conception of בטחון, trust, or reliance on God, which is found in Seder Eliahu, p. 90, in the phrase וכל מעשיו בטחון על אביו שבשמים. Comp. also, ibid., p. 91 and "Additions", p. 42.

One must assume that Sellars was not aware of the origin of creeds in Christianity when he says, "Unfortunately, Christianity had inherited a tradition of dogmatism and exclusiveness from Judaism and had added to it. Hence the strange conviction that incomprehensible dogmas, which were often mere forms of words, were a matter of salvation and damnation" (Religion Coming of Age, p. 23).

353 TE, p. 109., p. 32.

354 Above, p. 31.

355 Ibid., p. 32.

356 Ibid., pp. 36–7.

357 Ibid., pp. 37–9.

358 Cf. section on "The Study of Torah."

359 Above, p. 17.

360 Ibid., pp. 20–3.

361 Ibid., p. 23.

362 P. 105. We have noticed that "water" is among the Rabbis frequently a symbol for "Torah". Cf. TE, p. 128.

363 "Additions," p. 14.

364 Pp. 70–1.

365 P. 33. The J.P.S. Bible translates the verse as follows: "We will find Thy love more fragrant than wine."

366 P. 16. "In this passage מיעוטי is plene orthography for מְעוּטֵי, and means much the same as תלמיד קָטָן means in later phraseology — namely, the smallest, the insignificant among the scholars"— (L.G.).

Song of Songs 8:7 is similarly interpreted as referring to God's love for Israel manifested by Torah — p. 141.

367 Koheleth Rabba to Koh. 11:3. See Friedmann, p. 16, note #27. But "love" does not refer to the love of the learned for Torah or to the love of the learned for Israel expressed through the teaching of Torah, but to God's love for Israel manifested in Torah of which the learned are the transmitters, so to speak. The verse

in Koheleth speaks of "rain" which to the Rabbis spells "Torah", of course, because the metaphor for Torah is water.

[368] P. 139. The interpretation of the subsequent phrase of Ezek. 16:8 is unintelligible as given here due to a copyist's error. "מלכות שמים — gives no sense! The scribes misunderstood the abbreviation 'מש' which is משכן and not מלכות שמים. The erection of the משכן did away with the 'shame' of the golden calf (and thus ערותך is given meaning) — cf., for instance, Tanḥuma Ki Tissa, 4. The end of this *derashah* which is זו ישיבתו שנייה במשכן — that is, after the sin of the spies! — presupposes a previous reference to the establishment of the משכן"— (L.G.).

[369] "Additions", p. 21.

[370] TE, p. 109.

[371] See TE, Chapter VI.

[372] Ibid., pp. 176–7.

[373] Above, p. 81.

[374] On the emphasis laid by the Rabbis upon this world see Ginzberg, Students, Scholars and Saints, pp. 97–8.

[375] "Additions," p. 45.

[376] Ibid., p. 19.

The sayings on p. 22 of "Additions", given in the name of R. Simeon the son of Laḳish, are a composite of various sayings by various men, as Friedmann has pointed out (note #50). And here, too, the original interpretation was that he who studies Torah God protects him in this world and grants him also the World to Come.

[377] P. 128; "Additions", p. 4.

[378] "Additions", p. 18.

[379] P. 198. "Read מכאן instead of מנין; the *derashah* is based upon כל, which is taken to include Bible, Halakah, etc.; and cf. the parallel passage on p. 167. The statement (in the variant on p. 198 just above the passage we are utilizing) הרי הוא בן עולם הבא fits ill the verse quoted which would require רוה"ק שורה עליו as on p. 167. I believe therefore that the scribes erroneously quoted here the well-known saying (Niddah, end) כל השונה הלכות . . . שהוא בן עוה"ב. If, however, the text is genuine, the scriptural proof is based on II Sam. 23:4, which verse is taken to refer to the עוה"ב — cf. Pesaḥim 2a and Targum ad loc. Verse 23:2 is quoted in reference only to study (ומלתו על לשוני), and 'וגו refers to verse 4"— (L.G.). See also above, Chap. II, note 130.

[380] P. 127.

[381] Pp. 140–1.

[382] The italics in this paragraph are mine.

[383] Pp. 172–3. "Friedmann put something into the text of which there is not the slightest trace therein. What has the selection of Israel to do with the authority of the oral law? Did the Karaites deny the one because they refused to accept the other doctrine? Scripture has in hundreds of passages taught the Selection of Israel. The statement מיום שנברא העולם has nothing to do with the previous argument. The man simply stated that there is justice in this world; and our author agrees, saying that God takes reward (satisfaction) in this world, too. But, adds our author, for the worthy there is 'a double reward', in this world and in the next.

It is also *not* a Christian whom our author answers thus, for the former would not have questioned future reward"— (L.G.).

The phrase ובונין בית אחרון בצער struck me as a superfluous interpolation; it is not found in the application to Israel of God's condition. "ובונין וכו' is certainly out of place, but the application has likewise a double phrase — עשו . . . בצער and וצערו עצמן. It seems to me that a phrase like ומגדלין בניהן לתורה בצער has been corrupted. The difficulty of raising children for the Torah is often referred to in Seder Eliahu. It is, however, possible that our author dates the Mishnah from the time of the building of the Second Temple as does Saadia (in Schechter, Saadyana, 5). I believe, however, that on p. 173, line 3 שכר משנה=משנה ('double reward'). Israel received double reward for Torah and *mizwot.* Cf. Targum to Zech. 9:12 (where משנה is thus translated). Cf. also S. E. p. 196: שכר . . . כפול, and in the verses from the Bible there משנה is accented!"— (L.G.).

384 See the preceding note.

385 See TE, pp. 176–7.

386 P. 23.

387 P. 100; similarly on p. 155, except that in the latter homily the one guardian angel is given the man who has done "two or three good things". "On p. 100 מקרא cannot be correct since in S. E. it is חנ'ך, and it would be contradicting the sentence following. I think we must emend it to read מצות, for טובות=מצות on p. 155. By the way, the *derashah* is based on the singular בדרך in Exod. 23:20 — בדרך is taken to mean *'for* the fulfillment of דרך ארץ'— in contrast to Ps. 91:11 where בכל דרכיך (plural) is taken to mean *'for* all thy ways'. On p. 155 read ברו[ת]חה instead of ברוחה, and cf., for instance, Ber. R. 48.8 where הרתיח with regard to the sun=boiling sun"— (L.G.).

Note that angelology is used here in connection with two fundamental concepts, Torah and justice, in order to bring out the gradations of the rewards of justice in accordance with the amount of Torah engaged in. The highest award of justice here, however, becomes transmuted into an aspect of God's love, both homilies concluding with a parable of the father (God) who, with his own body as shield, protects his son from the hot desert sun. Cf. TE, pp. 90–95. "Every homily in Seder Eliahu that speaks of angels is an exposition of a concept"— ibid., p. 88.

On p. 93 (S. E.): He that labors in the Torah "will not see the retribution that is to come" (i. e., will not be included in it) — also in this world.

388 P. 69.

389 P. 107. The proof-text "Ask of Me, and I will give the nations for thine inheritance, and the ends of the earth for thy possession" (Ps. 2:8) also indicates that the "entire world" refers to this world. On "measure for measure" see TE, pp. 177–9.

"The proof-text (i. e., the first proof-text from the Psalms, 2:7) refers to אספרה אל חק which is taken to refer to the study of the חק, i. e., the Torah. In the reference to Lament. 3:27 עולה של תורה=עול. Cf. Midr. Ekah ad. loc."— (L.G.).

The man who labors in the Torah for its own sake — the whole world is regarded as worthwhile for him alone ("Additions", p. 15).

390 Pp. 96–7. See Friedmann, note #50. This and the preceding midrash are almost identical in wording except for their conclusions, hence their kinship is

easily apparent. Both begin by declaring that God chooses the learned and go on to say that he observes toward them the rule of "measure for measure" and then depict the earnestness and religious zeal of the learned in relation to study. "On p. 107 מקום is perhaps to be taken in the sense of 'opportunity', and מקום פנוי would thus mean 'a free opportunity'. For a similar use of מקום, cf. Mishnah Berakot 4, 2 — מה מקום לתפלה זו, 'What is the occasion for this prayer?' As this expression was not understood by the scribe, it was changed on p. 97 to יום; but קורין in this place (p. 97) is a better reading than וקורין in the second place (on p. 107)"— (L.G.).

[391] Pp. 115; 4.

[392] P. 70.

[393] "Additions", pp. 21–22. The child has read up to ויכלו and had thus read the section comprising our first chapter of Genesis. The division of the Bible into chapters took place long after Seder Eliahu had been compiled. "The old division of the Pentateuch, dating from the earliest tannaitic times was in *sedarim*, and the second *seder* begins with ויכלו. By the way, there is no indication in the text that ויכלו begins a new section, the point of the story being that the pagan king was greatly charmed by the story of creation which ends at ויכלו"— (L.G.).

[394] P. 93.

[395] P. 198. There is no difference between מתיראים ממנו and יראין ממנו. The former term is used with regard to the Nations of the World who "fear" the man in whom there is Torah, on p. 198, and the latter term in a similar context on p. 93. "ירא is very often 'revere' and יראה 'reverence' in S. E. as in many other rabbinic sources. Hence the well-known maxim that יראת שמים, reverence of God, leads to אהבה, love"— (L.G.).

[396] "Additions", p. 17.

[397] Ibid.

[398] P. 64. The twelve prerequisites are given above, pp. 47–8.

[399] P. 113. This rendering of the word יניח is explained by the following remark of Ginzberg's: "I do not think that יניח means here 'renounce' every possession but at times 'withdraw' his attention from his business to study. The point is made here that wealth as well as other worldly possession is a reward for study; and hence it would be senseless to tell a man to give up his wealth for study which latter is rewarded by wealth!"— (L.G.).

[400] P. 110.

[401] "It is to be noticed that the תפלה prayer, i. e., שמונה ע', contains *no* prayer for the individual but only for the nation, a point which has been noticed by the Gaon (Elijah Wilna) in his commentary on Mishnah Berakot 5:1"— (L.G.). See שנות אליהו in the edition of the Mishnah published in Warsaw, 1878.

Incidentally, it is somewhat anomalous for other-wordly religions to assign the very large place they do to petitional prayers for health and material prosperity. These matters, being transitory and unimportant in such a philosophy, should have as little attention given them as possible. The truth is that the salvationary religions of the West, springing out of rabbinic Judaism, have retained many of the popular features of that organic complex, and so possess elements incongruous to an out-and-out salvationary religion. Thomas Aquinas is more consistent. He defines prayer as the ascent of the mind (or intellect) into God, thus leaving little room for purely petitional prayers. "*Oratio est ascensus mentis in Deum*" (Summa Theol.: secunda secundae quaestio, lxxiii, art. 1), and again (in quaestio lxxxiii, art. 17), "*oratio est ascensus intellectus in Deum*". (Quoted from Anson, Spiritual Healing, p. 211). This definition as has been said gives very little room for petitional prayers for material things. But Maimonides, with all his attempt to make of Judaism a salvationary religion, remains happily inconsistent in this regard for he is steeped in rabbinic tradition, after all. See his Moreh, Part III, chapter 36. "The problem of prayer to Maimonides is metaphysical, as it assumes a change in the will of God"— (L.G.).

402 Above, pp. 43–4.

403 P. 195.

404 P. 37.

405 P. 115. Note also the use of the term in describing the spiritual satisfaction of Israel during the Ten Days of Repentance —"Additions", p. 38.

406 P. 132.

407 Above, pp. 16–20.

408 P. 37.

409 P. 139. "Read תשחיר ותעריב, and cf. Lev. R. 19, 1 ד"ת צריכין השחרה וכו' and parallel passages; תשכים of the text is due to משכימים in the preceding line"— (L.G.).

410 Ibid., — קלה [שבך] כחמורה שבחברך. See Friedmann note #32. This midrash certainly does not mean to cater to pride of learning or to the desire to be better than one's fellow any more than the midrash immediately following it. How the Rabbis look upon the pride of learning we have seen above, p. 51.

Ginzberg suggests another reading which disposes altogether of invidious comparisons as to one's fellow-student. "The reading שבחבירך is very doubtful, as the Venice ed. has שבך; I believe the correct reading to be קלה ש ב ה כחמורה שבה בידך — You will master the light as the difficult part thereof. Comp. also, on p. 97 קלות כחמורות. With regard to בידך cf. the phrase frequently used in the Talmud לא הוה בידיה, 'he did not know' "— (L.G.).

411 Ibid. See above, p. 65 for the entire quotation.

412 P. 137.

413 P. 104. *Shekinah* denotes God in-dwelling in man — see TE, pp. 53–56.

414 P. 84. "צדקה בסתר is, of course, to be taken literally, and hence תורה בסתר also means 'secretly', that is, not in the presence of others in order to show off" — (L.G.). Comp. the remark above, Chap. II, note 217.

415 P. 63. Note that this quotation is commentary material, as explained above, p. 48.

416 "Additions", pp. 15–17. "The world is created for the pious — a statement found in many places — and the man who occupies himself with the Torah is the one for whom the world is created: שכל העולם כלו כדאי הוא לו. The word סוד seems to refer to a certain secret. I am inclined to assume that סוד refers to דין, in other words, in judging, heaven will assist him by revealing to him the truth — in modern parlance, 'the true instinct'. והוי is very difficult; it does not mean 'and he is' for then the word would be והוא; and the imperative 'be' is out of the question here" — (L.G.).

[417] "Additions", p. 18.

[418] See TE, p. 25, note 30; ibid., pp. 46, 99–100, and p. 101, note 124. On terms and locutions evincing this tendency, see TE, pp. 43–44.

[419] TE, p. 202.

[420] P. 168. "Great and grievous" is the translation of גדול ורב.

Very similar to this ending of the Ḳasdir story is the homily on p. 96. There are also the same proof-texts. Since the Ḳasdir story deals with neglecting the *study* of Torah, there is a strong presumption that the homily on p. 96 also deals only with study, not with practice. Moreover, one of the proof-texts speaks of *understanding* the Torah: "Who is the wise man, that he may understand this (i. e., the Torah)?" (Jer. 9:11). The passages on p. 96 and p. 168 very likely were identical originally, describing the effect of the neglect of the study of Torah. In that case שלא חרב העולם בראשונה on p. 96 — the word בראשונה is missing on p. 168 — refers not to the Deluge, as Friedmann has it (p. 96, note #43), but to the destruction of the First Temple, for, as we know from other instances, עולם frequently refers to Israel. Comp. above, Chap. II, note 318. By taking both texts together we may, perhaps, obtain the text of the original statement. Thus: בוא וראה כמה גדול פשיעה של תורה (p. 96). שלא חרב העולם בראשונה אלא בפשעה של תורה (p. 96 & p. 168), ולא חרבה ירושלים ולא חרב בית המקדש אלא בפשעה של תורה (p. 96)—[נ"א] ולא חרבה ארץ ישראל אלא מפני פשעה של תורה (p. 168)—וכל צרות הבאות על ישראל אינן אלא מפני פשעה של תורה (p. 168). This statement, then, mentions the First Destruction, then the Second, then the troubles of Israel today, accounting for all by the neglect of the study of Torah.

Corroborating our interpretation of both passages are the proof-texts, all of which refer either to Jacob or Israel, and hence לא חרב העולם must refer to Israel. Finally, the Parma MS. definitely reads שלא חרב א"י בראשונה. See Friedmann, p. 168, note #5, where the Parma MS. is quoted.

Prof. Ginzberg doubts that the reading בראשונה is genuine, and states that in any case there is no reference to the Deluge here or even to the Second Temple. "There can, of course, be no doubt that E.R. 96 and 168 are two versions of the same midrash on the importance of study. There are two other versions — one in the Mekilta of R. Simeon, p. 98, and the second in the MS. reading of קנין תורה communicated by George Margoliouth in his Catalogue of Hebrew MSS. in the British Museum. You are quite correct in assuming that עולם=א"י; cf., for instance, Abot 5:11, concerning the seven visitations that come over the world as punishments for the seven sins, two of which are connected with מעשר which, of course, has reference to א"י only. If the reading בראשונה is genuine we would have to assume that the scribes have shortened the phrase from: לא חרב העולם בראשונה [ולא בשניה] ולא חרבה ירושלים וכו'. I do not think that בראשונה refers to the Flood, nor that לא חרבה ירושלים stands for the Second Destruction. It is likely that בראשונה is a slip of the author or scribe"— (L.G.).

[421] Pp. 12–13. Interpreting Ps. 29:1, the angels figure in this midrash on Torah, apparently by studying Torah in the place of men. But there are no doubt lacunae in this text. That the passage refers to the study of Torah is seen from the expression מבטלין מן התורה, for בטול תורה refers to study.

422 "Additions", p. 17. On *Bat-Ḳol* see TE, pp. 52–3. It frequently utters a verdict of some kind.

423 Ibid., p. 10.

424 P. 64.

425 P. 47.

426 "Additions", p. 8.

427 P. 137.

428 Prof. Ginzberg called my attention to a booklet by his great-grandfather ר' אברהם אחי הגר"א with the title מעלות התורה (Warsaw, תרפ"ב), which is pertinent to the material in this section and also to the "Efficacy of Torah". Though drawing in large part from rabbinic sources, the work also contains references to the Zohar; the rabbinic material, of course, is germane to our discussion..

NOTES TO CHAPTER III

1 Above, p. 69.

2 P. 112. "Read ו ע ל after עלינו"— (L.G.).

3 Pp. 171–2. The whole passage has been discussed above, pp. 33–5.

4 P. 72.

5 Pp. 72–3. See Friedmann, note #8.

6 P. 73.

7 Ibid.

8 Pp. 73–5. "Friedmann's explanation of גזל אח is very forced; it is quite evident that אח in Ezek 18:18 is synonymous with רעך in Lev. 19:13. I would suggest that אח is an abbreviation of אחרים, Gentiles, and the story given on pp. 74–75 seems to make this suggestion almost certain"— (L.G.).

9 P. 75.

10 Pp. 75–6.

11 "Additions", p. 19.

12 Ibid., p. 18.

13 Above, p. 74.

14 TE, pp. 69–70.

15 P. 144. "תורה" is out of place in this passage that deals with that true piety which makes one rejoice in doing charity. Read נדבתו (instead of תורתו), gift to the poor; and the three forms of charity are thus enumerated: נדבה, gift to the poor, תרומה, gift to the priest and מעשר, gift to the Levite"— (L.G.).

16 P. 130. The social significance of the Sabbath will be discussed shortly.

17 P. 124 (twice).

18 P. 131.

19 Pp. 53–4.

20 P. 80.

21 P. 92. Cf. TE, p. 183.

22 "Additions", p. 14 — דבר מצוה. Ginzberg corrects this expreesion: "I have no doubt that משנה is to be read instead of מצוה. The next statement by R. Simon, who undoubtedly refers to that made by the *ḥakamim*, contains the correct reading משנה. מקרא and משנה are often mentioned together in the Seder Eliahu"— (L.G.).

[23] P. 146.

[24] "Additions", pp. 42–3. Cf. TE, p. 157.

[25] Pp. 126, 138 (where the law of the blood of the paschal lamb is also found), 141 and elsewhere.

[26] Pp. 76, 79 and elsewhere.

[27] P. 86 and elsewhere.

[28] P. 65. Comp. TE, pp. 167–8. "The statement 'whether Gentiles or Israelite' etc. concludes the remark on the eleven *midot* which are purely ethical!"— (L.G.).

[29] P. 132. "The wealth of the entire world at one time" should not tempt a man to act as witness when actually he had not witnessed the transaction — p. 146. This statement has to do with false testimony, of course, and not with swearing falsely.

[30] Pp. 67, 69, 73, 138 and elsewhere.

This applies with equal force to Gentiles — comp. TE, p. 172. According to one view, taking things illegitimately from a Gentile is even more reprehensible than a similar thing done to a Jew, for in the former case there is profanation of the Name — Comp. TE, pp. 67–9.

[31] The Rabbis rightly take עמיתך to be "friend" not "neighbor".

[32] P. 109.

[33] Ibid. Jealousy or revenge one should never harbor, but these things should be forgotten even as the water which passes through in a river never returns — p. 105; also similarly, p. 109. In both the midrashim it appears as though the proof that the grudge is no longer held consists in not "withholding" Torah from one's fellow-man.

[34] P. 134. "חט is a misreading of חש=חלול שבת, which *must* be mentioned in this connection, and the Yalḳuṭ has the correct reading"— (L.G.). See Friedmann, note #25.

[35] P. 134. As the midrash points out, "mother" precedes "father" in Lev. 19:3.

[36] Ibid. The statement about God is strongly anthropomorphic and is therefore prefaced by the precautionary כביכול. See TE, pp. 43–4. Here the anthropomorphism makes the Fifth Commandment more vivid, and hence is in conjunction with Torah.

[37] Pp. 134–5. The passage closes with the phrase, "Therefore it says 'Honor', 'Thou shalt not murder'. . .'Thou shalt not covet' ", so that it seems likely that originally the Tenth Commandment was also coupled with the Fifth.

"You are quite correct in your suggestion that the last Commandment was connected with the Fifth, and the text most likely read: כבד ולא תחמוד מה ענין זה לזה אלא ללמדך יש לו נכסים הרבה בתוך ביתו ואינו מהנה את אביו ואת אמו לעת זקנתן כאלו חמד כל ימיו לפני המקום — in his greed he refrained from giving his parents their due — לכך נאמר כבד ולא תחמוד. The copyists shortened the text because the connection between the Fifth and the Tenth is fairly obvious.

"The structure of this homily is quite clear. The First Commandment is con nected with the three others of the same table (p. 132) as the Fifth with the five of the second (pp. 134–5). The Fifth is also connected with the Fourth for the reason that the Fifth connects the Commandments concerning man's relation to God with those that deal with man's relation to his fellowman. The view which sees in the Fifth the connecting link between the two *sets* of Commandments is frequently referred to in the Haggadah"— (L.G.).

[38] P. 135. The analogy of the King who rewards the son of his friends for having dealt kindly with them is given but the application is missing. "The entire passage is corrupt, and the connection between כבוד אב and the haggadic comment on והלכת בדרכיו is unintelligible. I suggest as follows: משל למלך . . . שגנזו לך אצלי כך בזמן שאדם מכבד את אביו ואת אמו הקב"ה אומר לו תהא לך קורת רוח בעולם שנאמר והיה אם שמוע תשמע . . . והאזנת למצותיו . . . כי אני ה' רפאיך (שמות ט"ו כ"ו) ואין מצוה אלא כבוד אב ואם שנאמר כבד . . . כאשר צוך ה' אלהיך (דברים ה' ט"ז). וכשהוא נפטר מעולמו הקב"ה אומר לו עכשיו בא וראה גנזים טובים שגנזתי לך אצלי שכן הוא אומר כי תשמר את מצות ה' אלהיך (דברים כ"ח ט') ואין מצוה אלא כבוד אב ואם ובסופו מה הוא אומר יפתח ה' לך את א ו צ ר ו (=גנזים טובים!) הטוב (שם כ"ח י"ב). ד"א כי תשמר את מצות ה' אלהיך והלכת בדרכיו וכו'.

"The scribes left out the *nimshal* (the application) and shortened the rest. On the *derashah* that at Marah — to which Exod. 15:26 refers — the Commandment of כבוד אב was given, comp. Mekilta ad loc.—שם שם לו חק ומשפט . . . זה כיבוד אב ואם (Mekilta de-Rabbi Ishmael, ed. Lauterbach, Vol. II, p. 94), and parallel passages. Attention is to be called to the fact that in several places in the Seder Eliahu only the *mashal* (parable) is given while the application is to be supplied by the reader; cf., for instance, pp. 31–2, 40, 69 *bis*"— (L.G.).

[39] P. 136.

[40] Ibid. "Comp. Ben Sira 3:13 and Ḳiddushin 30b"— (L.G.).

[41] P. 132.

[42] Ibid. See TE, p. 61; and comp. there the section on God's Kingship.

[43] Pp. 66–7.

[44] P. 59; p. 169; tithe of cattle mentioned —"Additions", p. 7.

[45] P. 29.

[46] Pp. 168–9. The law regarding *ẓarat ha-bat* prohibited a man whose daughter had married his brother from marrying any of his brother's wives if that brother died childless. On polygamy in rabbinic times, see Moore, Judaism, Vol. II, p. 122 and Vol. III, pp. 183–4.

[47] P. 113.

[48] See above, p. 97.

[49] P. 123.

[50] Ibid. Friedmann suggests that this passage really refers to the author's own day, when there were many Jews who sought to erase the sign of circumcision and who spoke Greek in preference to Hebrew — Introd. P. 117.

The passage has all the earmarks of mishnah and commentary. First there is the mishnah given tersely, merely stating: Israel in Egypt "made a covenant that they would do Deeds of Loving-kindness with one another, and keep in their heart the covenant of Abraham, Isaac and Jacob, that they would not forsake the language of the house of Jacob their father and learn the language of Egypt for fear of the manners of idol-worship." Then there follows a commentary introduced by the formula כאיזה צד —"In what manner," etc. Strangely enough, only the last statement of the mishnah given here is commented on, but other mishnah-like texts, also telling of what Israel did in Egypt, are first stated and then enlarged by commentary, one text even having a second commentary introduced by ד"א. This is not only proof supporting Ginzberg's theory regarding text and commentary, but confirms all he says about our Seder once having been very much larger than at present, for we cannot help realizing that this passage had a very much longer "mishnah" and "commentary" at one time, of which only fragments have remained.

[51] P. 72.

[52] P. 133.

[53] Ibid. "If thou callest the Sabbath a delight thou honorest the holy one of God"— ibid.

[54] P. 4.

[55] P. 15. The pilgrimages are again reflected in the Rabbis' attributing to Elkanah his going up with his family to Shiloh four times a year — p. 47. Sukkot is mentioned on p. 65 and p. 6 of "Additions".

[56] P. 149. This again shows that some parts of our Seder were written in the Diaspora, although other parts surely reflect a Palestinian locale: Cf. TE, p. 6 and p. 154, note 185, and p. 147, note 152; also above, Chap. II, note 108.

"A passage reflecting conditions in the Diaspora — Babylon! — is on p. 126 where the popular saying אפילו שבננים חביב וכו' is quoted. The beginning of this saying is undoubtedly badly corrupted — comp. below — but at the end it refers without doubt to the Persian form of punishment (cf. Selig Cassel, Wissenschaftliche Berichte der Erfurter Akademie, Erfurt, 1853) of hanging a man by his hand on a cross: חלוים על העצים ב י ד ן. The popular proverb is quoted as an explanation of כי יד על כס (Exod. 17:16) in which biblical verse כס is being taken to stand for קים, wood, cross (cf. Ginzberg's note in his article, Beiträge zur Lexikographie des Jüdisch-Aramäischen, in the Monatsschrift, 1934, p. 23); and the meaning of the verse is that Amalek will be hung with his hand on the cross, the most humiliating form of death. This punishment is not known outside of Persia, and hence refers to a popular saying in a Persian province, very likely Babylon. Of course, there is not the slightest evidence that from זהו to בדין (i. e., בידן) belongs to the text of Seder Eliahu; it is very likely a comment upon the old Baraita. The first part of this popular proverb is very likely a corrupt reading of אפל' נפל שבנוים — the נ was misread as ו and connected with אפל', and thus פל came to look like dittography. Cf., however, in Lam. 5:12, "Princes are hanged up by their hand"— (L.G.).

[57] See TE, pp. 125–6, where these institutions are discussed.

[58] TE, pp. 151–2.

[59] See TE, pp. 148–155.

[60] Of course, the other aspects of public worship were institutionalized as well so that, for example, seven men are called up to read from the Torah on the Sabbath in the morning, three at *minḥah* and three also on Mondays and Thursdays — p. 172.

[61] See above, pp. 77–9, where the "contradiction" between the practical efficacy of Torah and the experience of the Rabbis that men may know Torah and yet be scoundrels or not know Torah and yet be good men is resolved by the appearance of new — that is, other — concepts.

[62] P. 132. See TE, p. 126, note 65.

[63] P. 79. Cf. Friedmann's note #43. "The text is to be emended as follows: ר' מאיר אומר לא נאמרה פרשה זו—של זבה—אלא למצוות פרייה ורבייה שאפילו אכל כל מאכל ושתה כל משקה אינו נהנה כלום [אם כן למה אמרה תורה נדה שבעה אלא מתוך שהוא רגיל קווט—אני קץ בה—ואינו נהנה כלום] לכך נאמרה תורה שבעת ימים תהיה בנדתה.

"First an explanation is given for the prohibition of relations with a זבה — the section begins with ואשה כי תהיה זבה — the comment thereon being that it is on account of פריה ורביה which cannot be carried out with a זבה because: he may eat and drink as much as he likes but it will be no benefit to him — the husband, i. e., there will be no issue from such a connection. The same view is given on p. 75 with regard to the זב שאינו פרה ורבה. The objection is then revived as to why Scripture has prohibited נדה which certainly is in a position to bear children; and the answer is, as in Talmud Nid. 31b, that too frequent indulgence would 'cause disgust', and, as often, the very same expression — ולא נהנה כלום — is used as in the previous sentence, but with a different connotation. In the first sentence it means 'has no benefit', i. e., a woman in such a state is sterile; in the second, it means 'he has no pleasure'. נהנה in rabbinic sources is frequently used in both of these senses. Cf., for instance, זה נהנה וזה לא חסר (Baba Kamma 20b) —'one benefits, the other does not lose thereby'— and להנות בהן בני אדם in the benediction (see Berakot 43b) — 'to give pleasure to man'. In Seder Eliahu, the copyist skipped from the first לא נהנה כלום to the second while in the Yalkuṭ the phrase קווט came by mistake from the second sentence into the first instead of נהנה בה and, of course, שנ' שבעת ימים was added"— (L.G.).

[64] P. 4.

[65] "Additions", p. 32.

[66] P. 93. "The expression רפואה, as well as the remark towards the end of the page אינו רואה במידת פורענות, seems to convey the meaning that the *mizwah* will protect Israel against visitations in this world, in the days of the Messiah — חבלי מש' — as well as לעוה"ב when the wicked will be punished"— (L.G.).

[67] P. 132.

[68] For the implications of *Malkut Shamayim* see TE, pp. 58–64.

[69] P. 140.

[70] P. 170.

[71] Ibid.

[72] In an essay pertinent to our entire discussion of the ethical spirit of the *mizwot*, Schechter says: "Nor were all the laws actually put upon the same level. With a happy inconsistency men always spoke of heavier and slighter sins, and by the latter — excepting, perhaps, the profanation of the Sabbath — they mostly understood ceremonial transgressions" (The Law and Recent Criticism, Studies in Judaism, First Series, p. 250). The Sabbath, as discussed in the essay, is not merely ritualistic.

[73] P. 67.

[74] P. 136.

[75] Ibid.

[76] Above, p. 36.

[77] Ibid., p. 81.

[78] P. 4.

[79] P. 172.
[80] Above, p. 83.
[81] Ibid., p. 84. Note the discussion there on the matter of the "principal".
[82] P. 93. Cf. above, Chap. III, note 66.
[83] P. 134.
[84] TE, pp. 167–8.
[85] Ibid., p. 171.
[86] P. 184. Compare Ginzberg's remarks on this passage in תרביץ, IV, p. 306 (ירושלים, תרצ"ג). Cf., also, TE, p. 192. For the idea of corporate justice see ibid., pp. 179–84 and pp. 203–7.
[87] P. 73.
[88] See above, p. 95.
[89] Pp. 75–6.
[90] P. 72. "It is a bad sign for him", meaning, he will be punished.
[91] P. 134.
[92] P. 132. Ginzberg calls attention to the rationalization in the first part of this midrash by which the Rabbis arrive at the ultimate punishment of the wicked. "The strange phrase מביאין עצמן לידי פסול means: they cause themselves to become disqualified as witnesses; in other words, people lose faith in them with the result that they become poor (עניים עד יום מותן) as nobody wishes to have business dealings with them. Notice the rationalization! On the פסול of those who swear falsely, comp. Sanh. 27a, Mishnah Shebuot 7:1"— (L.G.).
[93] See TE, pp. 177–8.
[94] Ibid., pp. 178–9.
[95] P. 188. See TE, p. 181, note 84.
[96] מעשים טובים — pp. 38, 67, 92, and elsewhere.
[97] See above, pp. 69–70.
[98] See above, pp. 42–3.
[99] Ibid.
[100] See TE, pp. 129–132. This refers to sacrifices brought by the individual. Good Deeds alone is the symbolism contained in the peace-offering. The symbolism of the communal sacrifices involves the Patriarchs and Israel.
[101] P. 62. "Interesting is the statement preceding it which emphasizes that man ought to imitate God who spends the day in study and in dispensing justice and charity. By the way, the long passage (above on the same page) on the sport which the Lord will have when the wicked nations will be defeated is a later allegorical interpretation of an old mythological statement. Abodah Zara 3b quotes the Haggadah on the *daily* sport of God with *Leviathan* — Marduk's sport with Tiamat! — for later *Leviathan* was one of the many names for Satan, wickedness — this usage both among Christians and Jews — and hence the later Haggadah in the Talmud as well as Seder Eliahu on God's sport at the destruction of the wicked nations. The expression on p. 62, line 3 ואין לפני שחוק אלא שעה אחת cannot refer to one occasion but means that while God spends the day in serious work, as described, he gives to sport only a short time — שעה אחת — which, of course, refers to his sport with *Leviathan.* With אימתי begins the commentary which concludes with יושב בשמים ישחק"— (L.G.).

[102] P. 198.

[103] "Additions", pp. 1–2.

[104] P. 127.

[105] P. 13. See TE, p. 62, note 158.

[106] Pp. 91, 92, 93, 129, 197, and elsewhere.

[107] P. 196. See above, p. 69. "That מעשים טובים (Good Deeds) might refer to deeds of kindness and charity nobody doubts, but the question is whether it might not refer also to any other *mizwah.* The fact that in Seder Eliahu there never occurs a phrase like תורה ומצות ומעשים טובים would rather speak for the assertion that מע"ט (Good Deeds) is identical with *mizwah*, which is undoubtedly the case in the Talmud; comp., for instance, Berakot 32b where מצוה=מע"ט. The impression is that תורה ומע"ט=study and practice — in the Talmud, תורה ומעשה; cf. Ḳid. 40b" — (L.G.).

[108] P. 197.

[109] P. 104.

[110] Above, p. 42.

[111] Pp. 92, 93, 91 (twice). Israel, as well as the learned, are the recipients according to one midrash on p. 91.

[112] P. 19.

[113] Above, pp. 69–70.

[114] Ibid., p. 47.

[115] P. 68. Cf. above, p. 61.

[116] P. 129.

[117] P. 127.

[118] Ibid.

[119] P. 62.

[120] P. 198.

[121] P. 70.

[122] P. 104. See also above, p. 90.

[123] דרך ארץ — Pp. 56, 71, 103 and elsewhere.

[124] P. 158.

[125] I am guided here by Ginzberg's interpretation of the text. "I understand the passage as follows: Lot made two propositions — one to hand them his daughters, second not to hand over his guests. In Gen. 19:9, two answers by the inhabitants of Sodom are given — a short refusal of the first offer and a heated argument against the second. Yet the first was *natural*, and the second *against nature*, and they insisted upon the unnatural!"— (L.G.). See below, p. 120, where *Derek Ereẓ* is taken to mean *proper*, not only natural, sex behaviour.

The translation of the passage concerning the men of Sodom which was given in TE, p. 189, ought to be corrected and this rendering of *Derek Ereẓ* substituted. But the point made there, in connection with which this passage was used, remains unaffected.

[126] P. 30. That by "if a man marries" the Rabbis had in mind a learned man is seen from the conclusion of the passage which states that kind ought to marry kind.

[127] P. 185.

[128] P. 9. For the translation of the passage see TE, p. 81. "I am not quite sure that I understand this passage. As far as I am able to make it out it means that man will know that the reason why the stars are not crowded is not because God could not do it but because He wished it so; and the proof is the constellation כימה which has seven stars in close proximity. Accordingly, *Derek Ereẓ* here does not mean 'aesthetics' but the proper behaviour in thinking about God's might"—(L.G.). On *Derek Ereẓ* referring to attitudes as well as to overt behaviour, see below, pp. 121–2.

[129] P. 175–6.

[130] P. 182.

[131] P. 70. The translation of this passage given in TE, p. 113, needs to be slightly corrected in conformity with our rendering here.

[132] Pp. 62–3.

[133] This does not contradict the statement by R. Gamaliel in Abot 2:2 teaching the desirability of the study of Torah along with *Derek Ereẓ*, some worldly occupation, for our midrash above refers only to him who is completely engrossed in business. Incidentally, there can be no doubt that *Derek Ereẓ* in that mishnah of Abot refers to business or occupation of some kind since the phrase immediately following is "And all Torah without work ends in failure and occasions sin."

[134] P. 12. A parable similar in many ways is found on pp. 194–5. There also the king sends his sons to study Bible and Mishnah and *Derek Ereẓ*, and there, too, *Derek Ereẓ* refers to business.

"Business men" is the translation of בעלי משא ומתן. The whole phrase—"of whom there were some who knew Bible, some who knew Mishnah and some who were business men"—is found also on pp. 92, 163, 71. In all these instances the fact that "business men" are linked with those who knew Bible and Mishnah and the context in which the whole phrase occurs indicate the Rabbis' respect for business ability.

[135] P. 71. "In the text ובא is an abbreviation for ובאחרון which was later spelled out in full; נתן זמן ובָא is hardly possible. Cf. also Yoma 9b"—(L.G.).

[136] P. 58. Farther down on this page the Rabbis enlarge on the biblical account and put these words in the mouth of the priests of the Philistines: "Let us see what these (i. e., the men of Beth Shemesh) will do to their God whom we have thus honored." Friedmann misses the intent of the homily when he says (Introd. p. 104) that the reward of the priests of the Philistines consisted in their not being slain.

[137] Ibid.

[138] P. 59.

[139] Above, p. 70. *Derek Ereẓ* also stands for the relation between man and woman on p. 177 of our text.

[140] Pp. 56–7.

[141] Pp. 59–60. Cf. TE, pp. 191–2.

[142] Ethical *Derek Ereẓ* is not limited, of course, merely to the acts described above. "Pray for those who work with the community for the sake of Heaven, for the Holy One blessed be He pays them the reward of *Derek Ereẓ* in this world and the principal remains for them for the World to Come"—p. 103. Here *Derek Erez* consists of interested activity for the community.

[143] P. 177.

[144] P. 3.

[145] P. 69. That one who takes such an attitude will be punished is to be concluded from the phrase, "it is a bad sign for him."

[146] P. 177. Comp. TE, p. 173 and note 49.

[147] P. 74. See Friedmann's note #15. For *Ḥillul Hashem*, see TE, p. 64 ff.

"Cf. Erubin 100b, end — the statement of R. Johanan that nature, i. e., animals, have many moral qualities which ought to serve man as examples. It seems to me that Seder Eliahu takes not only ethics but belief in God to be ingrained in human nature and hence the use of *Derek Ereẓ* for ethics and religion. The seven Noachian laws, which include the one against idol-worship, likewise presuppose this view. Even *Ḥillul Hashem* is only a form of *Birkat Hashem* which is one of the seven Noachian laws"— (L.G.).

[148] Pp. 69 (twice), 82, 138.

[149] Above, p. 110.

[150] P. 71; cf. above, p. 120.

[151] P. 172.

[152] Friedmann (Introd. to "Additions", p. 3), who seems to be much confused as to the meaning of *Derek Ereẓ*, tries to distinguish *mizwot* from *Derek Ereẓ*, but to no purpose.

[153] See above, pp. 109–10.

[154] Ibid., p. 70.

[155] Ibid., pp. 73–4.

[156] Ibid., p. 75.

[157] Comp. the section on "The Efficacy of Torah" in the previous chapter.

[158] "Additions", p. 6. The righteous "come to Bible and Mishnah and to learn *Derek Ereẓ*"— p. 81.

[159] P. 84. "Twice Torah" refers to the written and the oral Torah.

[160] Above, p. 75. Practically identical with the reference cited there is the midrash on p. 56 of our text. The phrase אלא מדרך ארץ on p. 56 hardly gives any meaning. It may have been originally מ' ודרך ארץ (מקרא ודרך ארץ), and thus the passage would have the same sense as the one on p. 16. דרך ארץ ומקרא seems to be almost a stereotype phrase being found again, besides on p. 16, also on p. 13. So, also, Ginzberg.

The superiority of Torah over *Derek Ereẓ* is again seen in the passage on p. 100: He in whom there are *Derek Ereẓ* and *mizwot* has only one angel to guard him; he that has studied the whole Bible, two angels; but he that has studied thoroughly all branches of Torah, God Himself guards him. Note that *Derek Ereẓ* is apparently taken for granted in the two latter instances since Torah implicates ethical *Derek Ereẓ*. See Ginzberg's remarks on this passage, above, Chap. II, note 387.

[161] P. 103. The text here is faulty, but the correct reading can be determined by the help of a variant on p. 117 which is also in a corrupt state. The variant on p. 117 reads: וזרעו במים רבים אילו בעלי בתים שבישראל שבשביל דרך ארץ שיש בהן על אחת כמה וכמה הן ובניהן ובני בניהן. That this passage is indeed a variant of the one on p. 103 can be judged from the fact that the proof-text containing the word "waters", always a symbol for Torah, demands some reference to Torah, so that

the full proof-text —"And his seed shall be in many waters" (Num. 24:7) — supposes a statement concerning children engaged in Torah.

Ginzberg supplies us with the correct text. He agrees that the passage on p. 117 is only a variant of the one on p. 103, and adds: "In the first passage (p. 103) *one* word is missing, namely, בניהן. He asked for prayer for the business people who, though not occupying themselves with the Torah, live a moral life, and — he continues — pray the more for their children who study the Torah. The children of ב"ב occupying themselves with study is a favorite topic in Seder Eliahu. On p. 117 הן is a slip — הן בניהן ובני בניהן occurs very often — and by omitting this phrase here the two passages are identical. The present text is due to a misunderstood abbreviation; it read על אחת כמה וכמה ב"ב (=בני בעלי בתים) which the copyist read as בעלי בתים and, of course, *had* to leave it out"— (L.G.).

The translation of the passage in TE, pp. 141–2 and p. 179 should be corrected to conform with the interpretation given here.

162 P. 3. The interpretation hinges on the word מקדם which the Rabbis take in the sense of "precede".

163 Lev. R. 9:3; cited by Friedmann, p. 3, note #1.

164 P. 13. "Cf. Menaḥot 99b and Midrash Tehillim I, 8b (ed. Buber), which passages throw some light on these words of Seder Eliahu"— (L.G.). In Menaḥot, the recitation of the *Shem'a*, morning and evening, is regarded, for those who cannot occupy themselves with the Torah, as sufficient to fulfill the command, "This book of the law shall not depart out of thy mouth, but thou shalt meditate therein day and night" (Josh. 1:8); and in Midrash Tehillim, as sufficient to fulfill the conditions of the verse "And in His law doth he meditate day and night" (Ps. 1:2). Moreover, "his delight is in the law of the Lord" (ibid.) is interpreted there to refer to the six commandments given Adam (5b) and to the seven given Noah (6a), and, in the case of Israel, to the observance of the commandment regarding *tefillin* (8a–b).

165 P. 82. The other references have been cited above, Chap. III, note 148.

166 P. 59; similarly, p. 103. On p. 172: ". . . the reward of *Derek Ereẓ* is given him (in this world, apparently) and the principal is kept for him (in the World to Come)." *Derek Ereẓ* helps man to acquire this world and the World to Come — below, p. 129.

167 P. 13.

168 Pp. 175–6. Comp. TE, p. 194, note 143. The phrase which we called attention to there — ולהציל מידו מה שעשה — is similar to בשביל להצילם מיום הבא לקראתם used here.

169 Above, p. 49.

170 See "Additions", p. 18, and Friedmann's note #29. Friedmann also feels that the text as given here is sound. "I do not recollect any similar passage in the rabbinic literature where in the very same sentence a term is used with two different connotations. If Friedmann's assumption is correct that in מיעוט ד"א the meaning of ד"א is different from ד"א in במקרא במשנה בד"א then all we can say is that we have before us a text based on two different readings or sources, and that the one read במקרא במשנה ובד"א and the second במיעוט שינה . . . במיעוט ד"א"— (L.G.).

171 "Additions", p. 4.

[172] P. 128.

[173] Friedmann, "Additions", p. 4, note #18, suggests that the phrase is a summary of the preceding virtues, and may have possibly been originally, "through the labor of Torah, through the labor of *Derek Ereẓ*". It seems to me that the suggestion has merit. But the "the labor of *Derek Ereẓ*" would refer not to ethics but to work or business; and so I would suggest "through the labor of Torah, through *Derek Ereẓ*".

[174] P. 110. Comp. TE, p. 142.

[175] P. 112.

[176] See the views of the commentators on this mishnah as cited by Friedmann, Introd. p. 103.

[177] It was surprising to find that neither *Derek Ereẓ* nor Good Deeds are so much as mentioned by Schechter and Moore. Friedmann's attempt to analyze *Derek Ereẓ* in his two Introductions also throws very little light. He confuses the general concept with ethical *Derek Ereẓ*. And the talmudic dictionaries are not very helpful, giving only a few specific senses in which *Derek Ereẓ* is employed in a few specific passages. Higger has a useful list of the ways in which the term is employed in the Introduction to מסכתות זעירות (נויארק, תרפ"ט); but in his מסכתות דרך ארץ (New York, 1935) he says, "The ordinary meaning of the expression 'derek erez' is good manners, good behavior, or politeness. By politeness is meant whatsoever distinguishes us from barbarous nations" (Eng. Introd., p. 11).

[178] צדקה וגמילות חסדים — pp. 71, 90, and associated elsewhere frequently.

[179] Above, p. 120.

[180] Above, p. 110.

[181] Above, p. 98.

[182] See above, note 178.

[183] P. 170.

[184] Ibid.

[185] P. 53. This quotation from the Mishnah (San. 4:5) is given here in connection with charity.

[186] Not like *miẓwah* which refers to a *specific* action.

[187] "Additions", p. 2. *Ẓedaḳot* is also mentioned on pp. 181, 195.

[188] P. 182.

[189] P. 53. A variant is found on p. 139.

[190] See, for examples, on pp. 134–5, below.

[191] Cf. TE, p. 112.

[192] P. 4. We arrived at this conclusion by comparing this passage with the kindred one on p. 115. In the latter, God's justice is emphasized: generations and individuals who have "done" Torah are rewarded whereas generations and individuals that have done evil are punished with death. On p. 4, however, there is no mention of punishment at all. More, the verb קנסתי used on p. 115 in regard to both reward and punishment is not used at all on p. 4. The passage here, then has nothing to do with God's justice, but only with God's love. We are all the more convinced of this because of the latter part of the passage which, in contradistinction to the one on p. 115, states, "But I (God) do not remember the sins of Israel nor do they come to mind."

193 P. 136. "The reference is to II Sam. 8:15 where *ẓedaḳah* is attributed to David, which verse is explained in Sanhed. 6b as referring to acts of loving-kindness"—(L.G.). The passage in Sanhedrin, then, corroborates the view we have taken of *ẓedaḳah.*

R. Simon the son of Menasya takes ומצדיקי הרבים in Daniel 12:3 to refer to המאהיבים, "those who cause (men) to love (God)"—Sifre Deut. and Midrash Tannaim on Deut. 11:21.

194 "The word 'charity' never occurs in the A V in the sense of almsgiving, but always with the meaning of *love.* It comes from the Vulg. *caritas,* which was frequently used to translate the Greek *agapê*"— Hastings' Dictionary of the Bible (New York), p. 121, s.v. "charity". In later Greek ἀγάπη, Prof. W. R. Agard informed me, also means charity and alms at once.

The term *ẓedaḳah* in the sense that it is used here is already found in Ben Sira 3:14, where it epitomizes the aid to be given the father by his son. The filial relationship connotes the love of which such aid is the expression. In the commentary to Sirach, ad. loc., in Charles' edition (Apocrypha and Pseudepigrapha, Vol. I, p. 325), the term *ẓedaḳah* is misunderstood and is wrongly interpreted as "righteousness *par excellence*". *Ẓedaḳah* in the sense of "charity" is also found in Tobit 12:8–9, and elsewhere in that book.

195 Pp. 143–4.

196 P. 144; cf. above, p. 97. In the text this follows on the midrash just cited, and is, in fact, introduced by the phrase, "From this they taught."

197 P. 135. This may be another section of "commentary", for it is introduced by the phrase, "When a man honors his father and his mother when they are old," which is taken from a homily above on the same page.

198 P. 139.

199 P. 120. The law (Deut. 15:14 and 18) deals with a Hebrew slave, and the Rabbis interpret it to refer to the wicked who had been sold into slavery for theft; cf. TE, p. 172.

200 P. 84. See above, Chap. II, note 217.

201 Pp. 170 and 171. Charity and Torah are again associated, on p. 171, in that both bring man to the life of the World to Come; and the phrase "(Even) if a man has studied Bible and Mishnah and has done *ẓedaḳot* all his days" occurs on p. 2 of "Additions".

202 Pp. 169–70. Israel practiced "charity and Deeds of Loving-kindness" during the period of the First Temple, even though they were idolators — p. 71.

203 P. 53.

204 Pp. 170 and 171

205 Pp. 170–1. Some of the verses are made to speak of charity only by rabbinic analogy; but others such as Gen. 18:19, Hos. 10:12, Is. 32:17, Deut. 6:25, etc. contain the word *ẓedaḳah.*

206 P. 170.

207 See TE, pp. 123 and 204.

208 P. 181.

209 P. 144.

210 P. 74.

[211] P. 170
[212] P. 53.
[213] Ibid.
[214] P. 169.
[215] Pp. 170–1.
[216] P. 169. Note that, throughout this paragraph, most of the midrashim gave life in *this world* as the reward for charity, though it is also effective in securing the World to Come.
[217] P. 170 and 171.
[218] P. 84.
[219] P. 170.
[220] Ibid.
[221] Cf. TE, pp. 177–9.
[222] P. 34. "Suffer" is the translation of שמבזין את עצמן. For "(the lack of) My glory", etc. see above, Chap. II, note 129.
[223] P. 80.
[224] P. 167.
[225] Pp. 124 (twice), 123. Devotion to God and Israel, we saw, is associated with the practice of Deeds of Loving-kindness in the eulogy of Ezekiel's forbears.
[226] P. 89.
[227] "To be accurate, *gemilut ḥasadim* differs from *ẓedakah* in different ways; cf. the exact definition in the tannaitic statement found in Sukkah 49b. The strongest aspect of *gemilut ḥasadim* is the personal element"— (L.G.). The statement referred to declares that Deeds of Loving-kindness are superior to charity in three ways: The latter involves an expenditure of money, the former money or personal service; the latter has for its object the poor, the former both the poor and the rich; the latter can have reference only to the living, the former both to the living and the dead. Even on the basis of this statement, then, the two sub-concepts while not identical are certainly very closely akin.
[228] P. 167. The midrash goes on to give a proof-text that "waters" refers to Torah. "Al-Nakawa, ed. Enelow, Vol. III, p. 222 reads: בתורה ו ב מ צ ו ת ובגמילות חסדים"— (L.G.).
[229] P. 71. See above, Chap. III, note 135.
[230] P. 90.
[231] P. 195. On contemplations, see TE, pp. 155–9.
[232] P. 181. The text of this passage is faulty and repetitious. "The end ואין מצוקין וגו׳ is found in Tanḥuma, Bereshit, 1"— (L.G.). (The text in Tanḥuma reads: ומי הם מצוקי ארץ אלו שומרי התורה). This midrash reflects a period when Israel as a people must have been very poor. On the rabbinic version of the problem of evil, see TE, p. 203 ff.
[233] Above, p. 129.
[234] Instances will be given as these passages occur in our discussion. Friedmann has carefully compared all such parallels in his notes.
[235] P. 182.
[236] "Comp. Gittin 59b: כל התורה כולה מפני דרכי שלום"— (L.G.).

[237] P. 135. Friedmann, note #37, rightly points out that the qualities chosen for imitation are those mentioned in Exod. 34:6—"Merciful and gracious, long-suffering and abundant in loving-kindness."

[238] P. 65.

[239] P. 77; also in Derek Ereẓ Rabba, Chap. 2. See Friedmann, note #31. "The reading מוילי הרבים in Derek Ereẓ Rabba is not as good as ומליזין ברבים 'who in public make mock of people' "— (L.G.). As to the profaning of the Name being included in *Derek Ereẓ*, universal ethics, see above, p. 123.

[240] Ibid.; also in Derek Ereẓ Rabba, Chap. 2. The priests and Levites who borrow on their share traffic with religious things; those who raised small cattle (in Palestine) caused less land to be used for tillage, besides the loss involved in cattle straying over cultivated land.

[241] P. 78; also in Derek Ereẓ Rabba, Chap. 2.

[242] Cf. TE, pp. 185–6.

[243] P. 74.

[244] P. 92.

[245] P. 80.

[246] Cf. above, pp. 47–50.

[247] Ibid., pp. 51–2.

[248] P. 128. A parallel occurs on p. 4 of "Additions", from which the additional qualities in parenthesis were added above. See also the remarks on these variants found above, p. 129 and Chap. III, note 173.

[249] Cf. TE, pp. 69–70.

[250] "Additions", p. 8.

[251] P. 77; also in Derek Ereẓ Rabba, Chap. 2.

[252] P. 80.

[253] P. 78; also in Derek Ereẓ Rabba, Chap. 2.

[254] P. 138. The same expression occurs also on p. 118: "Let a man fear Heaven and acknowledge the truth and speak the truth in his heart". Here the ground for the virtue is the fear of God, man's reaction to God's justice. Comp. TE, p. 60. See also, above, p. 47.

[255] Pp. 76–7.

[256] P. 159. Idol-worship and arrogance are characterized as "abomination", the one in Deut. 7:20, the other in Prov. 16:5. Arrogance is tantamount to a denial of dependence on God, and thus corresponds to idol-worship.

[257] Ibid.

[258] P. 158.

[259] P. 157.

[260] P. 158.

[261] P. 159. The arrogant in Israel bring about even now the destruction of the innocent heads of families, an example of corporate justice — p. 103.

[262] P. 77; also in Derek Ereẓ Rabba, Chap. 2. See Friedmann in our text, note #29.

[263] P. 77. If he repents, he is healed.

[264] Pp. 103–4.

[265] P. 197.

[266] P. 178.

[267] A kindly, lowly attitude toward the members of the household is also the subject of a midrash on p. 156, and again such an attitude is derived from God's loving-kindness: The Holy One, blessed be He, say the Rabbis, urges that Israel do the will of their children and servants just as He does the will of His children and servants.

[268] P. 104. The midrash stresses *sacrifices*, in the plural. This advice and warning, the midrash continues, Jacob gave to Joseph.

[269] P. 143. "Have I caused you expense in the worship of Me" is Ginzberg's interpretation of the phrase כלום חיסרתי לכם. See also Schechter, Aspects, p. 92, note 1.

[270] P. 104.

[271] P. 197. A similar list of relationships is found below, p. 154.

[272] P. 84.

[273] P. 78; also in Derek Ereẓ Rabba, Chap. 2.

[274] Ibid.; also in Derek Ereẓ Rabba, Chap. 2. The proof-text, Is. 49:7, is to be understood in the light of the following explanation: "The Midrash takes נפש to mean 'oneself'; נְוָה=גוי, body, and used here in the same sense as גוף in later Hebrew. Hence the verse is to be translated: 'he who despises himself and who counts himself contemptuous'. יצר הרע=עבד; cf. Bereshit R. 22:7 (ed. Theodor p. 212) with reference to Prov. 29:21"— (L.G.).

[275] P. 146. The translation of Exod. 23:1 is in accordance with the rabbinic interpretation.

[276] P. 102. "According to the general view of the Rabbis לשון הרע ('the evil tongue') refers to spreading *true* reports calculated to do harm to a fellow-man, and only in a somewhat later use of the term does it refer to *false* slander"— (L.G.).

[277] P. 103.

[278] Pp. 107–8.

[279] "Additions", p. 37.

[280] Cf. TE, pp. 186–7.

[281] P. 77; also in Derek Ereẓ Rabba, Chap. 2. See Friedmann's note #30 in our text. "מעמיקי שפה — who use words with a hidden meaning suggesting something evil"— (L.G.).

[282] P. 107.

[283] "Additions", p. 6.

[284] "Additions", pp. 6–7.

[285] TE, p. 112.

[286] Pp. 156–7.

[287] P. 68.

[288] P. 106.

[289] P. 39. כירה in II Kings 6:23 is here taken to be "a term of peace, like the man who says to his fellow, 'Peace be upon thee, my master, כירי' ". "Friedmann did not understand this passage! פוסטון is the Greek φοσσετον from the Latin *fossa*= Hebrew כירה. The ditch which Elisha drew around the capital of the King of Israel protected him more than all the wars that the king carried on. It follows

that the sentence ואין כירה . . . כרה גדולה is a gloss which was later added to explain the reference to ויכרה . . . כירה. On כירי '*my* master' cf. Krauss, Lehnworter, s.v."— (L.G.).

[290] P. 167. Similarly on p. 104. "Inventive in fear (of God)" is found also there and once more on p. 63.

[291] P. 105. See above, Chap. II, note 287.

[292] Pp. 105–6. See Friedmann's note #107. Ginzberg offers a different interpretation of this passage which includes also the preceding midrash; in the latter case, however, his rendering coincides with that given above. His interpretation makes the proof-text far more understandable: "I do not altogether understand the passage on pp. 105–6, and I have no doubt that the text is incomplete. להשיב דברים וכו' can to my mind only mean 'argue in self-righteousness against God' in case of some evil that overtakes one, a teaching that fits very well with the sentence that follows: שאם יודקק לך וכו' — a well-known view of the Rabbis that nobody is righteous enough to claim anything from God. Then there follows a statement not to continue to confess a sin for which he had done pennance, which agrees with the view of the *ḥakamim* in Yoma 86b. The third statement is a quotation from the Mishnah not to put a repentant sinner to shame on account of his former deeds.

"The midrashic bearing of Prov. 25:8 on the admonition not to keep up a quarrel for long is not clear. Perhaps מחר=מהר, the equation of ה and ח being found in Seder Eliahu in other places (see, for instance, on p. 108 where הדרה in Is. 5:14 is made the basis for an interpretation concerning חדרי חדרים, and hence הדרה=חדרה). The midrashic interpretation of Prov. 25:8–9 in this passage appears to be as follows: 1) The first statement is based on מחר=מהר, hence לא ישמור עליו קנאה וכו'; 2) The second *derashah* belonging to this verse is לעולם אל תהי רגיל וכו' and refers to the second part thereof, namely to בהכלים אותך רעך (i. e., God) in which case אי אתה יכול לעמוד וכו'; 3) the third is a *derashah* on וסוד אחר אל תגל (Prov. 25:9), teaching that one must not be morbid in case of a sin — cf. Berakot 34b end"— (L.G.).

[293] P. 106.

[294] Ibid.

[295] Pp. 67–8.

[296] Pp. 143–4. See Friedmann, note #5.

[297] P. 77. Cf. TE, p. 178.

[298] "Additions", pp. 14–15.

[299] Cf. TE, pp. 191–2. This reward was in the nature of corporate justice.

[300] P. 60. See TE, p. 187, note 109.

[301] Pp. 60–1. Cf. TE, pp. 54–5.

[302] P. 89.

[303] P. 136. For the meaning of *ẓedaḳah* here, see above, pp. 132–3.

[304] P. 133.

[305] Cf. above, p. 54.

[306] P. 133.

[307] P. 133.

[308] P. 80.

[309] P. 79. See TE, p. 174.

[310] P. 62. On God's regimen, in which one-third of the day He studies Bible and Mishnah, one-third He judges His creatures, and one-third He provides sustenance for them, see TE, p. 38.

[311] See TE, pp. 179–80.

[312] P. 64.

[313] P. 61.

[314] P. 116.

[315] P. 78. The phrase "he that does the desire of his wife" also refers to sex matters — see Friedmann, note #37. These statements are also in Derek Ereẓ Rabba, Chap. 2, and elsewhere.

[316] P. 68. That the Rabbis were averse to that form of marriage described in Exod. 21:7 can be judged from their statement that such a sex-relationship will never make for satisfaction in the house, and is bound to lead to quarrels — p. 122. On polygamy in rabbinic times, see above, Chap. III, note 46.

[317] Pp. 100–1.

[318] P. 52. See Friedmann, note #31.

[319] "Additions", p. 22–3. On בפלטרי, see TE, p. 3, note (d). Cf. also ibid., pp. 14–15.

[320] P. 101 — אין הלכה כן, and ואף זו הלכה רווחת בישראל.

[321] Ibid. Deborah taught in the open, under a date-palm, for it is not meet for a woman to be with men in her home — p. 50.

[322] P. 101.

[323] P. 122. See the references cited by Friedmann on that page.

[324] P. 51 — אשה כשירה. "The Greeks' ideal of a good woman is about the same as that of the Rabbis"— (L.G.).

[325] Pp. 48–9. Barak, according to the Rabbis, was Deborah's husband. On Barak, see TE, p. 186, note 103 and the reference cited there.

[326] P. 49.

[327] See the next note.

[328] P. 128. אלך אוכל ואשתה אהנה [ואלך] מן העולם — By means of a slight correction, this statement is made to conform with that in the midrash immediately preceding. Moreover, the proof-text demands this correction. The same expression is also on p. 133. "The phrase ואלך מן העולם is very strange in this connection and I do not believe that it is influenced by Is. 22:13. I would rather prefer the reading ואוכל עולמי, meaning 'to enjoy life', a phrase which was later misunderstood. Cf. Gittin 68b: דליכליה לעלמא. The passage on p. 133 seems, however, to support the reading אלך מן העולם"— (L.G.).

To this midrash there are three variants in our Seder. The variant on pp. 112–13 lacks the first part found on p. 128, and also has different proof-texts. I take the selection on p. 128 to be the original because it is fuller without being repetitious, dealing both with the attitude of the ordinary man and that of the scholar; it thus conforms to the structure of the midrash immediately preceding; and it is further united to the preceding midrash by the parallelism in the manner in which both midrashim are introduced and by the identity of the statements attributed to the ordinary man. Hence, we have, apparently, to do here with a single passage having two sections parallel in construction, though on different themes, and, therefore, having all the earmarks of unified composition.

The variant on pp. 112–13 gives only the part dealing with the scholar. Besides minor differences, it has different proof-texts, referring not, as on p. 128, to the punishment in store for indifference, but to the need of the scholar to forsake his studies and go out to the people when the latter is in trouble.

329 P. 167. This variant has nothing to say of the attitude of the scholar, but gives the phrase, "Peace be upon thee, my soul" as being uttered by the ordinary man. It is, of course, much more fitting to the scholar who feels confident that, because of his devotion to Torah, the harm threatening the rest of the community cannot befall him; whereas in the mouth of the ordinary man it has little meaning, since such a man is included in the fortunes of the community as a whole. The parallel structure of the proof-texts also is lacking in this variant, only the verses characterizing the attitude of indifference to community trouble being retained together with one of the verses predicting punishment. But now, since the variant deals with only the attitude of the ordinary man, there is one characterizing verse superfluous. The variant, therefore, says that Is. 23:13–14 refers to the average man and that *ibid.* 56:12 characterizes the wicked's attitude.

On p. 198, there is still another variant. This is another version, apparently, of the one on p. 167, containing all the features in which the latter varies from the original, but inverting protasis and apodasis. It adds the feature of "angels of destruction" uttering the decree that "he who separated himself from the community shall not see the consolation of the community".

330 P. 17.

331 Pp. 86–7.

332 Above, pp. 121–2.

333 Pp. 127–8. I took the reading in the Venice edition, found in Friedmann's note #3.

334 P. 133. On ולא חבלתי, see Friedmann, Introd., p. 53. "I doubt the correctness of the reading חבלתי. Perhaps בטלתי in contrast to עמלתי —'I did not idle away my time' "— (L.G.).

A man's general character, according to the midrash, is confirmed or strengthened by the help of angels who deal with him as is the man's character: righteous and truth-telling, pious and resigned, or wicked and lying, or just average — p. 176. Here, too, the angels perform the work of God's justice, for they strengthen the bent or intention of a man. Cf. also Ginzberg's remarks on this passage in TE, p. 93, note 84.

335 "Additions", p. 12.

336 P. 147.

337 P. 77. Cf. also TE, p. 173. "Cf. Pesaḥim 50b. If Eliahu Rabba was composed in Palestine the objection to gaining wealth by traffic with other lands is to discourage emigration from the Holy Land"— (L.G.).

338 These are given above, p. 143.

339 Cf. above, p. 28 and p. 37.

340 P. 148.

341 "Additions", p. 8.

342 "Additions", p. 14. Ginzberg offers the following explanation: "Ethical laws have no place in the World to Come when all men will be completely ethical beings without evil in them. The ritual laws alone will have their *raison d'être*!"— (L.G.). This would explain why the ritual laws will be matters for discussion in the World to Come but does not account for the apparent preëminence of the ritual law in the characterization of the learned and in the description of the state of Israel's ignorance.

343 Yehudah Halevy, Kuzari, Chap. II, does attach preëminence to the ritual laws. He feels that in the ritual laws the element of divine fiat is most clearly apparent. He goes so far as to call the ethical precepts התורות השכליות (the rational laws) and the ritualistic התורות האלקיות (the divine laws), just because the ritual laws are confined to Israel. The former, he states, must be the prerequisite for the latter in conduct.

344 עבירה — pp. 13, 52, 112, 139, 188 and elsewhere; עבירות — pp. 38, 121, 168 and elsewhere.

345 עובר — p. 79; עברתם — pp. 130–1; לעבור — p. 132.

346 Pp. 18, 21, 64, 106, 122, 189 and elsewhere.

347 Pp. 130–1. Had Israel in the Wilderness not sinned with the golden calf, the Rabbis declare, they would have been immortal.

"It ought to be mentioned that this usage of עבר is biblical, in phrases like עבר תורה, מצוה, חק, ברית, את פי ה' וכו'"— (L.G.).

348 P. 132.

349 P. 79.

350 There is one instance in Seder Eliahu where '*aberah* refers specifically to sexual transgression — on p. 122. Out of a sense of delicacy, the Rabbis sometimes refrain from mentioning such transgression and refer to it by means of the general term for all transgression, '*aberah*. "This is not peculiar to our book but common to rabbinical literature. Cf. Sanhed. 70a. It is also very likely that in Mishnah Sotah 1:7 עבירה=זנות"— (L.G.).

351 P. 38.

352 P. 188. Comp. TE, p. 181.

353 P. 79. '*Aberah* is equated to '*awon* as the latter is found in a biblical quotation — on p. 21: Men who have committed many transgressions ('*aberot*) had death decreed upon them and their children unto the fouth generation, as it says, ". . . visiting the iniquity ('*awon*) of the fathers upon the children . . ." (Exod. 20:5).

354 P. 168. Comp. above, Chap. II, note 420.

355 P. 121. " 'Hundred' is a favored round number in our Midrash; cf. pp. 54, 89, 106, 107, 113, 121, 124"— (L.G.).

356 P. 104.

357 Ibid.

358 On p. 52. But see below, Chap. III, note 405.

359 See Moore, Judaism, Vol. III, p. 141, note 187.

360 P. 158.

361 P. 38; for the full quotation, see TE, p. 130.

[362] Such use of the word is found even in the Bible, as, for instance, in the statement "The soul that sinneth, it shall die" (Ezek. 18:4, 20).

[363] See Schechter, Aspects, p. 219 and Moore, Judaism, Vol. III, p. 142, note 190.

[364] Pp. 62, 105 and elsewhere — פושעי ישראל.

[365] P. 121 — פושעיהן.

[366] P. 189 — לישא לפשעיכם וליטול עוונותיכן ולהעביר חטאתיכם. מעביר is used again to express forgiveness for *ḥeṭ* and also for *'awon* — on p. 52. In the Bible, however, while the same words for forgiveness are found, they do not necessarily coincide with the manner in which the Rabbis appear to use them in connection with the three terms for sin. Comp., for instance, Exod. 34:7, Micah 7:18, Job 7:21.

[367] Pp. 12–13 — דברים מכוערים ודברים שאינן ראויין. Perhaps a better translation of the phrase would be "hideous things and things that are not seemly." It occurs again, among other places, on pp. 20, 36, 38. On p. 38, there is also a variant of the phrase: דרכין מכוערין ודברים שאינן ראויין — "hideous ways and things that are not seemly"— which may be merely a copyist's error. The variant occurs again on pp. 37, 101, 104; and in all four places the verb "*doing* hideous ways", etc. is certainly out of keeping with the variant phrase and entirely in keeping with the "original" phrase. As to the presence of the variant on p. 69, see Friedmann's note #8.

Ginzberg feels that the translation "not seemly" does not convey the full force of the expression in the original. "ראוי ל... occurs hundreds of times in the *halakic* terminology of the Mishnah and other tannaitic sources, and means 'fit.' Cf., for instance, הראוי לאשים and הראוי למזבח (Zeb. 9:1); הראוי לאדם 'fit for man', and הראוי לבהמה, 'fit for animals' (Sabb. 16:2). I believe, therefore, that דברים שאינן ראויין means 'something unworthy of a human being' and, like דברים מכוערים, refers to heinous sins like immorality, robbery, etc. The nearest rendering in English is 'unprintable' or 'unmentionable' while 'not seemly' is a very weak translation. Cf. Sotah 1:4 — דברים שאינה כ ד א י לשומען; and it seems as if דברים שאינן ראויין stands for דברים שאינן ראויין לשמוע or דברים שאינן ראויין לכתוב. דברים and not דרכין is undoubtedly the correct reading"— (L.G.). On the correction of the phrase טמנים דברין on p. 38 see TE, p. 129, note 75.

[368] See preceding note.

[369] P. 132 — מעשיהן מקולקלין ודבריהן שאינן ראויין.

[370] מן העבירה ומדבר מכוער — p. 139, also pp. 112, 115; מן הגזל ומן העבירה ומן דבר מכוער — pp. 67, 69 (twice), 82, 138, also pp. 136, 143.

[371] Pp. 176, 115 — דברים יתירים. "ד' יתירים is identical with ד' בטלים"—(L. G.). See also TE, p. 127, note 67.

[372] Pp. 3, 13 — דברים שלא כהוגן. "Thou hast not done properly" occurs on p. 103.

[373] P. 79. Cf. above, p. 168.

[374] Above, pp. 121–2.

[375] Pp. 69 (twice), 82, 138. This expression is a cliché as has just been remarked. *Gezel* is anything taken illegitimately.

[376] P. 107.

[377] Pp. 86–7.

[378] P. 67. For *gezel* see above, note 375. Almost identical is the passage on p. 139, omitting the mention of *gezel*.

[379] P. 143.
[380] P. 112.
[381] "Additions", p. 11 — יראי חטא.
[382] Above, p. 46 and p. 115.
[383] P. 115. The kinship between this midrash and the one on p. 112 is obvious.
[384] P. 132. But on חוזר במעשיו see TE, p. 126 and note 65.
[385] See TE, pp. 129–134 where the rabbinic passages on this subject are quoted and discussed.
[386] P. 132. Cf. TE, p. 61 and note 154.
[387] P. 136.
[388] See above, p. 149.
[389] Above, p. 170.
[390] See above, p. 158.
[391] See TE, pp. 67–9.
[392] See TE, pp. 114–18, 209–11.
[393] TE, pp. 120–22.
[394] Ibid., p. 127.
[395] Ibid., pp. 119–20.
[396] Ibid., Chapter V, sections III and IV.
[397] P. 104; similarly, p. 52.
[398] Above, p. 171.
[399] Pp. 139, 67.
[400] TE, pp. 127–8.
[401] Ibid., pp. 129–132.
[402] See above, p. 76.
[403] Below, p. 175.
[404] Pp. 12–13; above, p. 170.
[405] P. 104. This passage is much akin to the one on p. 52. Both begin by a laudation of him "in whom there is no sin" etc. and end with the idea of such a man being close to the *Shekinah.* As Friedmann suggests, however, the passage on p. 52 is incomplete. (Friedmann's note #34).
[406] Above, p. 172.
[407] P. 132. "I believe that the text must be emended to read על מנת לעבור על אחת מכל מצוות. To love and fear God but to transgress *all* its commandments sounds too strange!"— (L.G.).
[408] Ibid.
[409] TE, pp. 166–185; also pp. 185–193; and pp. 199–208.
[410] Above, pp. 93–4.
[411] Ibid., p. 112.
[412] Ibid., pp. 120–1, 136, 143, 147–8, 151–3, 158–9, 163.
[413] P. 79. "At the end of the passage is משחיר, a doublet to משכים; we have to read: משחיר ומעריב or משכים ומעריב. Cf. p. 52 where the same doublet was misunderstood and מעריב left out"— (L.G.).
[414] See TE, p. 127.
[415] See above, p. 150.
[416] P. 13.

[417] P. 20. God did not punish Israel according to their sins on a number of occasions, as was proved especially during that period before the (first) Day of Atonement — above, p. 149.

[418] P. 52; similarly, p. 4.

[419] Above, p. 168.

[420] TE, Chapter VI.

[421] Cf. the Index below in reference to the subjects not given separate treatment.

NOTES TO CHAPTER IV

[1] TE, pp. 112–13.

[2] Ibid., p. 89.

[3] Ibid., p. 113.

[4] Cohen, Reason and Nature (New York, 1931), p. 138. His noteworthy analysis of the importance of concepts is in the first two chapters of the book.

[5] See above, p. 7.

[6] See above, p. 8.

[7] See TE, pp. 209–11.

[8] TE, p. 211.

[9] See above, p. 81.

[10] Above, pp. 42–68.

[11] Ibid., pp. 68–79.

[12] Ibid., pp. 95–113.

[13] Ibid., pp. 113–117.

[14] Ibid., pp. 117–130.

[15] Ibid., pp. 131–140.

[16] Ibid., pp. 140–165. Incidentally, the general statements concerning Torah made at the outset of our discussion of the concept (Chap. II) will be found, on scrutiny, to be related to other concepts — to Israel, justice, the rabbinic view of nature, love, repentance, etc.

[17] TE, pp. 109–113.

[18] Ibid., pp. 137–161.

[19] Ibid., pp. 118–137.

[20] Ibid., pp. 166–185.

[21] Ibid., pp. 194–199.

[22] A few instances where these terms were used: the learned — above, pp. 76, 85; the ignorant — ibid., pp. 46, 127; the righteous — TE, p. 179; the wicked — ibid , p. 120; the Patriarchs — ibid., p. 133.

[23] See above, pp. 124–6.

[24] See above, pp. 136–8, and Chap. III, note 227.

[25] TE, p. 127.

[26] Above, pp. 75–6.

[27] TE, Chap. V, section IV, esp. pp. 127, 135.

[28] Ibid., Chap. V, section V, esp. pp. 140–142 and 159–60.

[29] See above, p. 78.

[30] Schechter in Aspects treats of Repentance and "The Zachuth of the Fathers" (which in our scheme would be an aspect of the sub-concept of corporate justice) in this manner, and Moore in Judaism deals similarly with Repentance and Expiatory Suffering.

[31] Quoted in TE, pp. 29–30.

[32] E. G. Coghill, The Neuro-Embryologic Study of Behavior, in Science, Vol. 78, pp. 131–8.

[33] Cited above, pp. 180–1.

[34] Cf. above, p. 120.

[35] Cf. TE, pp. 67–69.

[36] Ibid., p. 172.

[37] Ibid., p. 176.

[38] Ibid., p. 175.

[39] Ibid., p. 113.

[40] Cf. above, p. 92.

[41] Dr. M. M. Kaplan makes the pertinent observation that Philo with his allegoric method depersonalizes and makes of the concrete biblical stories and laws abstractions, but that the Rabbis with their midrashic method do just the opposite, rendering concepts that are themselves abstract into concrete teachings. (Jewish Quarterly Review, New Series, Vol. XXIII, No. 3, p. 291).

[42] TE, Chap. VI, section V.

[43] See below, pp. 197–8.

[44] Cf. above, p. 188, and Chap. IV, note 41.

[45] See ibid., Chap. III, note 227.

[46] Ibid., pp. 74–5.

[47] P. 19.

[48] See TE, p. 165.

[49] See TE, p. 109.

[50] Above, p. 184.

[51] Ibid., pp. 134, 136.

[52] Ibid., p. 53.

[53] Bergson, Creative Evolution (New York, 1911), Chap. IV.

[54] See above, pp. 57–8.

[55] Cf. TE, p. 181.

[56] See above, p. 140. In other midrashim, poverty is looked upon only as punishment — see ibid., p. 112 and Chap. III, note 92.

[57] See above, p. 22.

[58] Ibid., p. 21.

[59] Cf. TE, p. 168.

[60] Cf. above, p. 23.

[61] Cf. TE, p. 134.

[62] Ibid., p. 135.

[63] Ibid., p. 183.

[64] Ibid., p. 195.

[65] The degree of abstraction is also a matter left to the individual. See above p. 92, and Chap. II, note 418.

Nachmanides, among those who long ago recognized what we have called the fluid character of rabbinic thought, in commenting on Gen. 8:4, puts it thus: שבעים פנים לתורה ומדרשים רבים חלוקים בדברי חכמים (Commentary on the Pentateuch) This does not prevent him, however, from regarding rabbinic narratives on biblical themes as authentic history, as can be seen, for example, in his comment on Gen. 24:32.

The endeavor to harmonize "contradictory" haggadic passages, evident in medieval Jewish ethical literature, indicates that a profound change in mental outlook has taken place, despite the obvious dependance of this literature on rabbinic thought. An interesting example of this kind of harmonization is to be found in Sefer Ḥasidim, ed. Wistinetzki-Freimann (Frankfort a. M., 1924), pp. 29–34.

[66] Cf. TE, p. 67.

[67] Cf. p. 67.

[68] Cf. TE, p. 12.

[69] See above, p. 106.

[70] Cf. TE, p. 15.

[71] Ibid., pp. 167–168.

[72] See above, pp. 187–8, where we first demonstrated that the organic concepts are drives and that concretizations of the concepts of God's justice and His love are by no means inevitable.

[73] Cf. TE, pp. 119–120.

[74] Cf. above, pp. 167–71.

[75] See the discussion on the rabbinic attitude toward asceticism, above, pp. 53–7.

[76] See above, pp. 77–9.

[77] See ibid., pp. 104–7.

[78] Cf. ibid., p. 97.

[79] H. A. Wolfson, Crescas' Critique of Aristotle (Cambridge, 1929), p. 26.

[80] See above, pp. 39–41. Cf. also ibid., pp. 23–7.

[81] See ibid., p. 84, Chap. II, note 383.

[82] See TE, p. 120.

[83] Cf. TE, p. 89.

[84] Cf. ibid., p. 110.

[85] Cf. ibid., p. 83.

[86] Ibid.

[87] See above, Chap. III, note 37.

[88] Cf. TE, p. 43.

[89] Cf. ibid., p. 133.

[90] Cf. ibid., pp. 164–165.

[91] See above, Chap. III, note 161.

[92] Thirty-two *midot*, rules of haggadic interpretation, are given with R. Eliezer, the son of R. Yose the Galilean, as authority — cf. Bacher, Terminologie (Hebr trans.) I, 70 and notes 1–5. See Mishnat R. Eliezer, ed. Enelow (New York, 1933). A few additional principles are given by Krochmal, מורה נבוכי הזמן, Chap. 14, p. 240, ed. Rawidowicz, (Berlin, 1924).

[93] Cf. above, pp. 153–4.

[94] Cf. ibid., p. 61 and Chap. II, note 260.

[95] Pp. 68, 4–7, and elsewhere.

Since Seder Eliahu once had its "mishnah" and commentary, there is an instance left where two different comments explain one statement of the "mishnah", for the method of textual interpretation was general — see above, Chap. III, note 50. This confirms our statement above that Haggadah and Halakah approached texts with the same method.

[96] For examples of this, see Krochmal, Chap. 14, p. 241.

[97] See above, p. 191, and the reference. Note also how the directions for the observance of charity have to do with specific situations — ibid., pp. 133–4.

[98] Cf. ibid., pp. 60–2.

[99] Cf. ibid., pp. 47–57.

[100] Cf. TE, pp. 125–127.

[101] Cf. ibid., pp. 154–155.

[102] Compare for instance their description of arrogance and humility given above, pp. 147–51.

[103] Cf. above, p. 112 and Chap. III, note 92.

[104] Cf. ibid., pp. 108–9.

[105] Cf. ibid.

[106] Cf. ibid., pp. 33–5.

[107] See above, p. 187 and the references there.

[108] Another example of logical determination is given in the instance of the fisherman who was finally convinced that the concept of the study of Torah extended to him also — cf. ibid., pp. 45–6.

[109] Cf. ibid., p. 76.

[110] The combinations of concepts in which repentance is involved are given in TE, pp. 127–135.

[111] Cf. TE, pp. 103–104.

[112] Ibid., p. 105.

[113] Cf. ibid., pp. 190–191 and the references to Ginzberg's Notes on The Legends cited on p. 191, note 126.

[114] The great strain which accompanies logical thinking in general makes continuous interpretation of moment-to-moment phenomena impossible by that means. Maimonides describes this strain as follows: "Do not imagine that these most difficult problems can be thoroughly understood by any one of us. This is not the case. At times the truth shines so brightly that we perceive it as clear as day. Our nature and habit then draw a veil over our perception, and we return to a darkness almost as dense as before. We are like those who, though beholding frequent flashes of lightning, still find themselves in the thickest darkness of the night"— Moreh Nebukim, tr. Friedländer, (second edition), p. 3.

[115] Cf. TE, p. 80.

[116] See above, Chap. II, note 291.

[117] See Jewish Encyclopedia, Vol. X, art. "Rabbi".

[118] Cf. Krochmal, op. cit., pp. 242–245.

[119] Cf. TE, p. 67 and pp. 174–5.

[120] See above, Chap. III, note 101.
[121] Cf. TE, p. 186 and note 103.
[122] Ibid., p. 188 and note 115.
[123] Ibid., p. 189.
[124] TE, p. 88.
[125] TE, Chap. IV, section III.
[126] TE, Chap. IV, sections I–II.
[127] Cf. ibid., pp. 76–77. Comp. also the remarks on this problem, ibid., p. 78 and p. 98.
[128] Cf. ibid., p. 91.
[129] I am indebted to Professor Ruth C. Wallerstein of the University of Wisconsin for calling this poem to my attention, and for many other suggestions.
[130] See TE, Chap. III, Sections I–III.
[131] See ibid., pp. 43–44.
[132] Some of the passages in the Talmud on demons are — Ber. 54b, Shab. 67a; on the evil eye — Baba Batra 75a, Ber. 58a; on good luck practices — Pes. 109b; on witches — ibid.; on dreams — Ber. 55a.
[133] TE, pp. 81–82.
[134] Ibid., p. 81 and note 28.
[135] Ibid., pp. 129–132.
[136] Krochmal, op. cit., Chap. XIV, pp. 248–255.
[137] Critics of Judaism have always exploited both types of folklore for their purpose. See, for example, ספר מלחמות ה' לסלמון בן ירוחים, ed. I. Davidson (New York, 1934), Chaps. 14–17. The author, a Karaite of the tenth century, attacks first anthropomorphisms in the Talmud and then proceeds to cite gross anthropomorphisms in later works. The talmudic anthropomorphisms all belong to the organic complex; those in the later works invariably do not.
[138] See TE, pp. 34–38.
[139] A. B. Davidson, The Theology of the Old Testament (New York, 1904), pp. 166–169. Though Davidson makes the statement with regard to the Bible in general, he specifically proves this point by an analysis of the second half of the Book of Isaiah.
[140] Op. cit., pp. 174–175.
[141] Cf. TE, pp. 75 ff. As we suggested there (ibid., p. 83), the biblical descriptions of nature evince the greater interest and joy taken in natural phenomena. Nevertheless, these descriptions are given neither for their own sake, nor as Yehudah Halevy assumes (Kuzari, V, 8–10), to illustrate teleology in nature. The example he gives of the latter, Ps. 104, portrays rather the love or beneficence of God in providing for His creatures.
[142] See above, pp. 97–8. Chapter XIX of Leviticus is, of course, an excellent case in point.
[143] See TE, pp. 64–71, and especially p. 65, note 164.

The rabbinic concept of *kawwanah* has similarly been shown to be rooted in the Bible. Cf. Selected Works of Hyman G. Enelow, ed. F. A. Levy (privately printed, 1935), Vol. IV, pp. 256–260.
[144] Cf. TE, p. 178.

[145] Cf. ibid., pp. 189–190.
[146] Cf. ibid., p. 186.
[147] Cf. ibid., p. 110.
[148] Cf. ibid., p. 126.
[149] Cf. ibid., p. 211.
[150] Cf. above, p. 98.
[151] Cf. TE, p. 37.
[152] Cf. ibid., p. 141.
[153] Cf. above, p. 105.
[154] Cf. ibid., p. 42.
[155] Professor Louis Ginzberg has collected the rabbinic legends on biblical themes in his Legends of the Jews, Vols. I–IV (Philadelphia, 1913). His sources are not limited to rabbinic literature, however, rabbinic legends being found, as he states, also in the works of authors of the Middle Ages, in the older Kabbalah, in the Apocrypha and Pseudepigrapha, in the literature of the Church Fathers, in Philo and other sources. The many literary and historical problems occasioned by the utilization and comparison of all these sources are dealt with in his Notes, Vol. V (1925) and Vol. VI (1928). The student of Jewish thought can make proper and full use of this magnificent work now that there has appeared the Index to these volumes prepared by Dr. Boaz Cohen (Philadelphia, 1938). For a brief survey of the relationship of Jewish to non-Jewish legends, see Ginzberg, Jewish Folklore: East and West, in Independence, Converging and Borrowing in Institutions, Thought and Art (Harvard Univ. Press, 1937), pp. 89–108.
[156] Cf. TE, p. 88 and note 115.
[157] Cf. ibid., p. 190.
[158] Cf. above, pp. 153–4.
[159] Cf. TE, pp. 112–113.
[160] Cf. ibid., pp. 120–122.
[161] Cf. ibid., pp. 166–168.
[162] Cf. above, pp. 42, 45–6.
[163] Cf. ibid., p. 96.
[164] Cf. above, p. 182, and Chap. IV, note 22.
[165] Cf. ibid., pp. 57–9.
[166] Cf. ibid., pp. 104–7.
[167] Cf. TE, p. 143.
[168] Cf. ibid., p. 144.
[169] Cf. ibid., p. 160.
[170] Cf. ibid., p. 126.
[171] Cf. ibid., p. 124.
[172] Cf. above, p. 143.
[173] Cf. TE, p. 111.
[174] Cf. ibid., p. 115.
[175] Cf. above, pp. 132–3 and the references there.
[176] Cf. ibid., pp. 142–3.
[177] The rabbinic translation of the Pentateuch into the popular Aramaic of the day, known as Targum Onkelos, affords an excellent illustration of the difference

between the rabbinic interpretation and the simple textual meaning of the Bible. We owe much to the investigations along this line of S. D. Luzatto who embodied them in his אוהב גר (קראקא, תרנ"ה). Yet Luzatto was evidently by no means aware that the rabbinic interpretation is essentially something different as a whole from the Bible itself. Hence, while his remarks on linguistic matters are sound and his treatment of anthropomorphisms significant, a number of his categories are far too loose and his judgment, therefore, on many passages wrong. He recognizes that changes having to do with biblical anthropomorphisms are not due to philosophic tendencies but to a regard for the dignity and single majesty of God. But here, too, the category is too large, and there is no recognition of the part played by the new emphasis on God's love and His regard for the individual, both in reward and punishment. He places in his category of "changes for the sake of the honor of Israel and the Ancestors" such diverse matters as these: The Targum takes "and Jacob was a simple man, dwelling in tents" (Gen. 25:27) to refer to Jacob's studying Torah (p. 9); Rachel's statement translated usually "with mighty wrestlings have I wrestled" (Gen. 30:8) to refer to Rachel's having prayed to God (p. 9); "whom Thou didst prove at Massah, with whom Thou didst strive at Meribah" (Deut. 33:8) to refer to Aaron who, in its version, is thus declared to have been proved and found sound (p. 20). Now we recognize that such renderings are not made deliberately for "the honor of Israel" but represent concretizations of the new rabbinic concepts: The first conforms to the concept of the Patriarchs as that concept is affected by Torah; the second to the emphasis on prayer in rabbinic theology; the third to the concept of the righteous.

Luzatto does have one category wherein he places indiscriminately all changes "due to the oral Torah and to the interpretations of the sages" and which includes renderings like "the land of worship" for "the land of Moriah" (Gen. 22:2) and a number of rabbinic interpretations of biblical laws (pp. 9–10). But, not differentiating between rabbinic concepts, he is really not aware that the Targum represents a new theology and consequently new interpretations. Thus he states that the following changes made by the Targum are changes in language but not in content: For "Take all the chiefs of the people and hang them up" (Num. 25:4), the Targum has "and judge and slay those who are guilty" (pp. 15–16), a statement representing, we should say, the rabbinic concept of the justice due the individual; similarly the Targum takes "visiting the iniquity of the fathers upon the children" (Exod. 20:5) to refer to children who continue in the evil ways of their fathers (p. 17), again a concretization of the justice due the individual. There is hardly any need to add that Luzatto feels that a number of laws, distinctly rabbinic, which the Targum reads into the biblical laws are, in truth, biblical (p. 16, p. 18).

The considerations above, of course, merely indicate the need of a thorough analysis of Targum Onkelos. Such an analysis would certainly throw much needed light on the relation of rabbinic theology to the Bible.

[178] G. T. W. Patrick, cited in TE, p. 30.

[179] See TE, pp. 109–110 and 169.

[180] See above, p. 217 and Chap. IV, note 177.

[181] See above, p. 213 and Chap. III, note 101.

[182] M. Jastrow, Hebrew and Babylonian Traditions (New York, 1914), pp. 41–47.
[183] Ibid., p. 45.
[184] Cf. above, pp. 197–200.
[185] A. B. Davidson, op. cit., p. 514.
[186] More than two decades ago, Prof. M. M. Kaplan, in one of his courses, first gave an interpretation of the Bible from the standpoint of the Bible taken as a unit. In the last few years, the following books have appeared in which this position is taken with regard to the Book of Genesis: Volz und Rudolph, Der Elohist als Erzähler (Giessen, 1933); B. Jacob's translation and commentary, Das erste Buch der Tora, Genesis (Berlin, 1934); and U. Cassuto, La Questione della Genesi (Florence, 1934). See Martin Buber's article on these books entitled, "Genesisprobleme" in Monatsschrift, 80 Jahrgang, Heft 2, pp. 81–92. D. B. MacDonald, in his recent work, The Hebrew Literary Genius (Princeton, 1933), also assumes this position though not in so thorough-going a fashion as the others we mentioned. Though a consideration of these books would have strengthened the thesis developed here, they came to my notice after this section was written, and, since the thesis is in any case the same, I allowed the section to stand as it was.

I also benefited from a discussion of the entire matter with Dr. L. L. Honor of Chicago.

[187] See TE, p. 54.
[188] Ibid., pp. 34–38.
[189] Ibid., Chap. III, section V.
[190] Ibid., Chap. III, section VI.
[191] See above, pp. 223–5.
[192] See above, 225.
[193] Above, pp. 223–4.
[194] See ibid., p. 225.
[195] Cf. TE, p. 119.
[196] Ibid., p. 137.
[197] Ibid., pp. 194–195.
[198] See above, p. 81.
[199] Cf. ibid., pp. 43–44, 97, 105–6.
[200] Cf. TE, pp. 60–61.
[201] Cf. ibid., pp. 66–70.
[202] See above, p. 210.
[203] Cf. ibid., pp. 190–2.
[204] Wolfson, op. cit. pp. 26 f., has rightly pointed out that the method of medieval Jewish philosophy which consisted of a careful analysis of philosophical texts was at one with the talmudic method. In the analysis of texts the Rabbis, as we have pointed out, employed acute logical reasoning, and the method of talmudic textual analysis was no doubt carried over into the analysis of philosophical texts. Types of logical thinking being basically similar in method can be carried over from one field to another. But concepts of different types cannot be integrated without some change being effected. The *rabbinic concepts* were not at one with the *philosophic concepts*.
[205] See TE, p. 170, note 33.

[206] See above, Chap. III, note 343.

[207] See ibid., p. 69 and Chap. II, note 310.

See also S. Goldman, The Jew and The Universe (New York, 1936), pp. 116–125. I benefited much from discussing with Rabbi Goldman several of the matters taken up in this section.

[208] See TE, pp. 71–74.

[209] Cf. above, pp. 206–7.

[210] Cf. TE, pp. 72–74.

[211] Wieman, The Wrestle of Religion with Truth (New York, 1929), p. 154.

[212] Baron von Hügel, The Mystical Element of Religion, second ed. (New York, 1923), Vol. II, pp. 304–308.

[213] Ibid., pp. 283–284.

[214] See above, p. 214.

[215] Cf. TE, p. 3 and p. 7 ff.

[216] Introd., pp. 32–38.

[217] Cf. above, pp. 60–1. In this connection the Rabbis also stress coöperative study in the schools as against the private study of *Ma'aseh Merkabah*; the preference of normal study at schools is always maintained.

[218] See ibid., pp. 202–4.

[219] Cf. ibid., pp. 37–9.

[220] von Hügel, op. cit. II, p. 47.

[221] Ibid., I, pp. 367–368.

[222] חובות הלבבות, VIII, 3.

[223] Ibid., VIII, 4.

[224] Ibid., VIII, 6.

[225] Studies tracing the relation of any single rabbinic concept to the Bible, to medieval philosophy and to Kabbalah corroborate our analysis. Thus in Enelow's essay on *kawwanah* (op. cit., pp. 252–288), we find the information that: (1) The rabbinic concept of *kawwanah* — sustained devotion, intention, concentration in the recital of prayers and in the performing of *miẓwot* — is rooted in the Bible though the Bible does not contain the word itself; (2) Maimonides declares that *kawwanah* hinges on the proper metaphysical approach to God; (3) in Kabbalah, *kawwanah* comes to mean "appreciation of the esoteric significance of religious acts," a construction of the concept which Enelow characterizes as "the decadence of the idea." Incidentally, Baḥya, as Enelow points out, does not indulge in the fantasies of later abnormal mysticism, the Kabbalah. We purposely selected Baḥya because of his early date in order to demonstrate how abnormal mysticism, even in its less developed form, differs from rabbinic theology.

[226] See above, pp. 121–2. On the rabbinic concept of trust in God cf. also ibid., Chap. II, note 352.

[227] See ibid., Chap. III, note 147.

[228] See ibid., p. 123.

[229] Among the other instances are the way in which an Israelite may sanctify or profane the Name in his ethical relations with Gentiles and the way in which the scholar, especially, may do so in all his ethical relations — see TE, pp. 67–70.

[230] See above, pp. 190–2.

[231] Cf. ibid., pp. 133–4.

[232] Cf. ibid., p. 100.

[233] See above, pp. 191–2, and 205–6.

[234] See ibid., p. 125, and pp. 109–10.

[235] Cf. ibid., p. 110.

[236] Cf. above, p. 187.

[237] See ibid., p. 200 and TE, pp. 119–120.

[238] Drives are, of course, not necessarily positive. We tend to move toward physical pleasure and away from physical pain. So, too, whilst many of the concepts acted as positive drives, others, e. g. the concept of the wicked, acted as negative ones.

[239] Moore, Judaism, II, p. 81.

[240] Ibid.

[241] Cf. above, p. 78 and the references there.

[242] Cf. ibid., p. 126.

[243] Cf. ibid., p. 159.

[244] See TE, pp. 179–182, especially pp. 181–2; and pp. 203–207.

[245] See above, Chap. I, note 31.

The emphasis on the individual, by the way, also appears in the statement of Bereshit R. immediately preceding the one we have been discussing (53, 18). The Rabbis say there that when an individual who is sick utters a prayer himself it is more effective than prayers of others in his behalf.

[246] Cf. TE, p. 180.

[247] Cf. ibid., pp. 209–211.

[248] Cf. above, pp. 142–3.

[249] In formulating the analysis in this section, I was stimulated by discussion with Mr. Henry Kaiser, Mr. Benjamin Stephansky and Mr. Joseph Tussman.

[250] A. N. Whitehead, Science and the Modern World (New York, 1925), pp. 90–104.

[251] A. N. Whitehead, Process and Reality (New York, 1930), pp. 47–50.

[252] Ibid., pp. 138–139.

[253] Ibid., pp. 50–52 and pp. 136–141.

[254] See Dorothy M. Emmet, Whitehead's Philosophy of Organism (London, 1932), pp. 112–113 (and the references cited there) and p. 229.

[255] See Dorothy M. Emmet, ibid., pp. 116–133, especially pp. 132–133.

[256] A. N. Whitehead, Religion in the Making (New York, 1926), p. 88.

[257] Ibid., p. 87.

[258] Ibid., p. 16.

[259] Ibid., p. 89.

[260] Ibid., p. 32.

[261] Ibid.

[262] Ibid., p. 17.

[263] Whitehead, Process and Reality, pp. 73, 134.

[264] R. H. Wheeler, Organismic Logic, in Philosophy of Science, Vol. 3, No. 1 (January, 1936), pp. 26–61.

[265] See above, p. 195.

[266] John Dewey, Experience and Nature (Chicago, 1925), p. 271.
[267] Ibid., p. 261.
[268] John Dewey, A Common Faith (Yale Univ. Press, 1934), pp. 22–23.
[269] Ibid., p. 81.
[270] Ibid., p. 42.
[271] Ibid.
[272] See above, pp. 234–5.
[273] See the summary in Wheeler, op. cit.
[274] Lucien Lévy-Bruhl, How Natives Think, trans. Clare (New York, 1925), p. 126.
[275] Ibid., p. 109.
[276] Ibid., pp. 35–68, 76, 122.
[277] Ibid., Chaps. III and V.
[278] Ibid., pp. 106–109, 116–136.
[279] Ibid., pp. 35–38.
[280] Ibid., Chaps. II, VI, VII, VIII.
[281] Emile Durkheim, The Elementary Forms of the Religious Life, trans. Swain (Allen and Unwin), pp. 3–8.
[282] Lévy-Bruhl, op. cit., pp. 362–368.
[283] Ibid., p. 379.
[284] Ibid., pp. 381–2.
[285] Ibid., p. 386.
[286] See above, p. 193.
[287] "Reinterpretation is the process of finding equivalents in the civilization to which we belong for values of a past stage of that or another civilization"— M. M. Kaplan, Judaism as a Civilization (New York, 1934), p. 389. See Chap. XXVI of that book, entitled "The Functional Method of Interpretation," for his very suggestive and valuable theory of reinterpretation.

NOTES TO APPENDIX

[1] See TE, pp. 3–6. These views, adequately summarized by Friedmann in his Introduction, are to be found, as given by their authors, as follows:

(a) S. Rapoport, תולדות ר' נתן, note 43 and 44 (also published by Hazefirah, Warsaw, 1913).
(b) L. Zunz, Gottesdienstlichen Vorträge (Frankfort a. M., 1892), pp. 119–124.
(c) W. Bacher, Monatsschrift, 1874, pp. 266–74.
(d) D. Oppenheim, (וויען, תרמ"א) I בית תלמוד, pp. 265–70, 304–10, 337–46, 369–77.
(e) Z. Yawetz, (ווארשא, תרמ"ז) I כנסת ישראל, pp. 379–399. He bases his conclusion on more evidence, of course, than the single argument we cited.

We also discussed Mann's theory — comp. TE, pp. 12, 147.

[2] H. Graetz, Geschichte V (Leipzig, 1895), pp. 294–5.
[3] M. Güdemann, Erziehungswesen und Der Cultur II (Wien, 1884), pp. 52–55, 300–3.

[4] See TE, p. 16.

[5] S. Asaf, (ירושלם, תרפ"ט) תשובות הגאונים, p. 176; comp. ibid., pp. 153–4. My attention was called to this responsum by Ginzberg and others. Mann, who holds the dates in the Seder to be copyists' additions (H.U.C. Annual IV, p. 249, note 10), communicated to me a similar remark that he found afterwards in תוספות על מסכת ע"ז לרבינו אלחנן (Husiatyn, 1901), 9a.

[6] See TE, pp. 13–16.

[7] J. Mann, Genizah Studies, The American Journal of Semitic Languages, Vol. XLVI, No. 4, pp. 267–8.

[8] Ibid., p. 268.

[9] See Ginzberg's note 10, p. 199 of Genizah Studies in Memory of Doctor Solomon Schechter, Vol. I.

[10] See TE, pp. 8–9, and p. 15, note 47.

[11] See ibid., p. 14, note 39.

[12] Cf. TE: p. 15, note 46; above: pp. 48–9; Chap. II, note 237; Chap. III, note 38; Chap. III, note 50; Chap. III, note 101.

[13] Cf. the remarks and the references cited in Chap. III, note 56. Cf. also TE, pp. 9–10, and p. 12.

[14] J. Theodor, Monatsschrift, Vol. 44 (1900), pp. 380–4 and 550–61.

[15] A. Marx, Zeitschrift für Hebr. Bibliographie, Jahrgang VI, pp. 3–5

INDEX I

GENERAL INDEX

Page-numbers prefaced by "te" refer to the companion volume, *The Theology of Seder Eliahu: A Study in Organic Thinking.* Page-numbers not so designated refer to the present volume.

INDEX II

GINZBERG'S EMENDATIONS OF, AND REMARKS ON, THE TEXT OF SEDER ELIAHU.

Page-numbers prefaced by "te" refer to the companion volume, *The Theology of Seder Eliahu: A Study in Organic Thinking*. Page-numbers not so designated refer to the present volume.

Seder Eliahu (ed. Friedmann)

Seder Eliahu (ed. Friedmann)

Seder Eliahu (ed. Friedmann)